The Venus Syndrome

The Venus Syndrome

A FOUR-STEP PLAN FOR IMPROVING THE PEAR-SHAPED FIGURE

Eugenia Chandris

Illustrated by Mona Mark

CHATTO & WINDUS
THE HOGARTH PRESS
LONDON

Published in 1985 by
Chatto & Windus · The Hogarth Press
40 William IV Street, London WC2N 4DF

British Library Cataloguing in Publication Data

Chandris, Eugenia
    The Venus syndrome: a four-step plan for
    improving the pear-shaped figure.
    1. Reducing
    I. Title
    613.2'5'088042   RM222.2

ISBN 0–7011–3966–8

Printed in Great Britain by
Redwood Burn Limited, Trowbridge, Wiltshire

For Louise Mellor Gault
my friend, my editor, my guide

List of Illustrations

Figure 1 The Venus of Willendorf   Page 13

Figure 2 Figure of a Hottentot or Bushman of the
         Kalahari Desert in Southwestern Africa   16

Figure 3 Sexual Differences in Skin and Subcutaneous
         Fat Structure   25

Figure 4 What the Fat Distribution Score Looks Like   32–33

Figure 5 Diagrams Representing the Process
         of Fat Storage   54–57

Figure 6 Diagrams Representing the Process
         of Fat Release   59–61

Figure 7 Structural Differences Between a White and
         Brown Fat Cell   65

Figure 8 Fat Cells in Test Tube   70

Figure 9 Standard Measurement Points on the
         Female Body   159

Figure 10 Lines of Incision and Areas of Excision
          for Thigh and Buttock Reduction   230–31

Contents

*Foreword by Sami A. Hashim, M.D. Chief, Division of
Metabolism and Nutrition. St. Luke's-Roosevelt Hospital
Center, New York City.*   xi

Preface   xv

PROLOGUE   **xvii**

Chapter 1 A Voyage of Discovery   1

STEP 1 ANALYZING THE PROBLEM   **9**

Chapter 2 What Is the Venus Syndrome?   11

**STEP 2 UNDERSTANDING THE PROBLEM: ALL
            THERE IS TO KNOW ABOUT FAT**   **37**

Chapter 3 Mechanics, Myths, and Miracles: Some Facts on Fat 39

*Chapter 4 The Life History of a Fat Cell: When Is It Most
            Dangerous to Gain Weight?*   66

**STEP 3 TREATING THE PROBLEM: WHAT
            WORKS AND WHAT DOESN'T**   **83**

Chapter 5 Diets: A Matter of Calories or Confusion?   85

Chapter 6 The Only Diet for You   99

Chapter 7 Exercise: The Shape and Weight Solution   137

*Chapter 8 The Venus Workout: What You Can Do for the
            Bottom-heavy Figure*   172

Chapter 9 Drugs, Needles, and Nonsense: Some Desperate Remedies for Thinness   207

Chapter 10 Getting Slender by Surgery: The Most Drastic Approach to Getting Rid of Fat   222

STEP 4 HEALING THE PROBLEM   237

Chapter 11 Body-Mind: Re-creating an Essential Connection   239

Chapter 12 The Rebirth of Venus   254

EPILOGUE   263

Acknowledgments   267

Bibliography and Suggested Reading   271

Index   277

Foreword

From the days of Hippocrates, the father of medicine, who lived during the latter part of the fifth century B.C., to present-day molecular biology, humankind has gathered a staggering amount of knowledge about the human body. While the ancients spoke of the value of diet and ambulation as restorers of health and vitality, modern medicine is beginning to address the role of the hypothalamus and other parts of the brain in food intake regulation. Some of the great advances of the last hundred years have been in the area of nutrition. Many human nutritional requirements have been defined and many Nobel prizes awarded to the discoveries of the essential nutrients and the mechanisms of their interactions with life processes. The conquest of primary malnutrition, or at least the gathering of the know-how for such a conquest, is one of the highlights of this century.

It is apparent that despite the existence of a vast knowledge of nutrition, we in the United States have not been able to impart such knowledge to our own people, or even the guardians of the health of our people. A growing proportion of our people live in highly mechanized urban areas where the demands and opportunities for regular physical activity have diminished steadily. In this same environment, a variety of appetizing, calorically rich foods is increasingly available and readily procurable. The immense proliferation of mass communication has increased our awareness and consumption of supermarket foods. There are no signs of abatement in our relentless quest to please the palate while confined to our urban cages. The wisdom of the body calls for food through hunger and shuts off food intake through satiety. Such wisdom is bypassed through gluttony, not by choice but by force of habit. Our signals are crossed, and we succumb to the consequences: obesity, hypertension, diabetes, heart disease, stroke, and diminished physical fitness.

In 1894, Wilbur Atwater stated that "the power of a man to do work depends upon his nutrition. . . . A well fed man has strength of muscle and of brain, while a poorly nourished man has not." However, the distinguished American scientist did not foresee the day when more than 50 percent of Americans, ninety years later, would each harbor 100,000 to 1,000,000 excess calories in the form of fat. Astrand and Rodahl, the Scandinavian authors of a book on work physiology, remind us that "higher animals are basically designed for mobility." The capacity to move our bodies by use of our own muscles, joints, and bones has diminished markedly. The hard-working muscle can increase the process of burning fuel (nutrients including fat) to more than fifty times the level of burning at rest. Such an enormous increase in the rate of burning of fuel should work in our favor and facilitate our attempt to take advantage of our versatility in activating our musculoskeletal endowment. Whatever the individual's capacity is for burning nutrients, it can be improved upon by technique, motivation, tactics, training, and overriding the inactivity imposed on us by our own society. We can choose the activity that suits us best.

The laws of thermodynamics are still valid when it comes to energy balance. When energy intake is below energy expenditure, we lose weight. When energy intake exceeds expenditure, we gain weight. Thus the prescription for losing weight is not new to us. To abide by it requires a lifetime struggle aided by understanding and a sense of commitment. The mind must be tuned for moderation in eating, locomotion, mobility, action, fun, leanness, and good health.

Eugenia Chandris has given us much more than a personal account of her struggle with the Venus syndrome. Her book forms fascinating reading. Her experience with plastic surgery to restructure her bottom-heavy body led her not to revelations and dreams, but to a journey of research into obesity, adipose tissue, fat cell size, fat cell number, diet, calories, exercise, and motivation. She has condensed for us the knowledge about obesity and leanness interwoven with her own experience that led her, to quote her own words, to make a "lifelong commitment to knowing what you want." Her account should help make us immune to the bombardments we receive from blatant claims of a plethora of diet books. It is refreshing to witness her "work in progress." If it takes us twenty years to harbor twenty pounds of excess fat, we cannot expect to unload it in twenty days. The wheels of fatness move slowly and so do the wheels of leanness. The "inescapable reality of the energy equation" can be understood, accepted, and woven into a lifestyle characterized by freedom. To paraphrase Plato, this book teaches us not to be like cattle, with our eyes always looking down and our heads stooping to the earth (the dining table), so we fatten and feed and lust. Our eyes should look up, and our bodies should move on, toiling upward.

Eugenia Chandris started her voyage of discovery in search of the perfect body. While in other times, women with most of their fat on the hips and thighs inspired the artistic creativity of a Renoir or a Rubens, and while women today with the same body are looked upon with admiration in other cultures, Ms. Chandris sought to free herself from a body that "wants to change." While, in her case, the trigger for such a change was plastic surgery, this book discusses other treatments for obesity in other regions of the body. Thus, not only women but also men will find this book beneficial and relevant to their aspirations for leanness. "The way to a beautiful body is the result of an informed and utterly decided mind." Once the mind is made up, the ingredients for success will be a mystery no longer.

SAMI A. HASHIM, M.D.
Chief, Division of Metabolism and Nutrition
St. Luke's-Roosevelt Hospital Center
New York City
April 1984

Preface

I was told that when you write a book, there comes a time when the book takes on a life of its own. It chooses its form independently and seems to select the style of its choice. I began this book rather like an investigative autobiography. I wanted to share my experiences of having a disproportionate or bottom-heavy shape, and more important, to discover the reasons why women deposit fat on the hips and thighs. My original intention was to allow women with this shape to identify with me and to add a personal, human dimension to a medical problem.

The book, however, had slightly different although not incompatible ideas. While in my heart I knew I wanted to retain my understanding approach to this problem, my writing also wanted to pursue a factual path. All of a sudden I found myself researching all the medical facts on fat, attending conferences, and searching out the real specialists in the field. I was hungry to know what makes us fat, particularly in certain places. I could no longer tolerate old wives' tales on obesity. I wanted the truth and nothing less. *Obesity is a disease* and its mechanism is hard to follow. Yet refusing even to look at the complexity of overweight does not help, it simply makes us more blind to the solutions. Only by understanding the body will we ever attain the power to transform it.

From then onward, the book essentially wrote itself. It seemed to insist to me that it was more than just the sharing of a figure problem; it sympathized, but more important it answered questions. It was a chronicle of my inner and outer development as well as a definitive volume on obesity itself; a book containing almost everything I, and I hope, you, the reader, ever wanted to know about FAT.

E.C.

Prologue

1

A Voyage of Discovery

On My Way

The Venus syndrome is about fat on the hips and thighs. The most
ancient figures of women, known as the Venus statues, demonstrate
this bottom-heavy figure, and the problem has troubled women ever
since. For years I suffered because my figure was out of proportion.
My upper half was slim and shapely, my lower half much fatter.
Doctors and diet books were of no help whatsoever: their perpetual
advice was weight loss, not improvement of shape. And so, alone,
I set out for a solution, or at least an explanation of why my body
was shaped this way. I no longer believe I have to be a prisoner
inside a body that wants to change. I now know what works and
what doesn't. I want you to know as well so you can save yourself
danger, pain, money, and heartbreak.

Fat people generally are accused of greed and laziness, yet the
bottom-heavy woman seems to pose a special target for ignorant
and nasty remarks. Not even a passing thought is given to hormonal
influence and genetic makeup, which are actually most to blame
for bottom-heaviness. Neither can such judgments possibly take into
account just how difficult it is to lose a pound of fat and how much
more difficult it is to lose it from the right places.

An Arranged Marriage

In the past few years, everyone has been writing about being fat
and suddenly becoming thin as if it were a simple transition instead
of a major biological change. Everyone includes diet doctors, feminists, diet gurus, psychiatrists, and fat people. The diet doctors tend
to blind you with scientific theory (sadly not always accurate), while
feminists blur the physical reality of being fat with abstruse sociologi-

cal implications. The vision of diet gurus is dangerously blinkered by devotion to a particular (usually unbalanced) diet, and psychiatrists, even though they may have some ingenious ideas, tend rarely to surface from their analytic theories and give helpful advice. That leaves us with the fat people—reformed and converted fat people, who will tell you how they became thin and how they will never eat too much and become fat again. Their zeal is impressive, but sometimes their overwhelming conviction can actually alienate the reader.

What we have then are books that are either academic or purely personal, with no marriage between the two. It is now time for such a union of fact with feeling, of precision with passion. I know what it feels like to be heavy, but pouring my heart out was not enough. I wanted women to identify with me, but I also wanted them to be helped. Drastic physical changes and conversions in eating habits cannot happen instantaneously. Any book that suggests that they can loses credibility.

If you seriously want to lose weight and keep it off, and if you really are committed to having a more proportionate shape, you should not expect overnight success. If you remember how long it took your body to arrive at its present weight, you will see that it will take time to lose weight. If you make unrealistic demands of your body, the only result will be disappointment. I am not suggesting that you despair and see the situation as hopeless; just that you respect your body and have patience. I now know that my mind can inspire my body to become just the way I want and can give me the energy to bring about those changes physically. Both shape and attitude can change.

This book is partly autobiography and also a work in progress; hence its immediacy and its conviction. Most diet books are set in the past; their secret formula has already been arrived at. They contemplate weight loss in retrospect. To realize the sort of body in which you can be happy is not a one-day project. It involves a lifelong commitment to knowing what you want, getting it, and maintaining it. The body cannot be seen as a finished product: there is always room for improvement. Perfection is not a static state. This book is not so much about having the ideal body as it is about the process of creating a body that suits you.

I started *The Venus Syndrome* hating my body. As the pages

progressed, the dislike intensified as I was examining my physical being so closely. This made writing doubly difficult. I was also nervously aware that writing is itself a hazard to someone with a weight and shape problem. The immobility it necessitates and the neurotic nibbling it induces can be dangerous. Imagine promoting a book about improving your figure when the creation of that book actually ruined it! As a result, most of these pages have been composed in gymnasiums and swimming pools, while chopping raw vegetables, walking my brother's Schnauzer through the park, and gasping for air in aerobics class. When the book was nearing completion, I was surprised to see how I had changed. Writing it had been an exorcism and a catharsis for me.

The Belief in Miracles

In dieting there are no quick fixes, but there *is* one instant solution. Give up the struggle; cease to think of it as a fight. Obesity can, to a degree, be psychosomatic, but by that I do not mean unreal or imaginary. I believe that the way our bodies are reflects the thoughts we have about ourselves. Of course physical factors such as genetics, hormones, and metabolism are certainly involved, but we are the sum of mind and body; the one dictates, the other acts out our thoughts.

The way most people approach dieting, they immediately alienate body from mind. Feeling victimized, they immediately think of suffering, effort, and denial. This is a major mistake. If you are motivated by some desperate emotion, your body will resist your designs, for it can only react to violence with violence. If your mind is stuck in failure, your fat stores will win the siege. I am emphasizing this mental aspect because I found that it *really* worked. When I relaxed about eating, I lost weight. After I became thinner, people congratulated me on having suffered so much. When I blithely announced that my weight loss was the physical result of the new way I felt about myself, they were cruelly surprised; their ideas of martyrdom and abstention had been seriously undermined. For years we have been indoctrinated to think that losing weight was hard and changing shape impossible. It will take a little more than five minutes to undo all that.

A Dieter's Odyssey: My Story

My father's family comes from Chios, a Greek island in the northern Aegean Sea. Eating is a Greek national hobby, but in Chios it is the only hobby. To the inhabitants of Chios, your fat is your beauty, and even though aesthetic views are changing, the average plump Chios woman would think it nonsensical to worry over calories or carbohydrate grams. If I had been raised there amid succulently sticky desserts or mounds of moussaka, instead of being ashamed of my curves I might have learned to appreciate them.

Instead, I was born and raised in England, and though my father held the traditional Greek belief that a daughter should grow up to be an attractive commodity on the marriage market, he also held the totally Western belief that to be attractive was to be thin. It is therefore hardly surprising that, from the moment I was born, my father wanted my diet to be strictly supervised. He was of the opinion, as so many people still are, that fat babies always become fat adults, and he knew that I had a genetic tendency to gain weight. This had to be avoided. I was, after all, his only daughter, primarily destined to be demure and decorative; the last things I should be developing were my brain cells and my fat cells. Little girls may be made of sugar and spice, but they certainly shouldn't be eating either!

My future as an ornament seemed assured until one trying summer when I was eight years old. At that time I began to feel very insecure about growing up. There was no way I could express these fears or even understand them. So I repressed them, stuffing them deep inside the body's tissues. My eating habits went haywire. I promptly forgot my routine of a balanced diet in favor of life's goodies, especially grilled cheese sandwiches and french fries. These I managed to obtain by blackmailing my Greek governess. As my compatriots have an inherent conviction that even the plumpest child is a potential victim of anorexia, the governess began stuffing me with high-calorie foods to get me to eat. As a result, I very soon resembled the human incarnation of a barrel, much to my parents' horror.

From the age of twelve, I was subjected to diets, doctors, and despair. I remember visiting a particularly unpleasant and senile diet doctor whose understanding of the fat child's psyche was pitifully inadequate. He presented me with a diet sheet and assured me that if I adhered to it I would be thin. I was very excited at this prospect and, with a few occasional lapses, stuck to the regimen. When I returned to the office I was informed that I had been cheating and that's why I hadn't lost much weight. The tall, maddeningly thin doctor looked down his nose at me with glaring disapproval. In front of him, my mother, and the whole world, I felt accused and a failure. My crime was greed and my punishment was eternal dietary vigilance. I shall never forget how I felt that day.

As if alimentary deprivation were not enough, twice a week I was whisked from school to see a ferocious Australian physiotherapist, who would either pummel me with massage and shed several pounds herself, or goad me through a marathon of exercises. How much I hated the whole treatment was reflected in the results. I lost weight and inches only to put them straight back on again. I did not believe in what I was doing; therefore it had no hope of working. I remember that at about the age of fourteen most of my "puppy fat" melted away. I was delighted until I discovered what was underneath it. Sometime during my overweight childhood and adolescence I had deposited a very obstinate layer of fat on the lower half of the body. Ridding myself of this was to become my obsession for the next ten years.

Of course, the best-known diagnosis for this lower body fat was and still is cellulite. Such was my fanatical belief in its existence that I persuaded my mother to take me to clinics in France and Switzerland that specialized in the problem. This is fairly common practice for young European girls whose futures run the risk of being ruined by fat thighs. The doctors or cosmetologists who run these lucrative concerns knead, pinch, and prod you to diagnose the presence of cellulite. They then mumble something about poor circulation and prescribe a variety of painful or ineffective (or both) remedies, such as injections or potions consisting of plant extracts. The only reduction that took place as a result of these visits was that of my mother's bank balance.

When I left school, I decided that once and for all I was going to lose a lot of weight, and with it my bottom-heavy figure problem. I checked myself into the metabolic ward of a leading London hospital and remained there for almost two months losing weight, my sense of reality, and to a small extent, my mind. After another two months on the same mercilessly low six-hundred-calorie diet and a total weight loss of forty pounds, I found myself with little energy except the nervous kind. I was certainly thin but I was also unhappy. I was constantly afraid of regaining weight and I always felt obsessive and out of control around food. Today I can appreciate this crash diet phase as a large stepping-stone on my way to more complete awareness of my body. It required unbelievable motivation, which I had. It showed me what I could achieve: control over my body. At that stage, however, the control had been achieved only by force and deprivation.

Even with such a dramatic reduction, my lower body remained as out of proportion as before. At first I was unwilling to admit this but only after several years of the yo-yo syndrome, losing and gaining those same forty pounds, did I realize something. A shape problem cannot be treated as a simple lose-a-few-pounds weight problem. To alter your shape you need to lose body fat. Drastic dieting may be effective for losing weight in a hurry, but this weight loss is not true fat loss. Also, losing weight suddenly and gaining it back just as quickly could be more detrimental to shape than maintaining your normal weight. Every time I regained weight, most of it went back onto my lower half. This caused a stretching and then shrinking of the skin that left permanent stretch marks and reduced the skin's elasticity. This problem becomes more serious the older you get.

I cannot recall exactly what made me decide to take the most important physical step in the transformation of the lower half of my body: the decision to have plastic surgery. I suppose it was the result of both negative and positive influences: frustration, impatience, and desperation that the problem was insoluble combined with increasing certainty about the way I wanted to look and live. If I had not had the surgery there would have been no book. I was lying flat on my back in a room on the sixth floor at St. Luke's Women's Hospital in New York City, immobilized by five and a half hours of surgery. Though my interest in the ceiling was considerably enlivened by the haphazard antics of a pink helium balloon attached to an enormous flower arrangement, I spent the first day feeling nothing but boredom and backache. Then the phone rang. A friend of mine, the beauty editor of a popular magazine, was calling to ask how I was. When she realized how restricted my movements were, she suggested that I occupy myself by keeping a daily diary of my recovery and write it up as an article afterward. I did this with dedication, little realizing that I was writing the basis of a book. I continued the diary during my recovery at home, documenting not only my physical progress but also my hopes and anxieties.

At first I planned to write an article on plastic surgery, or body sculpturing. However, as I worked, I found my attention being drawn primarily to examining *why* women are bottom-heavy, and so I found myself researching far beyond the scope of the original article.

My surgeon's office was in Manhattan, on East Sixty-seventh Street, where I would waddle every week. Feeling stiff, swathed in bandages and multiple layers of clothing against the bitter New York cold, I found it hard to visualize myself as the svelte and limber individual I wished to become. Dr. Stark would answer most of my questions while removing my stitches. In retrospect, it must have been an amusing scene: Dr. Stark extracting electric blue strands of thread while elaborating on surgical terminology and anatomical details, while I lay there scribbling the answers, my squeamishness overcome by fascination for what I was hearing.

"With all that you know now, Jeannie, I think you'd better write a book," Dr. Stark suggested. After a split second of uncertainty, I realized that that was what I had wanted to do from the beginning; to write a book entirely devoted to women who have most of their fat distributed below the waist. I wanted them to possess the knowledge I had not had before my operation.

Plastic surgery figures prominently in this book, but by no means is it advocated as the only way out. Diet and exercise play other and, I believe, more important roles. I came to realize this only gradually. I spent two and a half years after the surgery working on this book without dieting or exercising. Not surprisingly, I couldn't write a word. As I was researching fat, I was actually getting fatter. My body was stiff and out of condition. It seemed that my thighs, which were spilling farther and farther over my desk chair, were trying to give me a message. Stop studying, start moving, then the writing will come. A special invitation accelerated the process.

An exceptionally generous friend of mine organized a week's stay at the famous California spa The Golden Door. He made sure to invite only his corpulent acquaintances, so that we could all lose weight together, although a few sylphs were allowed to slip in, too, presumably as incentives. (Does envy raise the metabolic rate?) I was prepared for a relaxing program and a mild weight loss. Instead

I found myself hiking up mountains at a preposterous hour, dancing my way through aerobics class, lurching on the volleyball court, and uncomfortably contorting myself into yoga postures. My weight loss was fantastic, but more important still was the change in my eating and exercise habits and in the way I thought about myself. What was even more lasting was the visit I made to my own inner self, to that quiet place inside of me that knows I can achieve whatever I set my mind to. That was the real transformation process and you don't necessarily have to go to a health spa to achieve it. You can create your own supportive atmosphere, though beautiful surroundings sometimes do help. Wherever you choose to effect your transformation, understand that it happens first on a metaphysical level, and that the physical will then follow. The change will occur first in your thoughts, then in your habits, and then in your body. I assure you that this will be effortless, not because it will be easy but because you will want to do it. The way to a beautiful body is not through a powdered diet meal or twenty daily push-ups. It is most of all the result of an informed and utterly decided mind.

Make the care of your body a priority, but not an obsession. The society we live in today places looks above all else. However, once you realize that beauty is more a state of mind than of body, you can relax. Most of us have other things to do with our lives besides calisthenics and calorie-counting. I believe that things gradually are changing and that a more tolerant aesthetic perspective will be found: the eye of fashion will refocus, this time with more realism. All shapes and sizes will be respected and regarded as physical expressions of each individual. But we are the ones who will bring this about, by accepting our bodies right now as beautiful in their present state and as perfect in their imperfection. Only then can we work on them positively and improve them.

1

Analyzing the Problem

2

What Is the Venus Syndrome?

Venus, the Goddess of Fat?

You have probably guessed by now that *The Venus Syndrome* is neither science fiction thriller, pulsating novel, nor mythological fantasy. It is a book about fat, more specifically about fat on the lower half of the body. But why the divine reference? What can a goddess have to do with flab? Can someone as identified with beauty as Venus have any connection with the sagging, dimpled flesh we so dislike? Yes, she can, for it is our present-day eyes that judge the bottom-heavy figure so harshly. Prehistory did not.

The Venus figurines, from which the Venus syndrome gets its name, are the very first artistic representations of woman. The most famous example is the Venus of Willendorf. In fact Willendorf is a poor example of what some of her lesser-known sisters exhibited— extreme bottom-heaviness—for Willendorf is round all over. However, she was thought to be first of a series of Paleolithic figures fashioned between 30,000 and 20,000 B.C. All across Europe as far as Russia, female statues from other places, over a considerable time span, continued to exhibit this pronounced pear shape. Predynastic Egyptian figures are excellent examples. So are those from Crete, the Cycladic islands of Greece, from ancient Anatolia, northern Syria, Bulgaria, and Malta. They all show women with hugely fat hips and buttocks. There are usually hardly any facial details on the figurines, some of them have no arms, and in most the legs just taper off with no suggestion of feet or toes. The whole focus is on the swelling lower half and, in some cases, the breasts. Overwhelming rather than vulgar, the statues seem to be saying that all woman signifies is contained in this bulbous form, her essence encapsulated in a perfect, abundant roundness. *These* heavy hips and thighs offer no apology; they are a celebration. But of what? Art historians, archaeologists, and anthropologists still wonder.

I first heard the term "Venus syndrome" when I was examined by a well-known professor of metabolism at St. Mary's Hospital, Paddington, London. The connection between Venus and lower body fat seemed to me a vague one until I began to research and reflect on it. Not until much later did I begin to appreciate and understand that the Venuses perfectly exemplify women's most common figure complaint. It is a deserved acknowledgment and no coincidence that the lectures given at each International Conference on Obesity are named Willendorf Lectures.

Art is a notoriously unreliable historian of the feminine shape. How do we know if the artists are using their eyes, their memory, their imagination, their desire, or perhaps all four? We can safely suppose that from the onset of Christian morality until the Mannerist period, a naked female model was inaccessible to the artist, who instead would have had to rely on young boys, making the necessary anatomical conversions. The society of our primitive sculptors, however, had no such restrictions; nudity is still common in tribal communities today. How do we know, however, what these primordial figures of women really represent? An ordinary woman? A goddess of a cult of fertility? Or the Paleolithic equivalent of a Playboy bunny?

An interpretation of the Venuses involves asking a fundamental question: what makes a woman attractive—her erotic desirability or her capacity to be fertile? One cannot help wondering why the two never seem to be mutually inclusive, but perhaps in these very first statues of women they were. (Some evidence does actually negate this view, showing that tribal societies did not equate sex with procreation.) In examining the original artistic representation of woman, we get a chance to analyze why women ever got fat in the first place.

Back to the Beginning: The Origins of the Curve

We live in a fat-hating age, but we fail to realize one very comforting factor: humans are naturally fat. That is what differentiates us, not only from the apes, but from most other animals. Even better news is that women are designed to be even fatter than men.

Why and when this fat developed remains uncertain. While any anthropologist lucky enough to find a fossil can deduce something

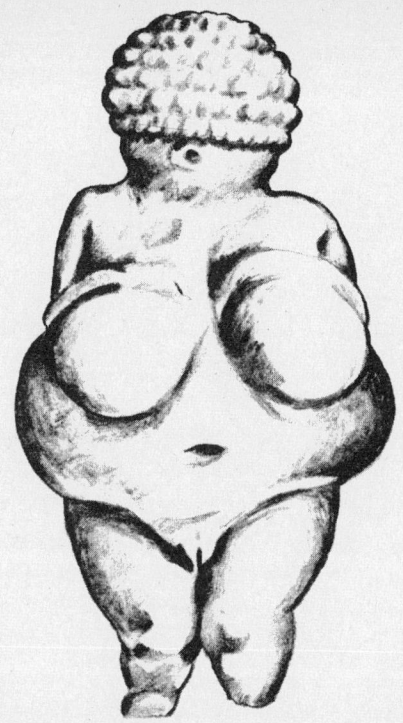

Figure 1 THE VENUS OF WILLENDORF

Limestone statuette (30,000–25,000 B.C.). One of the earliest artistic representations of the female form and regarded as a fertility symbol.

from the bony evidence, evidence of plumpness has long since disappeared. Possibly humans developed a layer of fat under the skin to
survive. In prehistoric society, with no organized agriculture, food
supplies depended on the hunt and would be sporadic. Moreover,
in climates that may have been more intemperate than the ones
we know today, when clothing was far less plentiful, fat would have
been deposited as a climatic safeguard.

Another favorite justification for female fat is that it helped women
perpetuate the race. Having enough fat is still of indisputable biological value. Onset of menstruation depends largely on the weight and
body fat of an adolescent girl. There is thought to be a threshold
weight under which women cannot become pregnant, and to lactate

adequately a woman must be able to produce from her energy stores enough to feed a baby and to maintain her own health. It would be wrong, however, to draw the conclusion that to be able to deliver children easily you must have the Venus syndrome. The shape of the bony pelvis, not the visible width of the hips, determines an easy birth.

Fat and fertility, however, are not necessarily friends. We are not sure that women's fatty layers developed to increase the birth rate; her scrawny relatives the monkeys were still managing to reproduce without them. Moreover, it is not likely that fertility was much revered in Paleolithic hunting society. Too many children would mean too many mouths to feed, and in a society that may have had to shift homes frequently, infants would have hampered the proceedings. A plump woman would be more popular and important as a survivor in times of famine and disease than as a baby machine.

Why then should women have developed a hip flask of stored food? Certain species of migratory birds deposit fat around the wings. Is this to make them aerodynamically efficient or because, as the fat stores are near the wings, they are particularly available to the circulation and can be drawn on more effectively? Why does the camel have its hump in the middle of its back, why do lizards and hibernating rodents store fat in their tails, and why is the rare South African fat-tailed sheep so named? There are other fascinating cases: the buffalo stores fat on its neck and so does the giraffe, presumably because of the length of the neck. The gorilla also uses this place, but does so to look threatening. The shark, on the other hand, keeps its fat reserves in the liver.

In most cases we can only guess at this evolutionary selection. Yet if the rule is efficiency, and an airplane's gasoline tanks are in the most important part, the wings, what is practical about a woman's hips and behind? If fat on a woman's lower half is a source of energy during pregnancy, could its proximity to the womb be of any help? Recent evidence suggests that during pregnancy and lactation, fat on the hips and thighs is more easily mobilized and might be specifically reserved for these purposes. Or perhaps the buttocks are a good place to store fat because they are, so to speak, out of the way and do not impede movement.

Another interesting explanation for the arrangement of female fat is a sexual one. Some anthropologists suggest that a woman's curves served as powerful sexual signs. Undoubtedly even today, most men would agree that a well-rounded figure has much more touch appeal than a very thin one.

Another fascinating theory suggests that during a prehistoric flood we were forced to adapt to life in the water. Humans lost their fur, developed a fatty layer for increased buoyancy and heat insulation, and began to mate face to face, belly to belly, as marine mammals do. In this case the development of fat for survival would naturally have led to a change in sexual preferences.

Fat Loses Its Popularity: When and Why

We may well wonder what happened to change people's minds and make them reject flesh and worship bone. It could have been the advent of Christianity, when the appearance of the Virgin Mary abolished mother earth. The change could also be attributed to that unfortunately vague principle, the socioeconomic factor. After the Neolithic period, with the arrival of agriculture, the hunting society gave way to a peasant culture, and mastery over the soil ensured that food supplies were comparatively regular. With this new and more self-assured society came class distinction: separation between those who owned the land and those who worked it. The owners wanted to look as different from the workers as possible. Natural selection and environmental influence had determined that the typical peasant woman was stocky, robust, and had a hardy, dark skin. Therefore, the land-owning class wanted their women to look just the opposite: pale, thin, and fragile.

An analogous example of uselessness is the Chinese foot-binding tradition, which ceased completely only at the beginning of the century. Tiny feet became the focal point of a sexual obsession far beyond a mere fetish. They were the body's most sexually exciting part and therefore veiled from view. The wife of a mandarin would not only not *need* to work, she would be rendered incapable of working and probably of walking also. Back in the West, with the advent of a more sophisticated society, fat began to lose its following and to be regarded as the mark of a primitive taste in beauty. Around this time, in the eleventh and twelfth centuries, women's clothes began to be laced in at the waist, indicating an increasing awareness

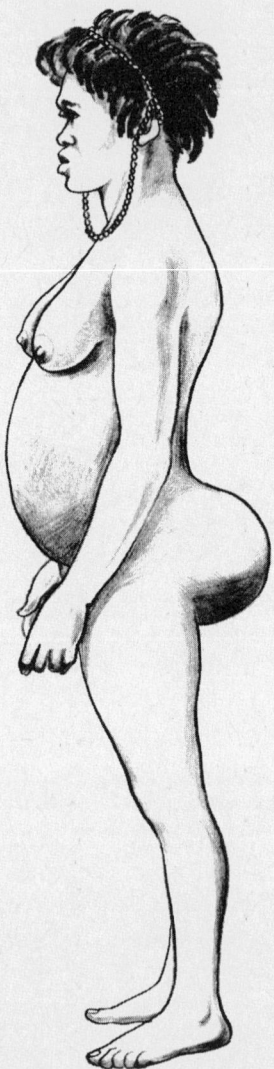

Figure 2 FIGURE OF A HOTTENTOT OR BUSHMAN
OF THE KALAHARI DESERT IN SOUTHWESTERN AFRICA

The excessive accumulation of fat on the buttocks causes a shelflike protru-
sion known as *steatopygia*.

of body curves and contours. Over the centuries the popularity of body curves and contours fluctuated. It was not that the shapeliness of a woman's body became unpopular but rather that taste changed continuously as to where the curves should be. In the nineteenth century the waist had to measure a merciless eighteen inches. Later it was allowed to relax, but bosoms and hips tended to become smaller. Only with the emergence of abnormally thin fashion models in the late 1960s did absolute skinniness become the rule. A refreshing example of a society where fat is still popular is the Hottentots in the Kalahari Desert in southwestern Africa. These people have always prized fat on the hips, thighs, and buttocks. Both the men *and* the women have buttocks that protrude so much as to form a shelf composed entirely of fat. This is known as *steatopygia* (meaning, in Greek, fat on the behind). The posterior shelf can become so large that objects can be balanced on it. Hottentot men have been known to line up their women and choose as a bride whichever woman protruded farthest from behind. In certain parts of Nigeria, girls who are to be married are closeted in fattening rooms where they are fed vast amounts of high-calorie food for several months. The girls are massaged frequently with fragrant oils and become extremely lethargic. Moreover, their cramped quarters are deliberately designed to keep them from exercising, and, consequently, they emerge very plump.

We probably consider the ritual admiration of fat in these parts of Africa primitive and absurd. We think of Western society as advanced and refined because we prefer thinness. Even now we are still suffering from the drastic effects of the development of agriculture and class distinction in favor of a hunting and tribal society. As absurd as the Hottentots may seem, it seems even more absurd in our "modern" society that there is no room to tolerate what for some women is their natural shape, even after weight loss and improvement of muscle tone.

Women with wide hips are characteristically viewed as good prospects for breeding purposes instead of attractive and sexual. Just like Paleolithic Venus statues, bottom-heavy women can be both. Yet in so many cases a man wants to be seen with a thin model and wants to marry a sensible, plainer, and sometimes fatter woman. The Greeks (some of whom to this day tend to do exactly that) were the first "civilized" society to categorize women into wives for procreation, concubines for everyday needs, and hetaerae for witty conversation as well as sexual fun. Yet the root from which the Greek word for woman, *gyneka,* comes betrays what they thought was woman's fundamental role. *Gyne-* means bearer of children.

This schism between women's roles and our consequent inability to think of ourselves as femme fatale *and* mother earth may be responsible for our yearnings and our dissatisfactions with our bodies. The sad truth is that women, in general, do not like their bodies, however slim they may look to others, and find it especially hard to cope with a shape like the Venus syndrome. The anthropological picture indicates to us that nature prompted women to deposit fat and that men's attraction to it was subsequently engendered. Now the picture is dramatically reversed. We, as women, tend to think that skinniness is preferred, but nature cannot be expected to cater to society's whims in a chronological instant. It took many millennia for the human body to evolve. The deposition of the subcutaneous fat layer was part of that evolution. Consequently, it cannot disappear overnight.

A Much-Neglected Problem

If every time you look down at your thighs, you feel like quoting the following line from *Hamlet,* probably you have the Venus syndrome. For women with this kind of figure, the tragic hero's lament, "O, that this too too solid flesh would melt," is directed most vehemently toward the lower half of their body.

With bookstores positively bulging with volumes on weight and diet, I find it amazing that no serious book has yet paid any amount of attention to explaining why some of us have too much localized fat. Most people, especially women, are interested not so much in losing fat as in losing it from the right places. It is not really surprising that so little has been written about lower body fat, for until recently relatively little has been known about it. When I interviewed doctors about fat on the hips and thighs, they were as interested and mystified as I was, but unable to offer me many answers on the causes or the treatment of the Venus syndrome. The answers that doctors could not provide I discovered from personal experience and from observing and interviewing women with this shape. I am glad to say that by the time I was finishing this book, the attention of many leading research centers for obesity began to focus on fat distribution. *The conclusion of my research is that weight is not the only, and in the case of many women, the real problem: therefore dieting alone is not an adequate cure. There is more to it than that. The issue we should really examine is shape.* So why are some women bottom-heavy?

The Heredity Factor and Racial Characteristics

The role of genetics in overall obesity is not yet fully understood. It would thus be even more difficult to trace the influence of genes on fat distribution. However, that influence is undeniable: the Venus syndrome is most often apparent in mothers, daughters, and grand-daughters. It is also true that women of certain nationalities and cultures have a far greater tendency to put on weight below the waist. Examples are women from Mediterranean countries such as Greece, Italy, and Spain, and Jewish women.

Perhaps over the years this shape has assumed a cultural signifi-cance. The Western obsession with thinness has permeated the Medi-terranean and Jewish aesthetic consciousness, but these societies are still to a great extent matriarchal. The bossy and obsessive Jewish/Greek/Italian mama is, by definition, fat. The women in these societ-ies tend to be "mother goddesses" in that they often have large families and are very protective of and assertive with their children. The racial tendency for bottom-heaviness seems to coincide with the ethnic image of the domineering mother. Similarly, in ancient times it was the earth mother that all people worshiped, and her fearsome figure was always shown as bottom-heavy, emphasizing her earthy domain.

Posture and the Spine

Posture has a peripheral influence on fat distribution. Almost all black women have an inward curvature of their lumbar (lower back) vertebrae. This causes them to have a "sway" back, with a protruding abdomen and a thrust-out behind. Many white women also have this posture, which is encouraged by wearing high heels. Whether this spinal structure is a cause of bottom-heaviness has not been precisely determined, but it is bound to exert pressure on the lower back and pelvic joint and could possibly affect circulation.

A Question of Hormones

Both sexes are composites of male and female hormones, but naturally in women female ones are most prevalent. When a girl reaches puberty, sex hormones such as estrogen cause her to develop curves and to get heavier on the lower half. Although estrogen is related to the production of fat in general, evidence suggests that it favors lower body distribution. Postmenopausal women, however, who secrete less estrogen, tend to develop a male pattern of fat distribution around the stomach, arms, and upper body. One common belief is that the sex hormones encourage the deposition of fat on the lower half to cushion and protect the reproductive organs; however, there has been some disagreement about this and the answer is still unclear. Scanning techniques that are now being used to estimate body fat show that women tend to have less fat around their internal organs than men.

In exceptional cases, when women are suffering from rare diseases of the endocrine (hormone) system, their upper half wastes away and the lower half becomes enormous. *Most women with the Venus syndrome are not suffering from some such disease.* It is far more likely, in pear-shaped women, that the tissues of the lower half of the body themselves seem to attract fat. There are several possible explanations. Fat in the thighs may be used up at a slower rate than fat elsewhere. Second, there may be regional differences in blood circulation, which may affect the tissue. Or the tissue itself may have a particular capacity for fat storage irrespective of the blood supply of the surrounding tissue.

An amazing case of "transferred fat" illustrates this. A twelve-year-old girl lost the skin off the top of her hand from a burn. A skin graft, with tissue taken from her abdomen, was performed on her hand. When the woman reached middle age, her abdomen became fat. The hand with the graft that had been transplanted so many years before fattened also and became hideously distended, like a boxing glove. The fat tissue in the skin graft was behaving exactly like the fat in its original site, the abdomen, and acting independently of the tissue in the hand to which it had been moved. In other words, fat seems to have a mind of its own. Or at least it looked that way in 1916, when this phenomenal case was reported. In Chapter 3, we shall be looking at some other fat cell transplants performed more recently.

A Safer and More Natural Shape

Fat distribution is not only an aesthetic matter, it can actually determine to which diseases you are prone. Top-heavy people tend to suffer more from high blood pressure, atherosclerosis, and diabetes; bottom-heavy people from poor circulation, underdeveloped muscles, and water retention. Bottom-heavies have a distinct advantage when it comes to diabetes. According to a recent study by Dr. Ahmed Kissebah and his colleagues at the Medical College, Wisconsin, top-heavy people have larger fat cells than the pear-shaped. Consequently, these cells have fewer insulin receptors on their surface, and thus their sensitivity to insulin is greatly reduced. To compensate, the body makes more insulin. A vicious cycle is thus set up, which is what causes the diabetes. Lower body fat, because it is stored in more numerous and smaller cells, with a greater supply of insulin receptors, is thus considered a more natural, safer form of obesity.

Though genetics, hormones, and the behavior of fat tissue itself are chiefly responsible for the Venus syndrome, to blame them entirely would be to fall prey to the trap of feeling victimized. Physiological factors do much, but they require our cooperation. For instance, most women discover they are bottom-heavy after they have gained weight, either at adolescence, as I did, or during pregnancy. When they do lose some of it, stubborn fat clings to the hips and thighs and refuses to be lost. It would be interesting to see if a woman who *does* have a history of the Venus syndrome in her family and who didn't suddenly gain weight would eventually develop it. It is possible she would, maybe during pregnancy, even without excessive weight gain. Moreover, a sedentary lifestyle certainly does not help bottom-heaviness. Lack of physical activity leads to weight gain and causes stiffness and immobility in the legs and hips. It is important to understand that eating patterns and lifestyle can work for and against latent tendencies to bottom-heaviness.

The Venus Syndrome: What It Is and What It Isn't

There are plenty of "authorities" who have very fanciful ideas about what is really ordinary fat on the hips and thighs. Even more hazardous to a woman with heavy hips are the many so-called specialists, doctors who claim to know everything about a subject that has baffled the real fat experts for years. To protect everyone from dangerous quacks and eventual bankruptcy, it is time the truth is told. Fat on a woman's lower half is precisely that, fat and nothing else. Researchers are not sure why some women deposit fat on their hips and legs, but they are sure about *what* they are depositing. Lower body fat is not water retention, a blockage in the circulation, dropped bowels, or cellulite. Let us see why.

First, the water retention myth. Fat on the thighs and buttocks has a dimpled appearance. It ripples like waves because it is oily and liquid, not solid. Water can be lost by sweating, by wearing plastic exercise suits, by taking saunas and Turkish baths, even by having the skin pressed with a steaming hot iron (believe me, I've even tried *that*). Fat cannot be lost in any of these ways; it cannot pass out of the pores of the skin. The body can only lose fat by burning it up internally. Because of gravity, any retained fluid tends to collect in the lower body, and this can be more of a problem for bottom-heavy women. Even though water retention can often be a symptom of lower body obesity, it is not its cause.

Now for the blocked circulation theory. If your circulation were blocked in the lower half or any other part of your body, your problem wouldn't be fat legs, it would be death. A blockage in the circulation causes the tissues to be deprived of oxygen and prevents the removal of toxic waste products. If your body is loaded with enough toxins that it cannot get rid of, you die. A sluggish circulation is a different matter. It could be either a contributory cause or a result of bottom-heaviness. Having heavy legs and sitting for long periods does not help either your circulation or your lymphatic drainage system, the network through which body fluids flow. However, circulation problems generally cannot be the cause of fat deposition.

The third supposed cause of bottom-heaviness is the most far-fetched. According to some doctors, it sometimes happens that the large intestine, the colon, suffers a ptosis; it falls from its correct position. This can cause disorders of the intestine and of the reproductive organs. The way it supposedly contributes to bottom-heaviness is by putting pressure on the arteries in the groin and impeding circulation in the legs. As we know, this has no real effect on fat distribution. Thousands, perhaps millions of women are bottom-heavy. It seems logical to assume that most of these women are perfectly healthy, they just have more fat below the waist than above it. A very small minority may have serious medical problems, but for the rest, such imaginative causes as these do not apply.

Cellulite

By far the best-known and most exotic diagnosis of lower body fat is cellulite. This has been eagerly promoted by magazine articles, a whole range of cosmetic products, and beauty clinics for several years now. A French word, "cellulite" has never been successfully translated and any attempt results in inaccuracy. Cellulitis, an extremely painful inflammation of the tissues, bears no resemblance whatsoever to it.

Cellulite is supposedly a condition caused by the thickening of the connective tissue that lies below the skin and above and around the layers of adipose tissue. The overgrown tissue forms gelatinous pockets that then trap toxic waste matter and water. The area is then supposed to become totally blocked off and the skin to take on a hard, lumpy appearance, which has been compared, ironically enough, to different kinds of food: "orange peel skin" or "the melted ice cream look."

The cellulite theory is not supported by any sound medical evidence. In fact, most doctors disdainfully deny the existence of cellulite: they say it is just ordinary fat. What is the truth?

The Reality Under the Skin
Studies done under a microscope, comparing fat from cellulite-prone areas with fat from other parts of the body, show that "cellulite" fat contained no greater amount of water than other fat cells, nor

did the area have thickened connective tissue. As for the claim that these tissues are laden with toxins, this is a prime example of how a cosmetic, money-making fad uses scientific information out of context. Our cells are constantly using up nutrients and oxygen. As a result they produce end products like carbon dioxide and urea, which are poisonous and must be eliminated. In that sense all our cells have a degree of toxicity. However, to suggest that cellulite areas contain a great amount of trapped toxins is ridiculous.

So why does the lower body look different? The distinguishing dimpled appearance of the fat tissues is caused by the way the fat cells are held in place by connective tissue and by the way that both the fat and the connective tissue are attached to the skin. On the thighs, fat is arranged in layers separated by connective tissue. The connective tissue acts as a kind of wine rack while the fat fills the spaces reserved for the wine bottles. In women the uppermost layer is thought to be arranged in compartments that are rectangular and upright. It looks as though these compartments are separated by strands of connective tissue, called septa, which run like a series of radial arches over and around them. At the top of the compartments, the septa attach themselves to the deepest skin layer, the corium. The fat cell compartments are also independently and directly connected to the corium by tiny extensions that protrude like little hooks into the upper areas of the corium and surround sweat glands and hair follicles. Thus the most recent theory that cellulite is caused by hair follicles has *some* truth in it.

What makes the skin on fat thighs look lumpy and dimpled and feel hard and granular is the amount of fat stored in the compartments and the amount of little hooks that dig in from the fat into the deeper skin levels, under the epidermis, the upper level. The familiar pitted appearance of the skin when subjected to a pinch test is referred to as the "mattress phenomenon" because it resembles the bumpy, stuffed surface of a mattress. This is all caused by the bunching up of fat under the skin. It is now thought that because women's fat is stored in such a way, and because their skin is finer in texture than men's, that 98 percent of "bumpy fat" sufferers are women. Their fat simply shows through more. As everyone has *some* fat on her thighs, even a small amount is evident, hence otherwise slender women's complaints that they have "fat" legs. In men the fat cell chambers are arranged at a tangent in a crisscross, honeycomb pat-

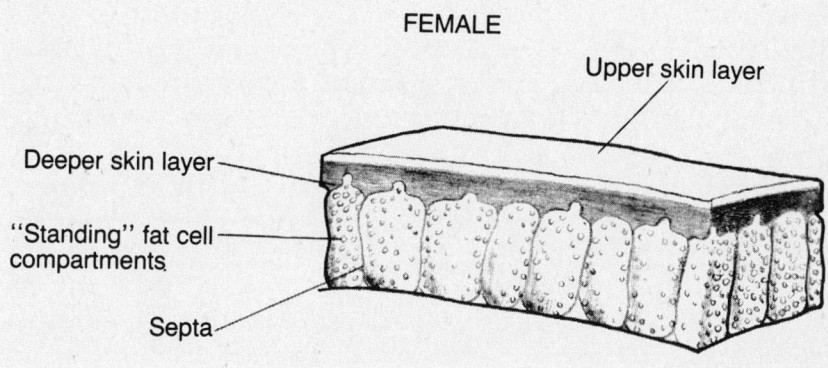

FEMALE

Upper skin layer

Deeper skin layer

"Standing" fat cell compartments

Septa

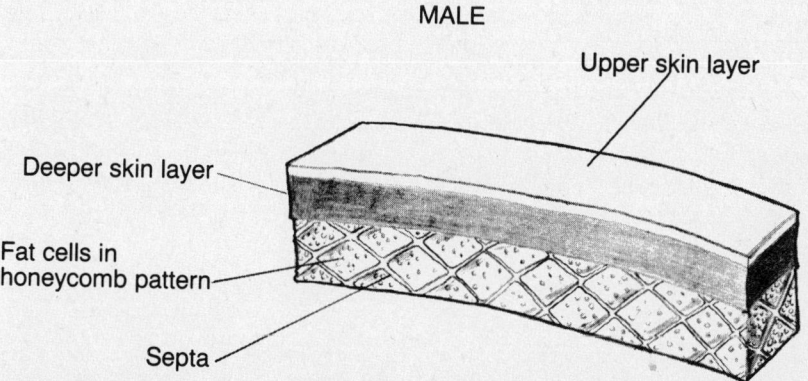

MALE

Upper skin layer

Deeper skin layer

Fat cells in honeycomb pattern

Septa

Figure 3 SEXUAL DIFFERENCES IN SKIN AND SUBCUTANEOUS FAT STRUCTURE

This figure gives us a much simplified view of the differences in skin and subcutaneous fat structure in the thigh between a woman (top) and a man (bottom). The woman's fat tissue is more plentiful and is actually attached to the deeper skin layer that overlies it. The fat, arranged in vertical compartments, protrudes upward into the skin layer, which is thus thinner than in men. When the fat compartments become full or when the skin is pinched, folds and furrows appear—the "mattress" phenomenon. In men, the fat cells are less numerous and instead of pushing upward are arranged in a honeycomb pattern. When the skin is pinched, only slight folds appear.

tern, so the problem does not exist as much; it takes more fatness in men to cause the mattress phenomenon. Men suffering from a deficiency of androgens (male hormones) and men who have been treated with female hormones for cancer sometimes have this type of fat because their skin structures have been affected hormonally. It is the subcutaneous fat structure and the skin texture that vary between the sexes rather than there being any fundamental differences between male and female fat cells.

Getting to Know Your Fat Stores

The theory just discussed, although not universally proven, seems to offer by far the most plausible explanation of the appearance of lower body fat. But before such specifics can be announced with confidence, we must know the basics.

The body has an average total of between 20 and 60 billion fat cells. These are located in many different parts of the body, not only the thighs. All fat is basically a yellow, oily substance. Fat is not restricted to certain areas of the body. Almost all cells have the capacity to store and release fat, except red blood cells and possibly nerve cells. Cells that have fat storage as a specific function (i.e., our fat cells) are collectively known as adipose tissue. They store fat in one large or several small storage droplets.

There are two basic kinds of fat. It is not yet clear which of our fat stores the body draws on when we lose weight, though gimmicky diets may suggest otherwise. Subcutaneous fat, the one we see, fight, pinch, and pummel, is by no means the only fat we have. It forms a layer underneath the skin, attached to it. Whether fat or thin, everyone has subcutaneous fat. Women tend to have more than men, though we don't know why.

Apart from its subcutaneous reserves, the body has many other ways of storing fat; for example, in the bone marrow and within the heart and the major organs and intestines. The only places that are fat-free are the eyelids, the scalp, the earlobes, the back of the hands and feet, the labia, and the penis and scrotum. There are a few storing places from which fat is never drawn: these are the eyeballs and soles of the feet, which are sort of locked deposits. Although we tend to think of fat as pinchable, a large percentage (though the exact amount is not known) of our adipose tissue is invisible, stored in internal depots that cushion some of the body's most important organs—the kidneys, the stomach, the heart, and the reproductive organs.

So far it has been impossible to trace which fat stores empty when we lose weight. The more researchers find out about where, how, and why our body stores fat, the nearer we will be to finding an answer. Progress in this field of research will probably also reward us with an answer about the female fat stores on the hips and thighs.

We have two different concepts to keep in mind when we think of fat. The first is body fat as a component of the body (body composition) and the second is the division of the body fat into various depots and different areas of the body (fat distribution). This selective deposition may serve a special function.

The Vital Facts of Body Composition—Ways of Measuring Fat Content

In the past fifty years or so science has been paying attention to the components that make up our physical body. Basically, these can be divided into fat and lean tissue, which includes muscle, vital organs, intestines, skin, water, and bone. At first this may seem of merely anatomical interest, but, in fact, the assessment of body composition is a far more important criterion for judging obesity than weight. Obesity is characterized not by excessive weight but by excess fat, even though when a person gains weight he or she will gain some lean tissue as well as fat. An athlete may weigh as much as a fat person, but his or her weight is not the result of the percentage of body fat but rather of the amount of muscle mass. The athlete therefore does not look fat.

It is not that muscle weighs more than fat—a pound of fat weighs the same as a pound of muscle. It is rather that muscle as lean tissue has a greater density than body fat. The equation used to evaluate body density is weight divided by volume. Say you have a pound of feathers. Each feather is low in weight, but together they take up a lot of room; that is, they have high volume. Low weight divided by high volume gives a low number. That is the density of a pound of feathers. On the other hand, a pound of lead would take up much less room than feathers, but for the volume it occupied would be heavier. A high weight divided by a low volume would produce a high figure. Lead has a higher density than feathers. In this exaggerated analogy, fat is the feathers and lead the lean tissue, although there is *much* less of a contrast between fat and lean tissue. Basically, pound for pound, fat occupies more space and lean tissue is more compact or tightly packed.

Body density has for a long time been one of the leading factors in assessment of body composition. Density actually determines floatability. In the water a person with a lot of fat will float because fat is less dense than lean tissue and causes buoyancy. It has for a long time been assumed that the fat and nonfat parts of the body had certain standard densities. These were worked out theoretically because, of course, it is impossible to investigate the total fat and lean content of a live person's body. However, recent studies on cadavers have not exactly corroborated these accepted figures. Many more studies will have to be done before the standard figures can be proved wrong, but if they are, it will completely turn the study of body composition upside down. Some scientists suggest that if what the cadaver studies show can be validated, the body will be shown to consist not of two components, fat and nonfat, but of four: fat, bone, muscle, and the remainder. Whatever the case, the studies on cadavers are unsettling evidence that the accepted figures may be wrong. If that is so, all the assessments made of whether people are too fat or not would be inaccurate.

One way of measuring body composition is by underwater weighing. Our body fat is what makes us float in the water because it is less dense than water. Our lean tissue, which is denser than water, makes us sink. To work out body density, we must have the values for body weight (in air) divided by body volume. What we are looking for here is volume.

The Greek mathematician Archimedes was the first to figure out that the volume of water that overflowed when he got into a full bath was equal to the volume of his submerged body. In that case one would only have to measure the volume of displaced water to measure body volume.

Another more practical way of assessing this is to measure the difference between a person's weight in air—on the scale—and his or her weight in water. Say a person weighed 90 kilograms (198 pounds) in air and 40 kilograms (88 pounds) in the water. The difference would be 50 kilograms (110 pounds). This difference in weight should equal the amount of water displaced, but the weight is easier to measure than the water. How do we turn this 50 kilograms of body weight loss in water into body volume? Because the density of water is 1, the weight of 1 gram of water equals the volume of 1 milliliter. As there are 1,000 grams to a kilogram and 1,000 milliliters to one liter, the weight loss in water of 50 kilograms represents a volume of 50 liters.

Once the volume and the body weight in air of a person are known, that person's density can be calculated by dividing weight by volume. By assuming the density values for pure fat and pure lean tissue to be 0.9 and 1.1, respectively, the percentage of fat in that person can be calculated from the total body density.

Another way of estimating body composition is to calculate the body's amount of water. Because around 70 percent of lean body mass is water, measuring the body's water tells you how much lean body mass there is and then the remainder must be fat. The amount of water in the body can be found out by drinking a known dose of heavy water (water that contains the stable isotope deuterium instead of ordinary hydrogen). This deuterium can be traced as it passes through the blood and urine. Thus the dilution of this abnormal heavy water in the body's own normal water allows one to measure total body water. Alternatively, lean body mass can be measured directly by a potassium test. An unusual, radioactive form of potassium exists in a constant minute amount in all the cells that constitute lean body mass and can be detected by a special machine called a total body potassium counter. Total body potassium relates to lean body mass.

The very latest way of estimating body fat is an electromagnetic machine, an invention similar to the machine used by butchers to estimate the ratio of fat to lean in joints of meat. Lean tissue has a greater electrical conductivity than fat. This is measured by the machine, which then goes on to calculate the amounts of lean tissue and then estimates fat. The electromagnetic counter is being developed by doctors working at St. Luke's Hospital's metabolic division in New York City.

All the above methods require complicated, expensive machinery that is not suitable for measurements taken outside the laboratory.

This being the case, several equations have been derived to enable total body fat to be calculated (not quite so accurately) for simpler measurements. The most commonly used are measurements of skin-fold thickness. This method uses a pronged instrument, calipers, which pinch the fat at selected sites (usually all on the upper body) and assess the skinfold thickness. Equations have been derived from skinfold thickness measurement *and* density values by underwater weighing of the same people so that skinfold thickness measurements alone can then be used to calculate percentage of body fat on other people when it is not possible to measure their density.

This method is becoming less and less popular as its disadvantages become more apparent. First, skinfold measurements may be reason-ably effective on normal weight and "ordinary" fat people, but in the very fat the skinfold measurement loses its accuracy. Second, if the skinfold thickness formula is based on the long-accepted body composition values that are now being questioned, the whole tabula-tion of skinfold thicknesses may be wrong also; some recent studies suggest this. Although standard information has been questioned, we do know the following facts about body composition:

MEN (average weight and height) have total body fat of around 15 percent; around 45 percent is muscle, 15 percent bone, and 25 percent accounts for the rest (organs, etc.).

WOMEN (average weight and height) have total body fat of around 27 percent; muscle accounts for 36 percent, 12 percent is bone, and the remainder is 25 percent.

These are *average* figures, although it is accepted that women do have more body fat than men. An average person's fat percentage can be anywhere from 14 to 28 percent. The fat could weigh between ten kilograms (twenty-two pounds) and fifteen kilograms (thirty-three pounds) but could go up to twenty kilograms (forty-four pounds). In a very obese person, the fat percentage and weight of fat could be much higher.

Getting to Know Your Curves: The Study of Fat Cell Distribution

Fat distribution is just scientific jargon for shape. It is a much more relevant criterion than weight and even body composition. Of course you care how much fat you have, but you care even more about *where* that fat is deposited. In research, far less attention has been paid to fat distribution than to body composition. The pattern of fat distribution has been, if anything, an interesting offshoot. More attention is now being paid to it. It has been discovered that women, even heavily trained athletes, have more limb fat than men, who tend to carry more weight on the torso. It has also been known for some time that men tend to develop a central pattern of fat distribution (on the torso, especially on the stomach) while women have peripheral distribution (more fat on the limbs).

One of the most exciting developments has been the use of computerized axial tomography (CAT scans) for assessment of quantity and deposition of body fat. This technique, principally designed to trace tumors, is now being used in England and Japan, among other places. One of their advantages is that CAT scans can measure minute increases, decreases, and shifts in placement in body fat during weight gain or loss and during growth. The results so far show that men do indeed have more fat on the central part of their body and that this fat is in the abdominal cavity; it is internal fat. Women have more fat on their limbs; on the upper arms, but especially the legs, in particular the thighs. This fat is subcutaneous, which seems to indicate that it is not deposited to protect the reproductive organs but is there for some other evolutionary reason.

Of course a CAT scan is an extremely expensive way to measure fat distribution. A more recent and more realistic method of assessing actual fat distribution is the fat distribution score. A group of researchers at the Clinical Research Centre, Middlesex, England, devised this score and used it on their patients. Patients were photographed in profile, and silhouettes drawn from the photographs. At standard sites, the waist and maximum thigh measurements were taken. The fat distribution score was based on the ratio of thigh to waist measurement. Bottom-heavy women, whose thighs were proportionately larger than their waists, got a lower ratio on the fat distribution scale. The opposite was true of top-heavy women, whose waists were proportionately larger than their thighs, hence they got a higher fat distribution score. Interestingly enough, although the women were measured before and after weight loss no significant changes in fat distribution were found. It looks as though shape cannot be that much affected by diet and weight loss, something

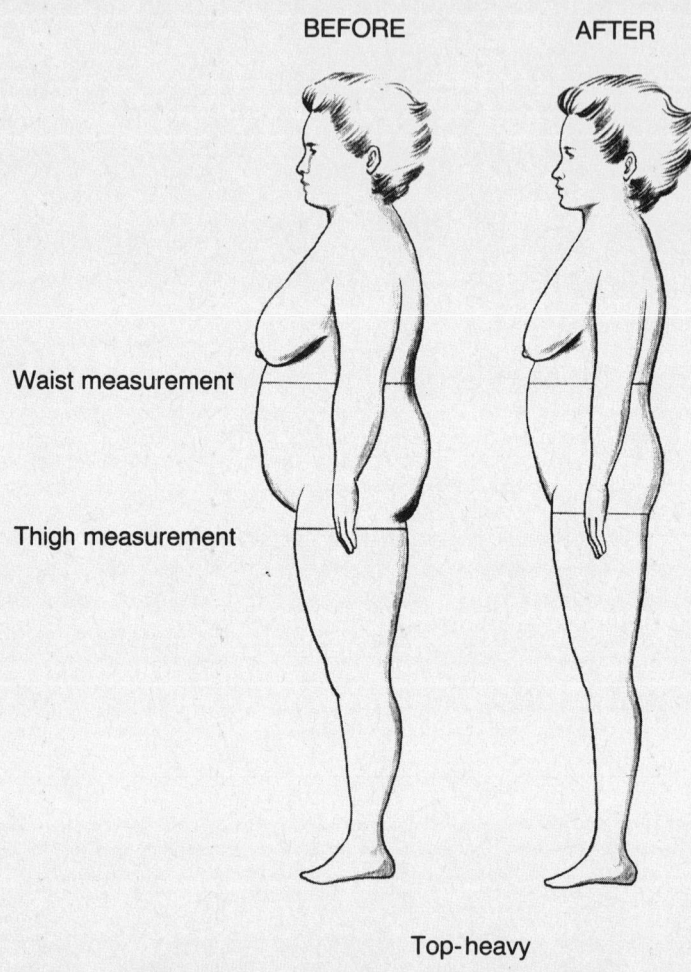

BEFORE   AFTER

Waist measurement

Thigh measurement

Top-heavy

FD score   5.4   4.3

Figure 4 WHAT THE FAT DISTRIBUTION SCORE LOOKS LIKE

Here is the silhouette of a top-heavy woman before and after weight loss. Her waist measurement is proportionately much larger than her thigh measurement even after losing weight, thus a high fat distribution score.

BEFORE   AFTER

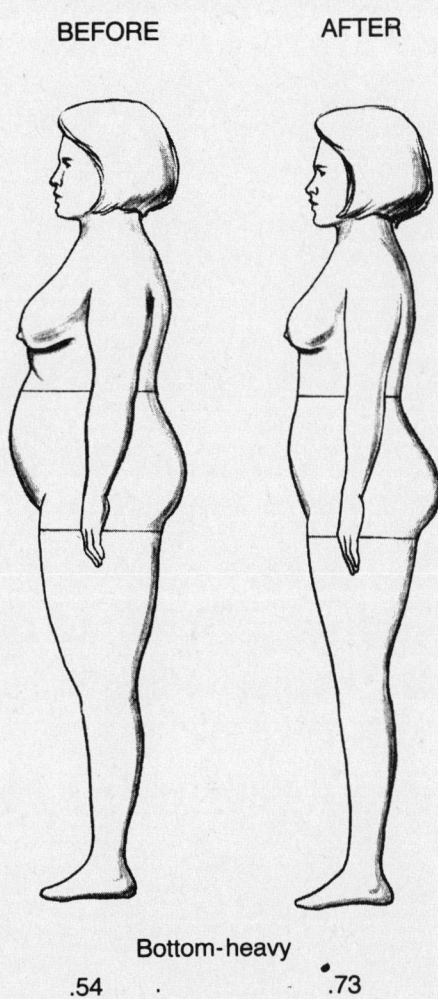

Bottom-heavy

.54   .73

The opposite is true of the bottom-heavy woman, whose thigh measurement remains high in comparison to her waist measurement, thus a consistently low fat distribution score.

to keep in mind before embarking on any dangerous and exaggerated
fad diets.

What You Really Should Be Watching Isn't Your Weight

When you dislike your body it is because it is too fat. But have
you really analyzed whether you are too heavy or too fat? For many
the answer is both, and an additional problem is that all the fat
seems to be concentrated on the lower half. When you have a figure
problem, there are three ingredients to it: weight, body fat content,
and fat distribution.

Our weight on the scale is a numerical assessment, it is not a
visual reality. After all, there are figures and figures. The one on
the scale tells us that we are overweight. The one in the mirror
tells us something else, something more real. That one shows us
our fat distribution. However heavy you may be, if you are fit and
your fat is well distributed, you do not *look* fat. If your fat is flabby
or unevenly distributed, you will *look* heavy even if the scale does
not indicate it.

Throughout this book, I shall be emphasizing the problem of shape
over weight. Weight is a consideration: it should not be an obsession.
Weight counts but it should not be an isolated criterion, your only
yardstick for assessing your figure. The aim is to lose body fat when
you lose weight and to *look* slimmer as well as be slimmer. People
pay a lot of attention to setting a target weight but a target shape
is just as important; it is much more individual and applies only
to you.

Treating the Problem Differently

What makes this book different from other fat books is its focus
on the specific problem of fat on the thighs. However, to know
about fat in certain spots, we have to know about fat everywhere.
To heal, we have to understand and to understand totally. The Venus
syndrome is the subject of this book but it is also a point of departure
for discussion of fat in general. This book really offers the story
on *obesity*.

We tend to assume that reducing the body is simply a question of discipline when it is really a matter of reversing the evolutionary dictates that cause our bodies to store fat: in short, of going against nature. I am not saying, "Do not reduce or improve your body," I am just saying, "Respect it." There was once a time when mind and body were in cooperation: when our thoughts about how our bodies should be did not contradict the reality of how our bodies were. Our aesthetic ideal today is an uncompromisingly emaciated, preadolescent girl, not a real woman. It is time that we begin admiring flesh and blood and no longer revere skin and bone. The next few chapters will illustrate how and why our bodies make fat. It will then be for you to decide why our minds, and the society created by them, blame us for doing so.

2

Understanding the Problem: All There Is to Know About Fat

3

Mechanics, Myths, and Miracles: Some Facts on Fat

At Last the Truth

To understand the process of depositing and storing fat, we have to understand a certain amount of biochemistry. In this book, while keeping the technical information as concise as possible, I have also avoided oversimplification because it benefits no one. To underestimate the complexity of overweight would be to lie. My intention throughout is to be as accurate and as comprehensive as I can be without essentially turning this into an academic textbook, useful but unreadable.

Thanks to the million-dollar diet industry, we are grossly misfed and misled. There is more fiction composed on matters metabolic than there is in Greek mythology, and fiction is harmful when it involves how we treat our bodies. The belief that fat is injurious to our health and that failure to lose weight merely indicates a lack of discipline has turned us into a guilt-ridden generation of anxious anorexics and amphetamine addicts.

Obesity and Overweight: Is There a Difference?

Almost everyone worries about his or her weight, but how do we draw the line between narcissistic obsession and genuine cause for concern? First of all, we have to define the problem we are talking about. Obesity and overweight are not the same.

Obesity is characterized by *excess* body fat. Overweight is a much more general definition and thus a much more inadequate one as it makes no distinction between fat, bone, or muscle. Weight is usually considered in relation to height, and often in connection with skeletal frame. Most diet books or magazines offer ideal weight charts for men and women. Finding your weight on these tables can be a depressing experience. Only when you have made vastly dishonest adjustments to your height and frame size can you arrive at a figure that resembles what you weigh. According to these tables you may be overweight, but that does not mean you are obese. If you are particularly muscular you will tend to weigh more, but if your body fat is not excessive, this "overweight" will not qualify you as obese. Some people may weigh a normal amount according to the tables yet look plump because they do not have much muscle. However, an extremely overweight person, who weighs more than fifty pounds over his or her presumed weight for height, will probably be obese also.

The weight tables are compiled by life insurance companies, whose statistics are responsible for giving fat a bad name. These companies compile statistics of the life expectancies of selected populations. They consider the effect of high-risk factors such as smoking and overweight. Their results show that fat people *may* have a higher risk of heart disease and fatal heart attacks, *may* have high blood pressure, and *may* be more prone to gall bladder disease, certain cancers, diabetes, and diseases of the joints. It is therefore *possible* but not certain that overweight people have a higher risk of dying younger. However, because these weight tables do not differentiate between overweight and overfat, their results are too often generalizations.

These insurance company statistics have recently been challenged. In 1983 a new study on ideal weight correctly pointed out that the previous statistics, compiled almost thirty years ago, were too severe. The new study suggested that most of the weights in the middle range of the charts could be increased by up to ten pounds. Many doctors, however, thought it was unwise to tell people they could weigh more because they feared that they would exceed the more relaxed limit and weigh too much. The insurance company evidence is contradictory. Some studies show that very fat and very lean people die younger and that the plumper people in the middle are healthy; other studies show even moderate overweight as a risk.

So how can you know if you are overweight or not? The best way of judging yourself as an individual is to think of how much you would like to weigh and can realistically achieve. Divide the

difference in pounds between your present weight and desired weight
by your present weight and multiply by 100. The figure you get is
the percentage by which you are "overweight," literally over the
weight you want. An example might be:

$$\left.\begin{array}{ll}\text{Present weight} & \text{150 pounds} \\ \text{Desired weight} & \text{135 pounds} \\ \text{Difference} & \text{15 pounds}\end{array}\right\} \quad \frac{15}{150} \text{ X } 100 = 10\%$$

Taking the Problem Seriously

The reason that there is such a hungry market for diets is that
none of them works. Yet nobody is willing to believe this. Delusion
after all is better than despair. That all commercial diets are useless
may be a bitter pill to swallow, but once it is, the problem of being
fat will be understood, accepted, and perhaps even solved. Obesity
is a *disease,* not merely a cosmetic nuisance, aesthetic offense, or
temporary condition. A disease to which there is no known cure.
Dieting may reduce the *symptom* of obesity, excess fat, but it does
nothing to cure what causes this excess fat. Any cure is impossible
when the cause or causes are unknown. Obesity is a chronic disease;
one becomes fat over a long period. Therefore any reduction will
take as long, if not longer, if it is to be permanent. While science
has finally recognized the severity of the problem, we, the general
public, persist in assuming that obesity is the result of greed, laziness,
and lack of willpower.

This misconception has stigmatized overweight people in our society to an inhuman degree. Bias is apparent even in the words used
to discuss obesity. *"Over*weight," *"excess* weight," *"over*eating" all
have quantitive judgments attached. For the sake of accuracy and
conciseness the English language forces me to use them, but keep
in mind that I do so in metaphorical quotation marks. To avoid
using awkward alternatives, I often use "fat" here to describe people
with either weight or shape problems or both. As an adjective it is
accurate; it is, after all, only society that has made it a dirty word.

In one of my interviews at St. Luke's Hospital, New York City,
with Dr. Hashim, a brilliant doctor of metabolism and a good friend,
he read out a startling fact from an advertisement he had received

through the mail. According to the ad, for every pound of excess
fat you carry, your body has to make an extra two hundred miles
of capillaries. A wave of disgust spread through me as I thought
of all the avenues and boulevards of little blood vessels *my* poor
body had had to lay down because of my greed and careless eating
habits. My self-judgment flared and once more I guiltily made a
resolution to purge and punish my body for the excesses I had inflicted
on it. Isn't that how most veteran dieters return again to the tortuous
path of semistarvation, through guilt and panic rather than positive
resolve?

I fled to my next interview, with Dr. John Kral, a world authority
on obesity and stomach and intestinal surgery. Once again I became
judgmental when I asked him what the point was of people having
stomach surgery if they continuously overeat, for surgery would not
cure the actual behavioral problem of gluttony. His reaction was
swift in defense of the obese. He made me see the complexity of
overweight and comprehend that gluttony itself may be a condition
caused by obesity rather than an indication of a lack of willpower.
He pointed out that what was missing was a book that took the
trouble to classify the different types of obesity that existed and
dispel the notion that overeating is the sole cause of overweight.
He asked me if I was going to include such a discussion in my
book. His commitment to dispelling that notion was infectious; I
gave my promise to do so.

Obesity: One Disease or Many?

Obesity is not purely the result of overeating: it may instead be
the cause. It is believed that there are three basic categories of obesity:
traumatic, genetic, and environmental, though of course these may
overlap. Traumatic obesity results from injury or damage to the
head. This can be induced in rats by operating on their brains and
thus altering their food intake. When we examine causes, we shall
notice the importance of the brain as the regulating headquarters
of our metabolism. In people traumatic obesity can be the result
of a serious head injury but can also exist even when there is no
obvious neurological defect. Biochemical abnormalities, once again
caused by physical or even severe emotional trauma, such as depres-

sion, can induce this type of obesity. A very common assumption is that endocrine disturbances, such as thyroid deficiency, cause obesity. Many overweight people would be relieved if the cause of overweight were that simple; however, such disturbances are probably responsible for only one in ten thousand cases.

Very little is known about genetic obesity, and unfortunately in human obesity no single gene can be isolated and blamed. Human obesity seems to be the result of several genetic conditions. It has been much easier to study the influence of genetics on obesity in mice. By crossing certain species, scientists have created strains of genetically obese mice. However, this has brought them no closer to understanding how genes can cause obesity. Even though so little is known about genetic obesity, if a child has fat parents, or even just one fat parent, his or her chances of obesity are much greater.

Some of the most convincing evidence on genetics is to be found in Swedish twin studies. Twins, because of their genetic similarities, are ideal material for this kind of assessment. In this particular study, monozygotic twins, produced from the same egg and thus genetically identical, resembled each other much more in body weight and amount of fat than dizygotic twins, produced from different eggs. According to another report, even when twins separated, became adults, and led relatively different lives, most pairs showed a weight variance of less than five pounds. One particular pair of twins, however, who separated and had drastically different eating and activity patterns, showed a considerable weight difference. More proof of genetics as a cause of obesity comes from studies done on adopted children. These children resembled their natural parents far more in body weight and build than their adoptive parents, with whom they lived and whose eating habits they must have acquired.

Two major influences determine obesity: genetics and environment. Our cellular heritage is one thing and the way we live our lives another. It has proved almost impossible for researchers to extricate the effects of environment from those of heredity. The usually indistinguishable interaction of these two forces is best illustrated by the question of nationality. The reason that it is difficult to quantify ethnic influence on weight and shape is precisely because the relationship is obscured by the common eating habits of a nation. For instance, the Greeks may tend to be obese because of their high-calorie diet, rich in sugar and fats, and their cultural habit of offering food as a sign of hospitality. They may well tend to have genetic tendencies that are emphasized greatly by the high incidence of intermarriage, especially on the islands. Even though the evidence for genetic obesity seems strong, it would be wrong to reject environment. One study in particular, which looked at the fatness of married couples, showed not only that a fat husband tended to have a fat wife, and vice versa, but also that the weight changes of partners over a certain time were always similar and in the same direction.

Environmental obesity is obesity caused by our habits. Also known as dietary obesity, it is extremely complex to assess because of its interaction with genetics. Children with one or two fat parents not only have a genetic predisposition to obesity, they will also be picking up their parents' eating habits. In the assessment of environmental obesity it is tempting once again to assume that the main reason for obesity is overeating. This is not only unfair to the obese, it may also be incorrect. If obesity were caused simply by eating more, normal-weight people would become fat if they increased their food intake.

A famous experiment conducted with prisoners by Dr. Ethan Sims in Vermont attempted to do this. Fattening up nonobese people by stuffing them with food proved very difficult in some cases. Although all the prisoners were fed the same high amount of calories,* some gained much less weight than others. After the experiment, some prisoners reverted to their normal weights more quickly than others. Excessive overeating caused a temporary weight gain that could not be sustained by the normal-weight subjects once they ate *normally*— and by that I do not mean that they dieted.

At first scientists thought two separate types of defects caused obesity. The first was thought to be in the body's regulatory system. As far as we know the brain's center of appetite regulation is located in the hypothalamus, a part of the brain situated at the base of the pituitary gland. This center is also responsible for the maintenance

---

* The famous "calorie" featured in all diet books is a kilocalorie—a unit of one thousand calories. A kilocalorie is a unit of energy trapped within chemical bonds. As with all forms of energy, when released it gives off heat. A kilocalorie can raise the temperature of one kilogram (one liter) of water by one degree Celsius. When calories are referred to specifically, as with caloric amounts, the word should, strictly speaking, be written with a capital C to indicate that it is an abbreviation of kilocalories. As the word now appears everywhere with a small c, that is how it appears in this book.

of temperature, water balance, and determining mood and sexual libido. By means of this mechanism our energy intake and output are so balanced that, under normal circumstances, once we finish growing our weight fluctuates within a narrow range. Obesity could well be a disorder somewhere in the hypothalamus that disrupts this balance. A second possible cause of obesity is a disturbance of the metabolism of the fat tissue itself. Originally, researchers saw the two causes as separate, but they are now thought to interact.

I hope that this information has done something to dispel the frequently unfounded accusations of greed against fat people. It has not been proved that the obese eat a lot more than lean people. Studies conducted both in hospitals and with the aid of food diaries have produced nothing but a battery of contradictory results. The painful reality is that however little fat people overeat they gain weight. If obesity were as simple a problem as is popularly suggested, why do fat people do the very thing that is supposed to worsen it? After all, if you have a tendency to sunburn, you simply stay out of the sun. You can't give up eating completely, as you can smoking. You must learn to eat less, but why is this so hard? While most fat people blame themselves for lack of willpower, few realize that when they *say* they feel hungry, they may actually be right. Real hunger may be the core of the problem. What is it and where is it located?

Thoughts on Hunger

There are three basic lines of investigation on hunger. The first examines the physiological aspects; the role of the brain, nerves, etc., and the eating stimuli of which we are unaware. The third line of investigation pursues external or cognitive eating stimuli, of which we are constantly aware. Somewhere between the physiological and the cognitive, the bodily and the mental hunger stimuli, is appetite, the second line of investigation. Appetite is a psychosomatic condition in that it is stimulated by both body and mind hunger.

Physiological Stimuli
Using rats, researchers were able some time ago to identify a hunger and a satiety center in the hypothalamus. In rats these are fairly

distinct and have been proved to influence eating behavior. In people, however, there is always the possibility that these two centers may be further developed and therefore not as clearly recognizable. The old theory that gastric contractions give *the* hunger signal to the brain is no longer accepted, but the hunger and satiety centers are known to influence the rate at which the stomach empties. The stomach has stretch receptors that transmit sensations of fullness, but whether they transmit the feeling of satiety is unknown. People tend to believe that the stomach shrinks after dieting and stretches again when food intake is increased. It is most unlikely that this actually happens; rather, dieters become used to eating less and thus feel fuller sooner. Another theory stated that blood levels of various fuels, such as sugar, protein, or fat, triggered satiety. This is no longer thought to be true.

Another theory that enjoyed some attention focused on the mysterious power of endorphins to stimulate hunger. Biochemical messengers found in the brain and in the gut, endorphins are the body's version of morphine. They seem to be involved in transmitting signals of either intense pain or pleasure. Drug addicts, alcoholics, and people in chronic pain have elevated endorphin levels and so also do obese rats and people. Although some studies suggest that certain endorphin-inhibiting drugs restrain feeding in humans, it cannot be proved it is the drugs' blocking of endorphins that causes this; the drugs may reduce food intake by some other method.

Appetite

It has been difficult to decide whether fat people eat out of hunger or out of appetite; out of need or greed. Appetite is the intermediary between physical hunger and hunger aroused by external cues. It is sensitive, therefore, to both our mind and body. Hundreds of experiments have been conducted on mice and people in an attempt to assess appetite. Unfortunately, the results have exposed many confusing contradictions and have divulged no definite answers. One thing does seem clear: both lean and fat humans prefer foods that are tasty and tempting. The obese, however, seem to have an increased response to these and eat more of them. It is possible that a disorder in the hypothalamus could cause this. Appetite as well as hunger may be partly under physiological control.

Lean rats return to their normal weight when they come off a highly palatable high-calorie diet, whereas fatter rats never get their weights down again. Is this true for humans? It seems to be if we return to Sims's experiment with the overfed prison volunteers who all returned to normal weight, having no history of obesity. However, this is probably not the case with obese people. It is far more likely that when people with a genetic tendency for weight gain are exposed to very tasty popular foods they will overeat, gain weight, and even if they return to a more restricted diet, never manage to remove the excess weight *permanently*.

Even though overweight people are often judged for having a sweet tooth, this is probably incorrect. In experiments that gave solutions of increasing sweetness to people, the sweeter the solutions became, the less the fat people liked them. If this were the case the development of palatable artificial sweeteners would aid successful weight loss, which they do not. Furthermore, it has actually been proved that obese people have fewer dental cavities than lean people. Instead of having a sweet tooth, fat people seem to have a "fat tooth"!

A study done of supermarket shoppers showed that fat women purchased more high-calorie items that were also high in fats than normal-weight women. It may be a craving for fat, not only for its taste but for its texture, that makes junk food such as ice cream, candy bars, and cookies so very appetizing to the obese and lean people alike. For the obese, this preference for fat may not be merely a whim but may have physiological roots. At the top of the list for taste appeal, above fatty and sweet foods, is a highly varied diet. Referred to by scientists as the "supermarket" or "cafeteria" diet because of the vast choice of foods that it includes, it is the one most guaranteed to make humans and rodents rotund. When faced with the increased palatability and interest of a *mixed* diet, fat people are far more likely to increase intake.

Taste is another factor that stimulates appetite. Taste is known to decrease the more you eat; thin people usually notice this and stop eating as it happens. The obese seem to be less aware and thus miss or ignore the "stop" signal. This apparent lack of control on the part of the obese may not be as much their fault as it seems. Studies indicate that it may be possible for people to inherit a greater preference for certain kinds of food that are mostly high in fats and carbohydrates, such as candy and cookies.

External Cues

A popular explanation for overeating is the externality theory: the idea that fat people are motivated to eat by cues outside themselves, such as the sight and smell of food, rather than by the internal stimulus of hunger. It has further been suggested that fat people, when stimulated by these cues, secrete more of the hormone insulin, which causes more food to be stored as fat. This theory has yet to be proved, and it does seem that thin people are just as affected by external cues as fat people.

The Mechanics of Metabolism

What exactly is metabolism? We hear the word bandied about in diet discussions, yet many people are not really aware of what it means. "Metabolism" is derived from a Greek word meaning transition or change. It is the body's chemical method of changing fuel into energy, which it uses for all its vital processes; breathing, digestion, fat deposition. Metabolism is a process that occurs in every one of our billions of living cells. Fat cells are no exception to this: metabolic activity does take place in fat tissue though at a less active rate than in lean tissue such as muscle. Men tend to have higher metabolic rates than women because they are more muscular. The combustion of food with oxygen produces energy and gives off heat as a by-product. Whatever surplus energy the body creates, after it has used all it needs to meet its requirements, is turned into fat and is stored.

The metabolic rate means the rate at which the body burns its fuel and uses oxygen. It is like a thermostat and is set at a certain rate that varies in every individual. People who gain weight easily might have a low metabolic rate and be able to maintain all their vital functions on very little food and store all the rest as fat. Their bodies are very economical, like a car doing the maximum amount of miles to the gallon. Naturally thin people, who do not gain easily, on the contrary, have an inefficient metabolism. Instead of their cells storing energy as fat, like a careful homemaker, their cells use up all the fuel and produce the by-product heat. In cellular terms, lean people are like big spenders, while fat people are much more careful and conservative.

Your metabolic rate does, as a rule, fall with age, but apart from this gradual change metabolism stays fairly constant. Very often I have heard people who have lost a lot of weight state that they can now eat whatever they like because their metabolism has changed. They are right about the change but not in the way they think. Dieting, if anything, lowers the metabolic rate. The body's automatic reaction to dieting is to reduce the amount of calories on which it can maintain weight. The idea of eating all you like after dieting is unfortunately a state of temporary euphoria. It lasts only as long as your body needs to adjust to its new weight and metabolic demands. After a restricted diet, you may feel you are eating a lot more because you are off the diet. When you gain a lot of weight, your metabolic requirements also alter. The increase of your total body mass (fat and lean tissue) exerts an increased caloric demand. You weigh more and need more to maintain weight.

Energy Balance, the Essential Equation

Our bodies are constantly trying to maintain a state of balance or homeostasis, staying in the same place. Whatever we may do our bodies will fight to maintain this balance.

No attempt can be made to understand the process of weight loss or gain without understanding the energy balance equation:

$$\text{Energy Intake minus Energy Output} = \text{Energy Stored}$$

When energy intake and output are balanced, there is no surplus and the body maintains its weight. If intake exceeds output, weight is gained, if output exceeds intake, weight is lost.

In the past, most obesity research pointed toward a disorder of the mechanism that regulates food intake as the primary cause of obesity. Now, however, there is an equal interest in intake and output. Energy intake means food; that means ostensibly the same thing for both fat and thin. Energy output consists of three factors: basal or resting metabolic rate, physical activity, and specific dynamic action. Basal metabolic rate represents our energy expenditure when we are not physically active. Resting metabolic rate is the same thing except slightly lower; it refers to the body's energy expenditure when it is in a complete resting state—when we are asleep. Physical

activity is self-explanatory, while specific dynamic action accounts
for the energy we expend in digesting food. Surprisingly enough,
basal or resting metabolic rate accounts for about 70 percent of
energy output: physical activity and specific dynamic action for a
mere 30 percent or thereabouts. *These figures may not be the same
for all people.* They will vary according to age, height, weight, and
body composition (percentage of lean and fat tissue).

It would be a mistake to ignore the contribution of physical activity
to energy output. Yet it would be equally unrealistic to expect activity
to perform metabolic miracles that an individual's physiology will
not permit. Even with frequent vigorous exercise, if your metabolic
rate is on the low side, you probably cannot eat freely and lose
weight, or perhaps even maintain it. If you were to abandon exercise
completely, you might have to be very careful with intake to keep
your weight even. Activity, that approximately 30 percent of energy
output, can be essential in tipping the balance in your favor.

The third factor of the energy equation is energy stored, which
means fat. You store fat and gain weight when you are in *positive*
energy balance: when you take in more energy than you expend
and have a surplus, which gets stored as fat. When you are in *negative*
energy balance, expending more than your intake, you incur a deficit
and your already existing stores are drawn on to maintain the balance.
You therefore lose fat and lose weight. Input and output are evaluated
exactly, the score is worked out, and the scales are tipped in either
direction. The system works like a bank account; at a bank, stores
are paid in and paid out continuously. The debit–credit process is
continuous, never static, and every time we weigh ourselves, we are
simply stopping the process for one brief moment, enough to assess
the bank balance of our body.

The system by which our energy input and output are equalized
takes into account any short-term variations and tends to work them
out over several days. That is why true weight gain or loss cannot
happen within a few hours or one day. The body needs time to
adjust. It takes an energy deficit of between 3,500 to 4,000 calories
to lose one pound of fat and an energy surplus of the same amount
to gain a pound of fat. If our *average* (and remember everyone's
equation will be different) energy intake is 1,800 calories a day and
an average expenditure 2,000 calories, the caloric debt to the body
would be a mere 200 calories. If that were the case, to achieve the

debt of 3,500 calories that we need to lose our pound of fat, we would take seventeen and a half days. Even if we were to create a larger caloric debt by drastically reducing intake and stopping up expenditure, it would *not* be possible to lose a pound of fat in one day. Neither would it be possible for the process to work in reverse fashion and for us to gain a pound of fat in one day.

What Fuel Does the Body Use?

Our diet is composed of three major nutrients—carbohydrates, proteins, and fats. In various combinations, using one, two, or all of these, the body creates its two usual types of fuel—glucose and fat. Glucose is used as an emergency fuel reserve while both glucose and fat combine to form the long-term fuel reserves of the body: fat. The name for stored fat is triglyceride. It is stored in fat cells known collectively as adipose or fat tissue.

As we shall see, some glucose is always readily available as an immediate reserve. Otherwise the body's fuels have to be extracted from the food we eat by a breakdown process. Digestive enzymes begin breaking down the food as soon as it enters the mouth. Starches, called complex carbohydrates because they have a more complex molecular structure than refined or simple carbohydrates such as sugar, are broken down into simple sugars such as glucose. Proteins are used by the body usually not as fuel but as building material to make and repair its muscles, bones, and other components. Proteins are metabolized by the body into amino acids. Finally, fats are converted into free fatty acids and glycerol. To sum up, we have the following:

Foods Ingested	Metabolites Produced
Carbohydrates	Glucose
Proteins	Amino Acids
Fats	Free Fatty Acids and Glycerol

Glucose is a short-term fuel reserve used by the brain and muscle tissues. Because it is drawn on short notice, it is stored, in the form of glycogen, in the liver and the muscles. As well as storing glycogen, the liver can synthesize fat, the body's other fuel, from free fatty acids, or from glucose or amino acids. However, the liver does not store fat. It acts instead as a sort of food traffic controller that sends the fat on through the circulation to the fat cells. There the fat combines with other metabolites to form the body's long-term store, triglyceride, which is stored in the fat cells. The liver can hold only so much glucose in the form of glycogen; 10 percent of its weight. This is because glycogen is bound with a lot of water. Triglyceride is a better storage fuel because fat cells can expand to hold unlimited reserves.

Although glucose is a short-term store and fat a long-term one, they are of equal importance. In fact, fat can be burned only in the presence of glucose, hence the common medical saying, "Fats burn in a carbohydrate flame." If for any reason no carbohydrates and thus no glucose are available, energy cannot be released from metabolized fats no matter how many are available. Glucose could be lacking because it has been completely used up in prolonged exercise, such as running a marathon, which would consume all muscle glycogen. Or it could be used up if a person were starving or on a very low-carbohydrate diet. Because of the lack of glucose, an incomplete breakdown of fat occurs, and highly acidic *ketone bodies,* made of two acids, acetoacetic and beta-hydroxybutyric, are produced, some of which are excreted in urine. The highly acidic content of the urine may harm the kidneys. Ketone bodies are used to fuel the brain in the absence of glucose, and because they require much more oxygen than glucose does to be burned effectively, they leave the brain shorter of oxygen. This in one way accounts for the exhilarating, euphoric high experienced with ketosis (an abnormal increase of ketone bodies). Its more unpleasant symptoms are nausea, dizziness, and vomiting.

How Does a Fat Cell Work?

Fat is our principal energy store. If it were not for our fat stores we would have to eat on a twenty-four-hour basis. In a world where cupboards, refrigerators, and supermarkets overflow with bountiful and appetizing provisions, we fail to understand that our bodies are probably obeying an evolutionary law of long ago. For prehistoric people feasting was a sporadic treat, starvation a more familiar reality. Because we spend our whole lives eating three meals a day, we cannot appreciate the safety value of fat. Without it, we could not have survived. According to the state of our energy balance equation, intake versus output, we either use fat as fuel or store it as potential energy. Most of our fat is stored in fat cells, collectively called adipose tissue, but it would be wrong to regard these cells as miniature dungeons in which our fat is locked away forever. The amount of fat we have is never really fixed or static: it is always circulating, involved in a complicated cycle of fat storage and fat release. With the exception of a few fixed deposits mentioned earlier (see Chapter 2), our fat stores are like a current account from and into which money is simultaneously drawn and paid. These simultaneous processes of fat storage and release are complex and take place in several stages.

The scientific term for release is lipolysis, which means freeing of fat. Lipogenesis actually means the synthesis of fatty acids that are needed to make triglyceride, stored fat. *Fat storage* is the actual process by which fatty acids are metabolically combined with glycerol phosphate to form triglyceride. Throughout the next few pages, please keep in mind that the words "triglyceride" and "fat" are interchangeable.

Fat storage and release are cyclical processes involving metabolites. The easiest way of picturing these metabolites is as steps along a pathway. These processes are constantly in progress. The chain exists because of the activation of the metabolites by substances that work on one another biochemically through a series of reactions, known as a "cascade." The first step is hormones acting on enzymes. The major role of these enzymes, which are complex proteins, is to act as catalysts that start activation. In turn, these enzymes act on the smaller molecular entities, the metabolites. Now we shall look at this in detail.

Fat Storage

The best way to understand how fat storage occurs is to picture a pool of dissolved metabolites (digested nutrients) that are circulating in the bloodstream around the fat cells, which are all clustered together. Drawing on these metabolites and building them up into a chain, each fat cell makes triglyceride, the form in which it can store fat. It does this in its storage droplet, a large "blob" that is the largest part of a fat cell. Triglyceride is synthesized from one glycerol molecule that acts like backbone chemically compounded with three fatty acid molecules that come from the free fatty acids circulating outside. How does the fat cell form this compound from the substances that are circulating around it?

The circulating pool outside the cell includes those elements that are synthesized to make fat and those that are released when fat is liberated. To synthesize triglyceride the fat cell needs fatty acids and glycerol, but these do not enter the cell ready-made. To simplify matters, let's take the creation of each of these substances separately, remembering that the processes described here in sequence actually happen *at the same time.*

Step One Let us begin with the synthesis of fatty acids, derived from fat. Fat is circulating around the fat cell in the form of chylomicrons (packets of fat formed after absorption through the wall of the small intestine). It is also present in the form of VLDL, very low density lipoproteins, which are protein-bound fats coming from the liver.

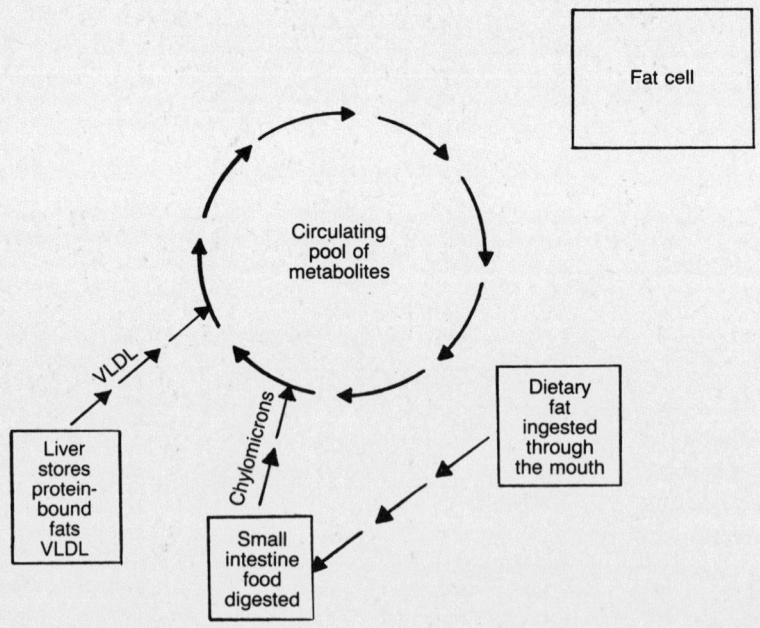

NOTE: Diagram not drawn to scale.

Step Two As we said before, the synthesis of triglyceride occurs through a biochemical cascade or chain reaction of hormones acting on enzymes and enzymes on metabolites. In this case, the uptake of these VLDL and chylomicrons into the fat cell is facilitated by the enzyme lipoprotein lipase. Nicknamed by one obesity specialist the "gatekeeper enzyme" because triglyceride cannot be synthesized without its activity, lipoprotein lipase is probably found in the walls of the blood capillaries. The production of this enzyme and the entry of the substances into the cell is originally stimulated by the hormone insulin.

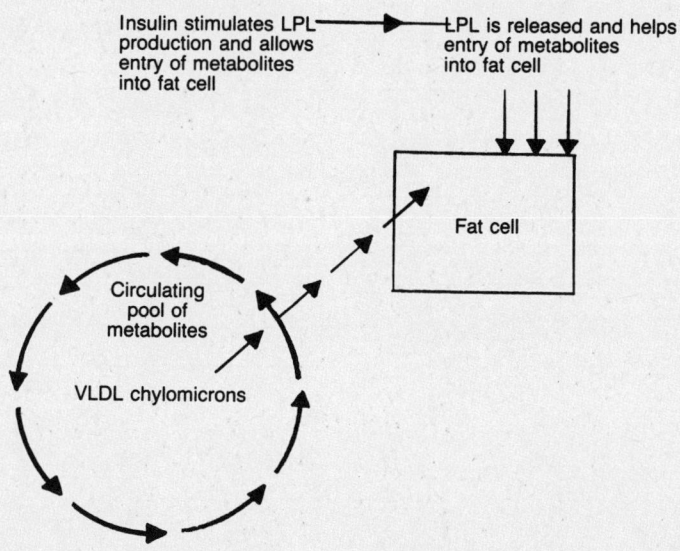

Step Three Once the chylomicrons and VLDL are inside the cell, they are acted upon by the enzyme lipoprotein lipase, which works on releasing or hydrolyzing the fatty acids. These fatty acids, which are chains of carbon molecules of various lengths, then join together with activating molecules known generically as acyl Co-A. The fatty acids are now ready to join up with glycerol.

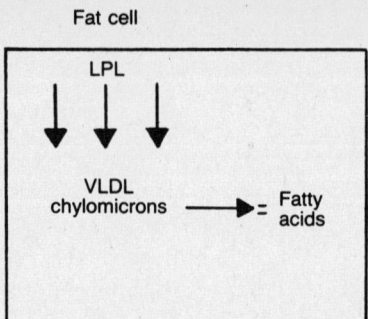

Fat cell

Step Four Now all the fat cell needs to make triglyceride is glycerol. Where does this come from? The triglyceride we store in our bodies is the same in structure as the dietary fat we eat; it consists of fatty acids and glycerol. So we have glycerol already present in our bodies. However, the metabolite glycerol cannot enter the fat

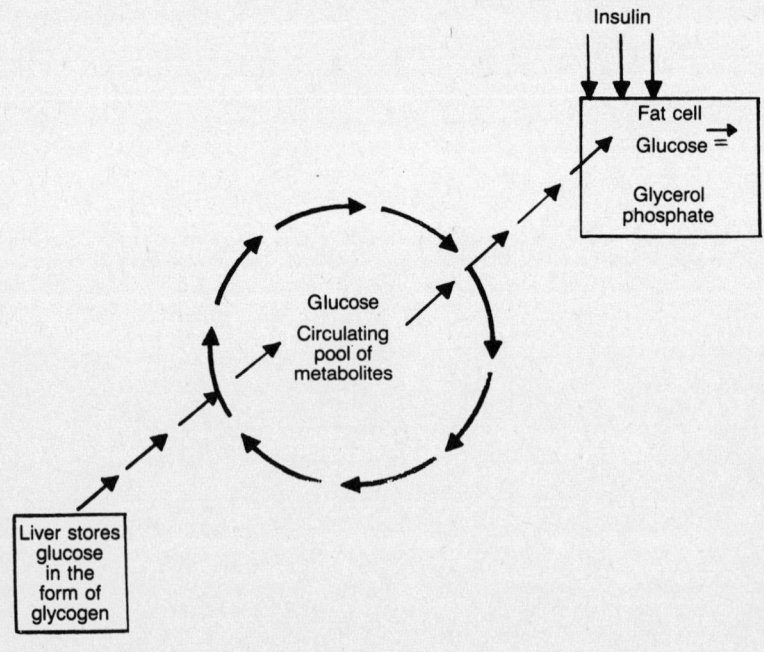

cell directly. Instead, it must be obtained from glucose, which enters the cell thanks once again to insulin. This glucose has come from the circulation, but originally it has been released from the liver where it has been stored as glycogen, the body's short-term fuel. Insulin actively promotes the uptake of glucose into *all* cells of the body except perhaps the brain, kidney, intestinal, and mucosal red blood cells. Fat cells cannot absorb glucose without it. Once inside the fat cell, glucose is converted via metabolic pathways to glycerol phosphate, the form in which it can combine with fatty acids.

Step Five Now the fat cell has everything it needs to synthesize triglyceride: three fatty acid molecules and one of glycerol phosphate. Once the glycerol molecule combines with the three fatty acid molecules, its phosphate molecule is released. The structure of triglyceride now looks like this: a backbone molecule of glycerol and three fatty acid molecules.

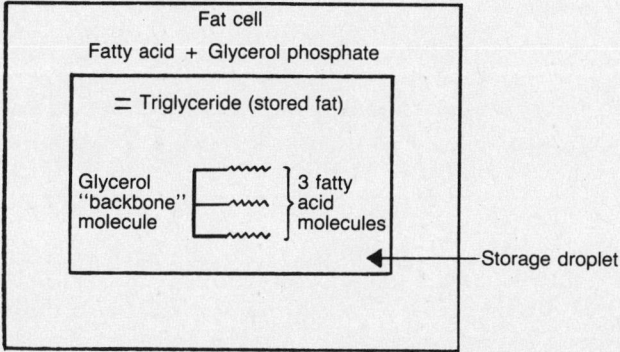

What Influences Fat Storage?

Though it is not known whether fat causes excess insulin or vice versa, what is known is that for the obese, insulin is bad news. Several other hormones either encourage fat storage or inhibit lipolysis or both. Examples are somatostatin and the sex hormones progesterone, prolactin, and estrogen. Another factor thought to influence fat storage is the level of glucose in the bloodstream. As the fat cell needs glucose to make fat, glucose levels in the blood possibly influence the degree of fat synthesis and fat release. Concentrations around and within the cell of other metabolites, such as blood proteins, also affect the metabolic processes that culminate in the storage of triglyceride.

Fat Release

Scientifically known as lipolysis, the liberation of fat, fat release goes on at the same time as fat storage. They are not happening in sequence but instead simultaneously. The fat cell can be synthesizing fat, releasing it, and if it is not used as fuel by the body's demands, turning it into triglyceride again. In step five, we were left with a fat cell that had synthesized triglyceride and stored it within its storage droplet. That triglyceride is released in lipolysis, but how exactly does that happen?

Step One This is how it is thought the signal for lipolysis is relayed. The initial messenger is thought to be the hormone epinephrine, which acts on the fat cell membrane or wall. This hormone is available in the blood circulating around the cells. Epinephrine stimulates a cell-wall enzyme called adenylcyclase to work on the energy molecule ATP.

Let us pause for a moment and examine what ATP really is. The initials stand for adenosine triphosphate, triphosphate because it has three phosphate groups. As we know, the fat cell stores fat as triglyceride. This is the fat cell's inert storage, rather like a bank balance. Transactions in and out of the cell have been stopped for a moment and you can survey how much you have. In the kind of fat we are talking about (I make the distinction because shortly we shall discuss an exceptional kind of fat), ATP is the *usable,* active energy molecule, not *inert* like triglyceride. ATP is like cash over the counter.

Adenylcyclase converts ATP into cyclic AMP (adenosine monophosphate). The cyclic AMP acts as an intracellular chemical messenger that goes on to stimulate hormone sensitive lipase, which then stimulates the release of triglyceride. This whole chain reaction of hormones, enzymes, and messengers is another example of what is known biochemically as a cascade.

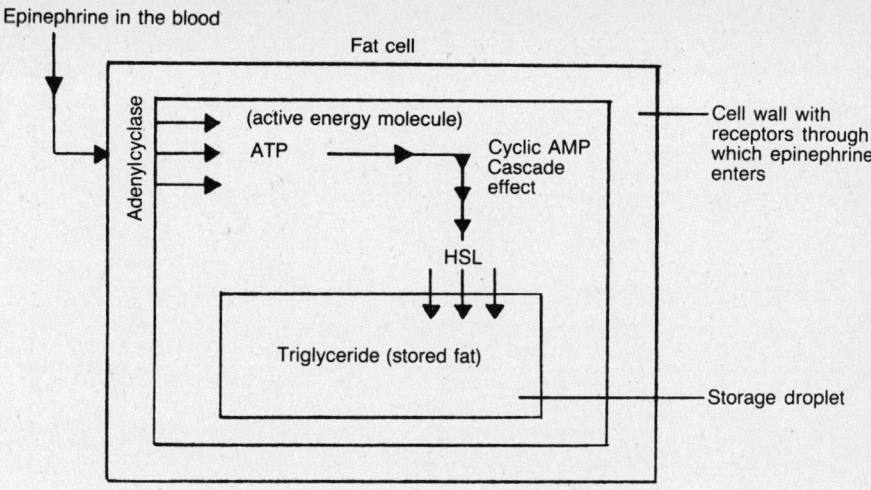

Step Two Triglyceride is broken down within the fat cell's storage droplet. The process releases fatty acids and glycerol. These are released out of the cell into the circulating pool of metabolites. This release is brought about by the action of the enzyme hormone-sensitive lipase.

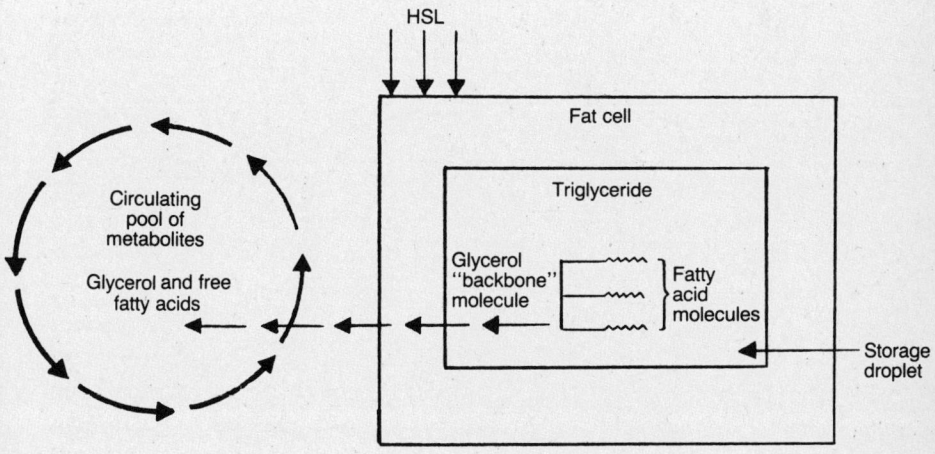

NOTE: Diagram not drawn to scale.

Step Three One of two things can happen to these fatty acids. They can pass into the circulation, thus becoming free fatty acids, for use as energy by all other cells except brain and red blood cells. Alternatively, they can be recycled and become resynthesized as fat in the process of fat storage. This process would be encouraged by insulin.

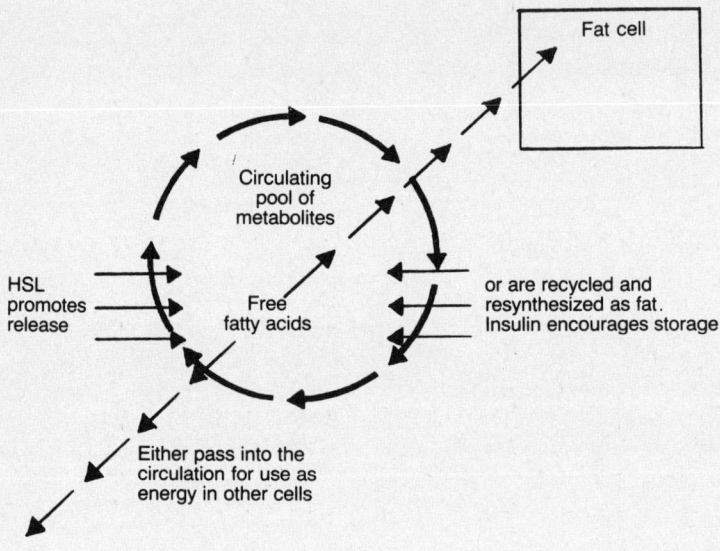

Step Four Glycerol has a similar choice. It can pass out of the cell and be converted to glucose in the liver by a process known as gluconeogenesis. Insulin aids this procedure, for when the liver turns glycerol into glucose, if the glucose is not used up as energy, it can be reused to make fat. As we know, insulin is the most important hormone for encouraging fat storage and actually preventing the mobilization of fat. Alternatively, glycerol passes into the circulation and can be used by the body's cells as fuel. This release is aided by hormone-sensitive lipase, the lipolytic or fat-releasing enzyme.

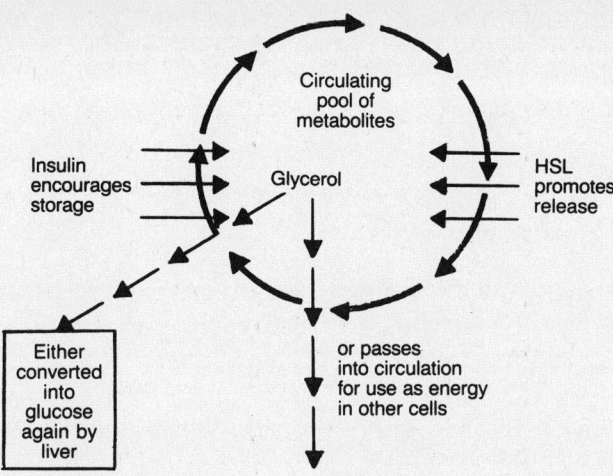

What Influences or Works Against Fat Release?

Insulin is a very powerful antagonist to the release and using up
of fat. It encourages fat storage and resynthesis. Fortunately, there
are contrary influences that encourage lipolysis and fat mobilization.
The most important stimulators of lipolysis are the following hormones: catecholamines, cortisol, glucagon, and ACTH (adrenocorticotropic hormone). The most important enzyme is hormone-sensitive
lipase. As its name suggests, its production is influenced by various
hormones, also by certain enzymes and other "messengers" that in-
form the cell that it must mobilize its fat stores.

Fat Release Does Not Mean Fat Usage

Triglyceride release or mobilization is the *release of triglyceride into
the bloodstream, not the actual burning of it*. Once the fat has been
liberated into the bloodstream it can be used. Some fat is always
being burned even if we are not making drastic energy requirements
on our body through physical activity. This is because living cells
constantly need energy to maintain their vital processes.

Even as fat is released, some of that fat is immediately taken
back and re-stored as energy. Of course the more energy we burn,

by creating a caloric deficit (eating less and moving more), the more fat will be used and the less fat will be stored again. Certain drugs are claimed to act as fat mobilizers. Fat mobilization does not guarantee fat use or the burning of fat that results in weight loss.

A Clue to the Cause of Obesity

Obesity is the result of increased fat storage, but fat release itself may not be impaired in fat people. Instead, they may have a metabolic tendency to *re-store* their released fat. Up until about 1972 it was suspected that obesity might be caused by a primary defect in a fat cell enzyme. However, as with all obesity theories, it is very difficult to determine whether the condition is the cause or merely one of the symptoms of being overweight. Maybe excess fat causes certain enzyme levels to rise or fall and thus make more fat.

The data on a certain enzyme, though, were particularly mystifying. For a long time it had been thought that lipoprotein lipase, the main lipogenic enzyme, was the only enzyme whose levels did not normalize after weight loss. This implied a losing battle for the obese, suggesting, as the setpoint theory had, that however much one dieted, the body would seek to reestablish its predieting level of fat. Fortunately, recent studies from Finland have shown that lipoprotein lipase levels do stabilize in the obese after weight loss.

A Tale of Two Tissues: Are Some Fat Cells Different from Others?

In trying to ascertain why we gain weight in certain places, what we are really asking is how independent is a fat cell? Is it affected by its environment, that is, by the blood supply, the nervous system, the hormones and enzymes that work upon it? Or is there some inherent defect within the cell itself that causes it to have a greater propensity for fat storage? The idea of regional cellular differences was previously somewhat discounted by doctors. It is now becoming increasingly clear, however, according to the evidence from not one but several eminent sources, that certain fat cells do behave differently.

Several factors are suspected of causing regional differences in fat cell formation and behavior. These may be responsible in some way for different patterns of fat distribution. One is the differences in innervation (nerve distribution) of fat tissue in different regions. Blood supply, or vascularization, is closely linked to this factor. Although there is much work to be done on these aspects, experiments on animals involving the denervating of adipose tissue have shown that in the part of the body where the nerves were cut, fat gain was easier and fat loss slower than in other parts of the body. In partial facial paralysis, the paralyzed side of the face is usually fatter and will not empty its fat stores. Current research also implies that differences in blood circulation in different adipose areas of the body might be important, because hormones and other critical substances may have greater access to some fat depots than others.

Obesity is a complex matter at the best of times, but work on cellularity is further hampered by the inaccessibility, in humans, of any but the most surface fat. While fat cell biopsies (in which fat is sucked up through a needle) are useful, there are also problems. It is impossible to tell whether the needle sucked up a representative sample of adipose tissue. Also, test tube experiments cannot always mimic all that is going on inside the body; enzyme reactions, hormonal cues, signals from the fat cells themselves.

Much recent work has been done on regional cellularity by Dr. Ahmed Kissebah, whom I met at a leading hospital in London and is now based at the Medical College of Wisconsin. His findings led him to suspect that fat tissue in various sites is of different morphology (form) and varies in metabolic behavior. As we saw in Chapter 2, he found top-heavy women more prone to diabetes. Moreover, he partly attributes the abnormally high insulin, sugar, and fat levels in the blood that characterize diabetes to top-heavy women's enlarged fat cells.

What was previously an uncharted area in obesity research has now become the new "hot" topic. Although no solution has yet been discovered, the idea remains certain: fat cells are susceptible to many influences: age, diet, environment, genetics, and perhaps others of which we are still unaware.

Brown Adipose Tissue: A Furnace for Fat

We have looked at the process of fat storage and fat release in an ordinary fat cell. Now we shall look at a different kind of fat: brown fat. Up to now when we have been discussing adipose tissue, I have been referring to the white kind. Most of our fat is white, which is characterized by the presence of the large storage droplets that form the largest part of the cell.

Brown fat differs from ordinary white fat in several ways. There is much less of it: brown fat accounts for barely 1 to 2 percent of body weight in most experimental animals. In human beings, the amount and even the existence of brown fat tissue is still uncertain. Calculations range from a skeptical 5 percent of total body fat in babies to a zero amount in adult human beings. One of the reasons brown fat differs in color from white is that an increased amount of blood vessels runs through it. The other reason is that brown fat cells contain many more mitochondria than white fat cells (see Figure 7). These mitochondria have the unique capacity to burn up or waste calories as heat. It seems that those animals with a tendency to get fat have a different type of mitochondria, which cannot waste calories as heat, and therefore more energy is stored in the traditional white fat.

We are fairly sure that brown fat works like this in small mammals. Does brown fat really account for the successful energy deficit in lean people? If so, do obese people have less brown fat or is it defective? The very existence of this rare and different adipose tissue has not yet been proved in humans, and if indeed it does exist, its action will vary widely from one individual to another.

WHITE FAT CELL

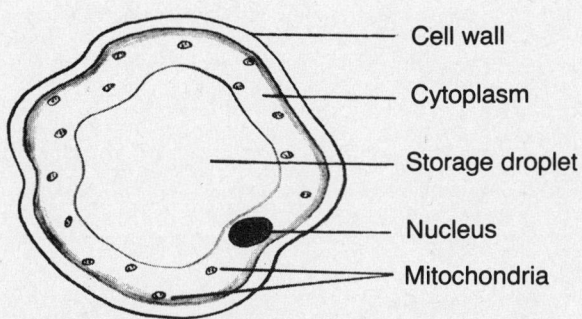

Cell wall

Cytoplasm

Storage droplet

Nucleus

Mitochondria

BROWN FAT CELL

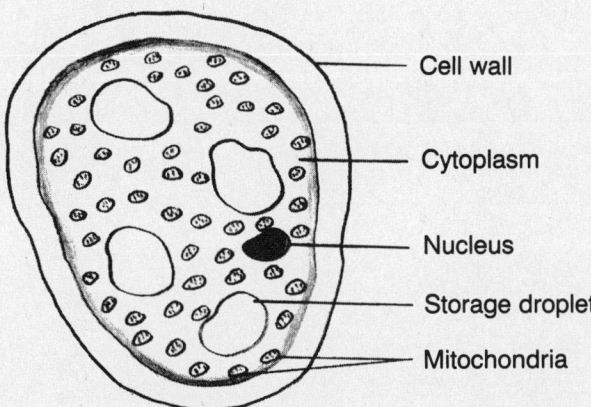

Cell wall

Cytoplasm

Nucleus

Storage droplet

Mitochondria

Figure 7 STRUCTURAL DIFFERENCES BETWEEN A WHITE AND BROWN FAT CELL

NOTE: Not drawn to scale.

4

The Life History of a Fat Cell: When Is It Most Dangerous to Gain Weight?

The answer to the title of this chapter is "Anytime." The body gains weight only when it is in a state of positive energy balance—when you are taking in more energy than you are expending. At no time are you exempt from weight gain, whatever you may have thought in the past. There are no magic fat-free moments, let alone years. We must always pay attention to the energy equation, energy input minus energy output equals energy stored.

When people actually gain weight continues to be one of the most important clues to the cause of their obesity. A certain weight gain at particular stages of life is part of the natural process of growth; for instance, as a child grows, he or she gains weight; as a woman's pregnancy progresses, her weight increases also. Apart from these normal stages of growth, there are other periods when the body's hormones and enzyme secretions encourage fat deposition. At those and indeed anytime, additional psychological pressures can trigger overeating and favor increases in weight that have no connection with skeletal and muscle growth. These periods of weight gain are caused by increased body fat. Such periods are adolescence (though this is also a period of growth), the taking of oral contraceptives, and menopause.

Cellular Expansion: How Do Our Fat Cells Grow?

Up until the 1950s most obesity research was centered on the regulatory mechanisms in the hypothalamus. Since then the development of experimental techniques has made it possible both to measure fat cells in the body and to watch them grow in laboratory conditions.

Obesity is a disorder characterized by an excessive accumulation of body fat. This excess fat is stored in the body's fat cells. The average person has between 10 and 20 kilograms (twenty-two to forty-four pounds) of body fat. This amount is not out of proportion with the other tissues that make up our body: skeleton, skin, and muscle. There is one big difference, however. Whereas our other body parts fluctuate very little in their size and degree, our adipose tissue can expand within a range of a factor of one thousand: a tenfold increase in diameter of each cell entails a thousandfold increase in volume and therefore weight. No other cell in the body can fill up and expand quite like that. Fat cells are unique, their capacity almost infinite. The way they work can explain to us when and why we gain weight.

One's adipose tissue mass can enlarge in two ways; fat cells either grow larger in size or increase in number. The first process is known as hypertrophy; the second as hyperplasia. Only in the 1970s did scientists start debating how the processes interact in obesity and more specifically *when* either process is most likely to occur.

Although fat cells can now be successfully grown in culture, some uncertainty still exists in the measurement of fat cell size and number. The results are always open to interpretation. In humans, although techniques have been developed to study subcutaneous (under the skin) fat with a fair degree of accuracy, fat in the internal depots is buried too deep to be accessible. There is no way of measuring it except in samples acquired during operations and now increasingly by the CAT scan. It is hoped this new technique will reveal some answers. Whether internal fat depots are larger or smaller than subcutaneous ones is a question that for the time being remains unanswerable.

Babyhood: Is Weight Your Fate?

Doctors are obviously most interested in infant obesity because it may provide some clues to the condition in later life and also because it is a period not complicated by social pressures. It is, moreover, easier to assess food intake in babies and to examine their eating behavior, which is comparatively free from psychological stresses. Because fat deposition begins in the womb, a study of babyhood includes the period of intrauterine growth. Even then, the baby's development is the result of genetic tendency and environment.

One of the most common assumptions, widely accepted until very recently, is that fat babies become fat adults. This hypothesis was the result of some experiments conducted on rats. The experiments involved rats reared in small litters, with access to more milk during suckling than those reared in large litters. The small litter differed from the large litter in that they not only increased fat cell size but increased fat cell number as well. Studies in humans followed. They seemed to indicate that people with the most fat cells had been obese from childhood, implying that overfeeding in early life causes the production of an "excess" number of fat cells (hyperplasia), which predisposes the baby to obesity in later life. Because obesity, after approximately the first year of life, was thought to be *solely* the result of fat cell enlargement (hypertrophy), the person who had too *many* fat cells from babyhood, all of which could enlarge later on, had a much higher risk of obesity.

The scientists' assumption soon became the popular belief that fat babies were doomed for life. Thankfully, this did much to prevent mothers from overfeeding their babies, but it also sounded like a fatalistic pronouncement of irreversible obesity for veteran dieters, encouraging them to sit back and succumb to moaning and munching because they had been fat babies.

Fat Need Not Be Your Future: Some Recent Discoveries

It *is* true that most fat is deposited shortly after birth and that nutrition at this time will affect the production of fat cells. *But, according to more recent evidence, having an excess amount of fat cells does not mean you will always be fat.* Research proved that it wasn't because people had been fat as babies that they had an excess amount of fat cells. Their increased number of cells was just as much the result of the extent of their obesity as it was of its age of onset. Obesity could happen at any time as long as a person was in a state of positive energy balance, eating more than he or she was expending. Whereas some people early in life established a stable complement of fat cells that never increased, other people could increase fat cell number at any time if they incurred a positive energy balance.

Some Problems with Fat Cell Experiments

It is known that adult animals can increase fat cell number. Although it is not 100 percent certain, there is now evidence to suggest that the number of fat cells also increases in adult humans.

Our number of fat cells *is never static.* There is a constant turnover of fat in the body: fat is stored, released, and burned in a never-ending cycle. We have no way of finding out *exactly* how many fat cells a person has at any one given time. We can only guess. As with the estimation of percentage of body fat, the method is indirect and involves dividing total body fat by average cell weight. The word "average" is fraught with uncertainty in this case, for fat cells from different areas could vary tremendously.

To complicate the issue even further, recent evidence has indicated that even if fat cell number increase is detected, it cannot be established that the extra cells are new cells. Fat cells can only attain a certain critical size. After this has been achieved, any more excess fat has to be accommodated in new fat cells. By what process do these come into existence? One possibility is that existing cells split and make new ones. Perhaps it is even possible that completely new fat cells are synthesized from DNA. Or is there another explanation?

The Fat Cell Pool: How Our Bodies Can Always Make Fat

This idea speculates that actual increase in number of the fat cells themselves probably takes place in the early stages of life but that fat cell number can increase at any age through the filling and subsequent increase in size of newly recruited fat cells. How this recruitment occurs can best be explained if we imagine ourselves in a laboratory studying fat cells.

The concept of a fat cell "pool" suggests that adipose tissue contains several different types of cells. Previously, scientists were working with only two cell classifications. Using an enzyme to separate fat cells from the connective tissue that holds them together, they identified cells with single large lipid droplets as mature fat cells or adipocytes. These cells would float to the top of the test tube. The remaining cells, with insufficient lipid, would sink to the bottom. These cells were known collectively as stromal vascular cells. Vascular cells are the cells forming blood vessels that run through adipose

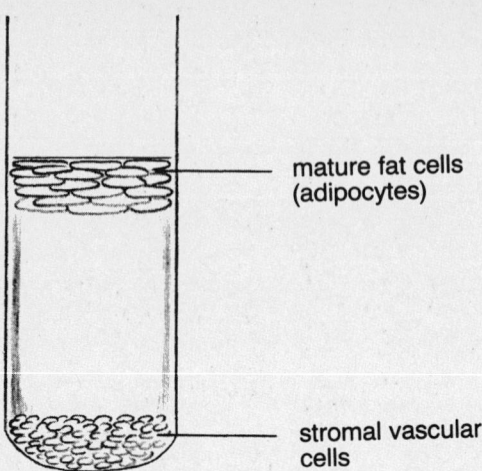

Figure 8 FAT CELLS IN TEST TUBE

The larger, mature fat cells float to the top; however, it is the small cells at the bottom of the test tube, the stromal vascular cells, that are now attracting attention.

tissue. Stromal cells are the cells of the connective tissue that hold together the mature fat cells like a string bag holding onions. It was the investigation of what these stromal cells consisted that was of great interest.

At the bottom of the test tube there seem to be cells at varying stages of development. First there are cells that have not yet assumed a particular function in the body. They are therefore still capable of division. Generally known as fibroblasts, they could become any sort of cell in the body; for example, a skin cell or a vascular cell. These cells are small, less than fifteen micrograms in weight, and do not have the necessary enzymes to store and release fat. Under certain circumstances, however, these cells could turn into preadipocytes, so they are also known as adipoblasts because of their possible fat storage potential. Eventually these cells become differentiated: they receive instructions on what their job is. These cells, weighing fifteen to thirty micrograms, are called preadipocytes or adipose precursors, cells that have been elected to become mature adipocytes (fat cells) when the body needs them and once they reach a certain size.

So in our pool there are adipoblasts, preadipocytes, and mature adipocytes. There may also be some empty fat cells. These are former fat cells that are now redundant. Their lipid droplet has emptied and so they are no longer fulfilling a storage function. Because they are empty they are extremely hard to detect with microscopic techniques; thus there are more queries about the existence and location of these cells than of any others in the pool.

Fat Cell Recruitment

Although it is still open to debate, scientists are fairly sure of the events involved. The first and most important prerequisite for fat cell increase is positive energy balance. If you are taking in more calories than you are expending, all the fat cells, at their various stages of development, will start to grow. First, the adipoblasts, still undifferentiated, will become more numerous. Next, if they receive a signal, these adipoblasts grow large enough to become preadipocytes. Then the preadipocytes themselves will achieve a size large enough to convert into mature fat cells. The precise signal that starts off this recruitment is still not certain, though it is thought to be transmitted via the circulation either regionally or locally in the fat tissue itself. One possible factor is the size of the mature fat cells themselves. Once they reach a certain optimum size, which may well vary from one person and one area of the body to another, they start to recruit new fat cells from the preadipocytes.

As with fat storage and fat release, a combined cascade effect of hormones working on enzymes and enzymes in turn affecting other factors is probably responsible for fat cell recruitment. Other factors may be genetics, type of diet, and environmental exposure, such as extreme cold. In the light of this theory it is possible to see that fat cells are not merely passive receptacles for storage. They may well influence metabolism and even degree of food intake by their size and number.

Do Fat Cells Ever Die?

For adipose tissue to decrease, we need to be in a state of caloric deficit, taking in less than we expend. Once this has been achieved, do fat cell size and number both decrease? It is fairly certain that fat cell *size* decreases, but no mechanism by which fat cell number decreases has been identified. As a fat cell empties its lipid droplet, it shrinks and therefore becomes redundant. What is more worrying to fat people's chances of ever becoming permanently thin, however, is that fat cells never die. They empty and lose their storage *function*, but they never seem to lose their storage *capacity*. That means that every time you gain weight new fat cells are filled; when you lose weight your fat cells never disappear. Thus with weight gain you are constantly increasing your storage capacity by expanding your amount of adipose tissue. This will always retain its potential, even when empty, to fill up again.

Practical Advice: How to Feed Your Baby

Even though there is no need to panic about dieting your baby, it is advisable not to stuff him or her with very rich and fattening food or with large quantities. First, because it *is* possible that fat cell number in babyhood is not only increased by quantities but also by the composition of the food. Second and more important, overfeeding in babyhood forms eating habits that are difficult to reverse later on.

Factors Affecting Your Baby's Appetite

Genetics

When children were fed a lactose formula, babies with heavy mothers, who tended to be bigger babies, consumed more than those with lean mothers. Whether this suggests that a genetic factor determines food intake or that heavy babies' caloric demands are higher still is open to question.

Birthweight

In another study done at the same time, babies were fed several solutions of varying sweetness. Babies with lower birthweights, who were also leaner, consumed less of the sweeter solutions. This indicates that birthweight can possibly influence food intake or liking for palatable food, which may become a problem later on. It has also been noted that birthweight is the direct result of the mother's weight during pregnancy and even before.

Eating Habits

Babies are the most helpless victims of their environment. They must rely on their mother's interpretation of their needs. If she misunderstands their signals, thinking they are hungry when they simply want to be cuddled, she may be encouraging a tendency toward obesity. If you force-feed them, they will correlate satiety with an artificially high level of intake; "artificial" in that it has not been induced by the babies' appetite center. The appetite setting will thus be raised and will remain high.

Breast-feeding is still a matter of controversy in infant nutrition. Research seems to indicate that bottle feeding itself is not a cause of obesity. However, breast-fed infants may be more aware of when to stop feeding because they are thought to develop an appetite control mechanism based on variations in the taste and texture of human milk. Formula foods are constant in texture, so no signals are given to the child to stop. In addition, human milk is thought to be less rich and better balanced than formula varieties. More important is the difference in eating behavior observable in breast-fed infants. They seem to feed more frequently, maybe because they take in less air than bottle-fed ones. This type of eating behavior may be significant for determining future obesity, for it has been suggested that fewer, larger meals result in increased fat storage. Moreover, breast-feeding mothers have the advantage of direct physical communication, as well as fostering their babies' psychological security, which forms through this bond.

Childhood

Children will gain weight for two reasons. The first is growth. This is of course a natural process: the skeleton and the muscles are growing along with the adipose tissue. Weight gain is the combined effect of the growth of *all* these body components. What naturally concerns parents is that it is very hard to differentiate between the normal development of body fat and excess development that signals overweight. Doctors most commonly assess the child's growth by the habitual weight/height index. As I said in Chapter 2, "ideal" weight tables are neither realistic nor individual. They are a means of classification designed for the average person, whoever he or she may be! We are naturally concerned with ourselves or our child as an individual. The best way to check that your child's development is proportionate, that he or she is not getting too fat, is to have your physician, or you yourself, take a good look at the child. In the end this type of estimation is probably just as effective as the skinfold thickness test, which has proved not to be very accurate.

The other reason children gain weight is that their body fat is expanding out of proportion to their lean body mass. They are becoming obese. As with babies, this doesn't mean they are doomed to a lifetime of overweight. Studies show that significant percentages of obese children successfully lose their weight some years later. However, evidence also indicates that fat children run a far greater risk of becoming fat adults than lean children. Studies vary enormously, some showing that large percentages of fat children stay fat, others that very few obese adults were that way when children. However, it seems likely that a person who becomes fat in early life will be more likely to continue these faulty habits in adult life.

The age at which a child puts on weight is irrelevant when it comes to the consideration of whether he or she will lose it again. *How* is your child likely to develop obesity? Heredity must not be overlooked. Genetic traits could possibly have metabolic consequences that might endanger even normal-weight children if they have obese parents. Two studies showed that four- to five-year-old normal-weight children with obese parents ate considerably less than normal-weight children of lean parents. What was astonishing was that their overall energy expenditure was lower too, indicating a lower metabolic rate. That meant that the children of the obese parents maintained their weight on *less food*. If these children, even though normal weight, were to eat even a little bit more at some point in their lives for whatever reason, they would immediately gain weight and run a high risk of becoming obese.

Environment is also a key issue. Overeating and underactivity could be to blame, but unfortunately it's not that simple. The reliable studies on children's food intake show that some children eat twice as much as other children and that not all of them are obese, while some are. Studies on energy expenditure are equally unclear; some show that fat children are just as active as lean ones, others that they are slightly less so. Even if this were the case, fat children's *total* energy expenditure would probably equal that of slimmer ones because they need more calories to move their extra weight. Childhood obesity may well be the most difficult kind to examine because it is hard to monitor a child's eating habits out of the home. It may also be the hardest to understand and ascertain: some children are very sensitive to obesity, while others seem totally unaware of the problem.

How Can You Help Your Child?

If you were fat as a child, or are fat now, you will be tempted to prevent obesity in your child. How you carry this out is of prime importance. If you suspect that your child has a genetic tendency to weight gain, try and introduce a healthy lifestyle early on. Encourage your children to be as active as possible. Introduce them to sports that they like; there is a good chance that if they associate activity with fun the habit of exercising will persist into later life, where it certainly does make a difference in controlling weight gain. Or get your children interested in something—music, crafts, books, etc.—since eating often comes from boredom. As far as diet is concerned, it's up to you to control it as much as possible with logical explanation, tact, and understanding and to let the children eat what they like sometimes, but in moderation. If you want to find out how many calories your children need and whether their diet includes all the vitamins and minerals essential for their growth, it is best to have a personal assessment done by your doctor.

On a psychological level, every child, thin or fat, requires a positive self-image. If you let your children know that they are totally loved and accepted unconditionally, however they may look, you will be helping them inestimably toward having high self-esteem. I think the reason that so many fat adults have been fat since childhood is their chronic negative body image. If you grow up with a fat consciousness, you may always be perpetuating it and increasing your chances of further weight gain or regain.

Adolescence

This is the most critical time for weight gain in terms of biological development, as the biggest period of growth takes place at this time. Adolescent boys tend in general to become leaner, but with girls this growth spurt involves the deposition of a good deal more body fat. In girls, the attainment of a certain weight, thought by a leading authority to between 47 and 48 kilograms (103.4 pounds and 105.6 pounds), is essential for menstruation to occur. This weight gain includes a 120 percent increase in body fat, from 5 to 11 kilograms (11 to 24 pounds), so generally body fat accounts for around 24 percent of body composition. This increase in body fat continues, most girls gaining a further 4.5 kilograms (9.9 pounds) until they reach eighteen years of age, fat then accounting for between 26 percent and 28 percent of body composition. Body fatness may then decrease as the girl enters her twenties.

Reproductive functions depend on body fat because it is suspected that adipose tissue encourages the secretion of estrogen, one of the main sex hormones secreted by the ovaries. Moreover, estrogen is one of the hormones most responsible for fat synthesis, so the two are really very interdependent. Girls with the disease anorexia nervosa, which involves self-starvation, and dancers and athletes all have decreased body fat and therefore menstruate later than normal or have amenorrhea (cessation of periods). Many female joggers find the same problem. However, if a woman is *too* fat it will also cause infertility. This may possibly help explain why women's weight fluctuates the way it does during the menstrual cycle. In midcycle, during the few days when pregnancy could occur, the appetite may tend to normalize because the body "knows" that being either too thin or too fat would not encourage fertility. As menstruation approaches, however, and the chance of pregnancy has been missed, appetite may flare up again and weight will consequently be gained. All this still rests in the realm of speculation, though.

This is when the Venus syndrome originates. One of the main reasons for this is the dramatic hormonal flux that takes place in adolescence. The increased secretion of the sex hormones fashions a woman's curves. The process by which such hormonal secretion can influence fat deposition in *particular* areas has not yet been traced exactly, but it is now known that thigh fat stores are more responsive to storage and less so to release during all phases of the menstrual cycle. Certain fat depots or local areas of subcutaneous fat could easily be more susceptible to estrogen, which is a lipogenic (fat-creating) hormone.

To isolate the action of these hormones, one can observe body shape changes in patients who are receiving them as drugs. Men with cancer of the prostate are given diethylstilbestrol, a form of female hormone related to estradiol, the main hormone produced by the ovaries. They tend to develop a more feminine shape as a result. On the other hand, women being treated with male hormones such as testosterone or having testosterone-secreting tumors lose weight from the hips and thighs and may deposit it on the stomach. Male eunuchoids, suffering from endocrine disorders that inhibit male sex hormone secretion, tend to be bottom-heavy. Animal studies show the same results: castrated roosters get fat and when injected with testosterone become slim again. This suggests that the *absence* of the male hormones, as well as the secretion of female sex hormones, causes lower-segment obesity.

Adolescent Anxiety

Most teenagers are very sensitive about body development. The body changes for a girl are total and therefore traumatic. Instead of having a flat chest and linear body, a new form has to be adjusted to. With these unfamiliar curves also comes the threat of impending sexual advances. No wonder the risk of anorexia nervosa is highest in girls who are approaching sexual maturity. Menstruation also causes anxiety in young girls for many reasons, one of which is that it causes weight gain from fluid retention.

Because increased adipose tissue is normal and necessary for the development of a teenage girl, it is difficult to distinguish between acceptable amounts of fat and excessive or disproportionate fat distribution. The Venus-syndrome shape is far from abnormal in this context. It is an exaggeration of the normal female shape. It is important to adopt this attitude of common sense toward a teenager who is developing lower body obesity and worrying about it. Panic and starvation are *not* solutions. Obviously, controlling weight through sensible dieting is most important, since, if overall weight gain is prevented, there is less chance that the hips and thighs will get overly large. Yet, as many teenagers find to their dismay, any excess intake may turn to lower body fat. Here exercise can be very important. If a teenager exercises, the maintenance of a certain degree of muscularity in her legs will prevent them from being too fat and flabby. Apart from these preventive measures, there isn't anything that one can do at adolescence to control the flood of hormones. It would be dangerous and stupid to try and tamper with the hormone balance at this or any other time. Adolescence is the peak time for awareness that the body *is* the self, that the outward expresses the whole. It is therefore very important to instill self-esteem in overweight teenagers, to assure them of your love at all times, and to help them feel innocent about their bodies. Then they can improve them.

The Pill and a Word on Water Retention

Many girls and women complain of weight gain when they take contraceptive pills. There are two basic kinds of pill; estrogen- and progesterone-based. Both these hormones can promote fat storage, partly because they make you retain fluid. The best thing to do is to find out, with your doctor's advice, which is the least troublesome pill for you in terms of fluid retention.

Water retention can occur for several reasons: a very rich or high-salt diet obviously bloats you, as does too much alcohol. Fatigue, stress, and air travel all promote water retention. In the latter part of pregnancy, water is retained as part of the body's storage function for the fetus. As each menstrual cycle is a simulated pregnancy from midcycle on, in the later part a woman's tendency for water retention will be particularly marked. The best ways to prevent fluid retention are avoiding not only salt but even moderately salty foods if you are very sensitive, drinking as much water as you can (at least one glass every half hour), not eating too late at night, and exercising a little while after dinner to avoid sleeping on a full stomach. If your feet tend to swell, which mine do badly, either wear support stockings or sleep with an elasticated support sock (ensure that it is not too tight and that it just grips you comfortably) and elevate your feet as often as possible. I find lying down flat on the floor with both my legs upright resting against a wall very refreshing and effective.

Pregnancy and Lactation

Science has established the dangers to the baby of a seriously under-weight and malnourished mother, but very little is known about pregnancy and nutrition in normal-weight and especially in obese women. It is hard to establish how much gain is the right gain. For a start, very little is known about the energy needs of a pregnant woman. One study has calculated that the average extra energy expenditure resulting from pregnancy is only 9 calories a day during the first three months, 84 during the second, and 216 during the last. The same study also established that as much as 90 percent of the calories consumed in excess of these requirements was stored as body fat.

The average weight gain during pregnancy is supposed to be around 12.5 kilograms (27.5 pounds). The pregnant mother stores around 3 to 4 kilograms (6.6 to 8.8 pounds) of the average weight gain as body fat. This is enough to provide the fetus with the calories it requires should its mother not be eating adequately during the last three months, which are so vital to its development. The fat bank may also contribute to providing energy for lactation.

There is enough evidence to suggest that for a thin woman the average weight and fat gain is necessary but that in a well-nourished obese woman, who already has plenty of fat, the average weight gain may be too much, both for her and her baby. Not only will the fat be harder to lose afterward but obese mothers also have heavier and fatter babies. As we know, a fat baby needn't become a fat adult but does have an increased risk of that happening.

If a woman does gain weight, the level of certain hormones will ensure she gains most of it on the lower half. If she incurs a slight energy deficit, her fat can be more easily mobilized and released during pregnancy. Most important is to sensibly limit food intake after carefully planning your diet with your doctor and to get as much exercise as you can. The amount of exercise you can take depends on how active you were before pregnancy.

Some of the best news on bottom-heaviness comes from a Swedish study. Scientists found a greater rate of fat mobilization in thigh fat during lactation than at most other times of a woman's reproductive life. If a woman can incur an energy deficit while lactating, and breast-feeding can account for up to one thousand calories of daily expenditure, not only will she lose weight but probably will lose it from her hips and thighs. It goes without saying that if she eats more than she needs, no weight or fat loss will occur despite the high fat mobilization rate. Obviously many more studies are needed before this theory can be confirmed, but the rate of fat mobilization in thigh fat during lactation does seem to suggest that our bottom-heavy fat stores were destined for this very function.

Menopause and After

For some women, from this time on fat on the hips and thighs decreases and the tendency is more toward depositing fat around the waist and sometimes on the upper body. This more masculine pattern of fat distribution is caused by the lessening secretion of hormones such as estrogen.

However, it is possible to gain weight at any age; in fact, body fat does tend to increase and lean body mass to decrease with age. The metabolic rate also decreases slightly as you get older. It is difficult to assess exactly how many more calories per pound of body weight are burned by a woman of twenty-five than by one of fifty-five. Metabolic rate depends more on genetics, body weight (you expend more calories moving a heavier body around), and activity than on age.

How Do Fat Cells React to Dieting?

The purpose of this chapter was to let you see that adult obesity is not purely the result of overfeeding in early life. If you have a genetic tendency to obesity, a childhood period of eating more than you need will be enough to trigger that. If the weight is lost and a sensible diet plus exercise program maintained, however, there is no other reason why the fat child should become a fat adult. If it looks as though you have a genetic tendency for weight gain, you *have* to be careful. There is evidence to suggest that once fat cell number goes up, weight loss is more difficult to maintain and weight is regained faster. However, another interesting discovery is that if positive energy balance is achieved only for a short time, the fat cells merely increase in size. If it is maintained for a longer time, increases in cell number are more likely to happen. Two conclusions can be drawn from this: first, that it is not the end of your dieting world if you go out to dinner and gorge one night providing you are careful again the next day. Second, it is best to lose weight as soon as you gain it. It's like scoring a goal as soon as you've had one scored against you in soccer.

If you do manage to maintain a negative energy balance, your body fat will decrease, but it is thought that probably in the first two years of dieting, fat cell size *alone* will decrease. Fat cell number requires an energy deficit to be maintained for a longer period than two years before it will change.

As the fat person's body does everything in its power to preserve flesh, you might think the stricter the diet, the better the results. This is incorrect. The more sudden the trauma you impose on the body, the more it will go into a state of fat preservation. A sensible and gradual diet is the best way to lose body fat, and it may even be markedly more effective if you are bottom-heavy.

3

Treating the Problem: What Works and What Doesn't

5

Diets: A Matter of Calories or Confusion?

The Reasons Diets Fail

A great many people love talking about diets, reading about diets, and thinking about diets. Very few people love going on them. In the United States, approximately 20 million diet pilgrims annually tread the path of self-denial and realize that the promised miracle at the end of the way has bitten the dust while they have been biting on not much more.

The real problem with dieting is perseverance. Motivation constantly comes under attack. Media advertising never leaves us in peace. It tempts us with a succulent cupcake just after our meager lunch of colorless cottage cheese. Every direction we look in, pictures and posters proclaim what we already know: food is delicious!

There is a simple reason why there are so many diets around: not one of them is permanently effective. Each one may work for a few people for a few weeks, perhaps even months, but eventually none can be claimed to be entirely successful. Diets designed for the masses cannot possibly suit every individual's metabolic requirements or eating habits. There is also a psychological reason why "designer" diets fail. They take away the control you have over what you eat. Following someone else's dietetic dictates, you obtain no knowledge of nutrition yourself. Because you lost weight thanks to someone else, you have no confidence in making your own choices.

Why Diet at All?

Even though medicine does not yet seem decided on whether a moderate degree of obesity is a health risk or not, there is a view that being ten to fifteen pounds overweight is perhaps not dangerous after all and is certainly not fatal. What is more important than medical data is how you feel about yourself. Do you remember being lighter and feeling more alive, more as you wanted to be? If the answer is yes, that is the most vital criterion for deciding to lose weight, and that improved image of yourself is your greatest motivating factor. Once the decision is made, half the battle is won.

Your mind can make you believe anything, so make it believe what will benefit you most. Diet is a principle and a *lifelong way of life*. If it is seen as tedious deprivation, that is how it will feel and fail. If it is felt as exciting, as a challenge, as giving *yourself* the most you can out of life by being good to yourself, it will work *forever*. It is just a question of attitude, and only you can change that.

Is There a Diet for the Hips and Thighs?

Losing weight from the lower body is a difficult proposition but not impossible. Even though it is your body that decides where weight will be lost, when you lose enough weight you *will* lose fat from the lower half. That can happen only on a carefully balanced diet. A sensible calorie-controlled eating plan is the most effective way of treating a weight and shape problem.

A popular concept, much publicized by some diets and the cellulite industry, is that eating certain foods causes you to put on weight on your hips, thighs, and buttocks. If you eat too much of any kind of food, especially a high-calorie one, you gain weight, and if you have a tendency for the Venus syndrome, you will gain most of it on your hips and thighs. Cutting these foods out means you lose weight in general. The elimination of these foods can *in no way* guarantee fat loss from the lower half. There is no scientific proof of this idea.

Those of us either with the Venus syndrome or with an ordinary weight problem did not become that way overnight. We are not going to remedy either problem immediately by sensational and temporary weight loss. Successive bouts of losing and maintaining weight can be very damaging, psychologically and physically. Moreover, it can be depressing and disorienting to cope with losing and regaining the same forty pounds ad infinitum. Finally, some studies have indicated that with each successive attempt at dieting, the metabolic rate, which decreases during dieting anyway, goes a little lower each time. It also takes progressively longer after each bout of dieting to return to its predieting level. Furthermore, even though there is no medical evidence to prove this, I found from experience that whenever I lost weight rapidly my body always lost fat from its upper half; my face became gaunt and my hips and thighs remained untouched. This of course made me look even more out of proportion than ever.

What Happens to Your Body When You Diet?

Many people, encouraged by what popular diet books tell them, assume that all weight loss is fat loss. Not so. If you experience very sudden weight loss, anywhere from two to eight pounds overnight, most of that weight is water, some of it is glycogen, and some of it is fat.

The weight loss happens in exactly that order. Water is lost first, then glycogen, and then fat. Water is the most easily lost. This is because when you start reducing intake, your body automatically gives up the excess fluids. As soon as you reduce calories, especially carbohydrate calories, the body draws on its short-term energy reserves of metabolized carbohydrates, glucose. This is stored in the liver and muscles in the form of glycogen that is bound with water. As soon as glycogen is used up, the water is lost. You don't always need that much of caloric deficit to lose water; it happens fairly automatically, though a certain caloric reduction *is* necessary.

What we really want to lose is fat, as obesity is a condition characterized by excess body fat. While the body's short-term energy store is limited, fat reserves are vast, and these are what the body usually draws on after a few days of dieting. Fat is more difficult to lose than glucose in the form of glycogen or body protein, which I shall discuss later. One gram of protein or carbohydrates contains only four calories; one gram of fat contains nine. When we lose a pound of fat, it isn't pure fat. If it were it would take a caloric deficit of 4,032 to lose it. Here's how the calculation works:

> 1 gram of fat = 9 calories
> 28 grams = 1 ounce, and 16 ounces = 1 pound
> therefore 9 × 28 × 16 = 4,032 calories

Roughly 85 percent of that pound of body fat is pure fat; the rest is protein and water. Therefore, we can perform a simple calculation:

$$\frac{85}{100} \times 4{,}032 \text{ calories} = 3{,}427 \text{ calories}$$

We see that to lose a pound of fat we need a deficit of 3,427 calories, let's say 3,500. It is impossible to incur this in one day. Even if you starved all day and jogged for hours, you probably could not achieve it. Therefore when you hear promises such as "Lose ten pounds in one week" you can be sure those ten pounds are not fat pounds, but mostly water and body glycogen pounds.

One final component of weight loss is body protein. It is most undesirable to lose this. Protein loss occurs when the diet is very low in calories and contains neither enough protein nor enough total calories to maintain the body's lean tissue. You require far fewer calories to lose one pound of protein than one pound of fat.

1 gram protein = 4 calories
28 grams = 1 ounce, and 16 ounces = 1 pound
$4 \times 28 \times 16 = 1{,}792$ calories

When you lose a pound of protein you are not losing pure protein—73 percent of lean body tissue is water. Therefore, if you take the remaining 27 percent, the calculation looks like this:

$$\frac{27}{100} \times 1{,}792 \text{ calories} = 483 \text{ calories}$$

It requires a deficit of only 483 calories to lose a pound of protein. Protein loss, which can happen so much more quickly than fat loss, is not desirable and can be extremely injurious to your health.

The short-term glycogen stores do not last long; usually they are exhausted after twenty-four hours of starvation. Once glycogen is depleted, the body must look elsewhere for carbohydrates, its most accessible form of fuel. If you are not ingesting enough carbohydrates, the body will have to make its own. It does this by breaking down protein and synthesizing the resultant amino acids into carbohydrates in the liver. This process is known as gluconeogenesis, the new creation of glucose. If it continues for too long, it could be fatal, as the body would break down too much protein that is essential for tissue repair and maintenance. It may also start to break down vital muscles such as the heart.

To prevent this from happening, the body switches from burning carbohydrates to burning fat. From this fat are released fatty acids and glycerol. To prevent protein from being converted to carbohydrates, the brain switches from its usual fuel, glucose, and uses ketone bodies instead, which are formed from the metabolism of fats. This may seem a foolproof system except that these ketone bodies are incompletely metabolized fats and are highly acidic. An excessive buildup of ketone bodies results in ketosis, which can cause unpleasant symptoms such as dizziness and vomiting. Ketosis can lead to excess uric acid in the system, resulting in gout and kidney stones, and can also cause loss of calcium.

How does the body react to all this burning of its stores? Unfortunately, it automatically lowers its metabolic rate, which means that the longer you are on a diet, the more slowly you lose fat. Basal or resting metabolic rate may start to decrease even twenty-four to forty-eight hours after you start restricting intake. This happens even more when one is on very low-calorie diets because the body breaks down its protein-rich stores. Because protein or lean tissue has a higher metabolic rate than fat, the less body protein you have, the less energy you burn.

Fad Diets: The Lean, Hungry, and Sometimes Dangerous Truth

Do you think that most of the world's diet authors really follow their own diets? I spotted one famous one in the most exclusive dining club in London. Do you think that she was pecking away at the meager allowance of acidic fruits she proposed for the masses? If so, you would be wrong. Instead she was tucking in to a substantial portion of pasta. The truth is that fad diets do not satisfy you any more than a normal, balanced, calorically controlled diet. They may look and sound more attractive but the majority of them are nutritionally deficient and unbalanced. They are also monotonous: would you rather stay on bananas and milk for the rest of your life (which may be considerably shortened as a result of vitamin and mineral deficiency) or learn to eat a selection of healthful foods like a human being instead of a lactating monkey? As we know, to lose body fat we have to decrease caloric intake. What should make one immediately suspicious of these fad diets is that in most of them calories are either not mentioned or not emphasized as the basis of the diet.

High-Protein Diets

Well-known examples of this diet are Dr. Atkins', Calories Don't Count, Stillman's, Scarsdale, Drinking Man's, and Magic Mayo (also known as the Grapefruit Diet). These diets allow dairy products and fat in various amounts; alcohol is another main attraction but only on the Drinking Man's Diet. What they all have in common is an unnecessarily high protein content, encouraging you to eat mostly unlimited amounts of eggs, meats, and cheeses. Carbohydrate intake is strictly limited. There is no advantage to eating excess protein: the body needs a certain daily amount and cannot store any more. Also, many of what we think of as healthy, high-protein foods such as steak or hard cheeses contain a higher percentage of fat than protein. One hundred grams or 3.5 ounces of mostly lean, grilled sirloin steak, worth 387 calories, contains 23 grams of protein and 32 grams of fat: 100 grams of Cheddar cheese worth 398 calories contains 25 grams of protein and 32.2 grams of fat. The dairy products advocated on these diets are usually limited to cheese alone, though a little milk is permitted. Healthier low-fat and low-calorie sources of calcium, such as yogurt and low-fat cheeses, are not even mentioned.

Excluded completely are carbohydrates, both refined ones such as sugar and much more essential, complex ones such as whole wheat breads, cereals, grains, and potatoes. As we saw before, the body breaks down its other tissues or forms ketone bodies in the absence of essential carbohydrates. Yet almost all these diets have carbohydrates as the dieter's enemy. Carbohydrates are no more fattening than protein and less fattening than fat. Unless you have something drastically wrong with your metabolism, and very few people do, you should have no problem breaking them down.

The immediate weight loss on these diets is impressive but it *cannot* be fat loss. No matter what you eat, to lose a pound of body fat your caloric deficit must be around 3,500 calories. These high-protein diets are *not* calorically controlled, portions are usually unspecified, and as there is so much fat in these diets, and fat per gram has more than *double the amount* of calories of carbohydrates or protein, these diets are likely to be high in calories. What you are really losing is water. As we know, in the first few days on a diet, the body uses its glycogen stores and as glycogen binds three to four times its own weight of water, much water is lost. This explains why men sometimes have a greater success with high-protein diets than women. Men tend to lose water much more easily than women. Unlike women they have no hormonal water-retaining tendencies, and their bodies contain more water than fat anyway. Because of this water loss, high-protein diets have a quicker *weight* loss than high-carbohydrate or mixed diets of the same caloric value. But remember the difference between weight loss (in this case mostly water loss) and fat loss. Fat loss is what to aim for and it takes time.

High-protein diets can also be extremely dangerous by inducing ketosis. Moreover, with all the protein on this diet, you will be excreting vast amounts of the waste product nitrogen. Normally healthy kidneys should be able to cope with this, but if they are even slightly under strain, it could be dangerous. Additionally, in the absence of carbohydrates, the body runs the risk of burning protein tissue to turn into carbohydrates. There is also a possibility of dehydration. Severe water loss is accompanied by the loss of valuable electrolytes—minerals such as potassium, sodium, and chloride, which, in solution, convey electrical impulses in the body.

Another problem is the amount of butter, animal fats, and cheeses. This may lead to a rise in blood cholesterol (see Chapter 6) if you have a genetic tendency for it. Also, because no complex carbohydrates are allowed, the fiber content on these diets is low and constipation may result. Even though your body needs only small amounts of sugar, as many of these diets limit or exclude even fresh fruits you may get a craving for something sweet and feel weak and dizzy from low blood sugar.

Even if you manage to stick successfully to a high-protein diet, coming off it can cause problems. As soon as carbohydrates are introduced, glycogen stores are rapidly replenished and therefore water is regained. Your weight will probably increase as a result. Also, such diets do little to educate you in balancing the types of foods to eat and teach you little or nothing about portion control.

For these reasons, these diets are not sensible. Those of us who are bottom-heavy may be as encouraged by rapid weight loss as anyone with a weight problem, but the water loss and subsequent gain once the diet is stopped can be uncomfortable and demoralizing.

High Complex Carbohydrate Diets

Leading examples are Kempner's Rice Diet, the Macrobiotic Diet, and the Pritikin Program. They all encourage consumption of unrefined carbohydrates, such as rice; the macrobiotic diet stresses the importance of brown rice as a perfect nutrient. They allow large quantities of raw vegetables and fruit as well as cereals and grains. So far so good. What is seriously deficient is protein intake, which is essential for the body's cells. These diets do allow protein from animal sources (mostly fish) and also permit protein intake in the form of nuts, cereals, and legumes such as peas, beans, and lentils. However, the diet is bland and monotonous and it is doubtful that protein needs are met. The fat intake is so low (about 10 percent of *total calories* on Pritikin's program) that the skin may become rough and hard.

Because of the lack of fat and protein, these diets are essentially quite low in calories. They are so unappetizing because of their low fat and low sodium content that one tends to eat less than the amounts allowed. Because of the absence of fat, this type of diet is generally much healthier than the high-protein types. The restriction of alcohol, salt, tea, coffee, and sugar is very strict and rather unpleasant to follow but the benefits are considerable. Cereals, the basis of the diet, are high in vitamin B, which is useful in combating stress. The diet is simple to follow because it is so restricted and monotonous.

Now for the disadvantages. Number one on the list is boredom. Imagine eating only rice, fruit, and vegetables—easier perhaps for a Buddhist monk in the Himalayan heights, safely isolated from the wonders of Baskin-Robbins than for you and me. Socializing is hard on these diets and they require a lot of willpower. They are probably of great value in cleansing the system of toxins for a few days, but as a long-term strategy for losing body fat, they are deficient from a nutritional standpoint. As these diets are high in unrefined carbohydrates, they are also high in fiber. Too much fiber can cause bloating and gastric discomfort. Also, because of the limited use of dairy products, you may be at risk of calcium deficiency. Because salt intake is reduced, some people's blood pressure may drop too low. Finally, these diets are deficient in some vitamins and minerals, so you should take an appropriate supplement with them.

High-Fiber Diets

The most well-known example of fiber diets on the market is The F-Plan. This is a calorie-controlled diet, specifying energy levels, including fats and proteins in measured quantities but emphasizing complex carbohydrates that contain fiber. Menus include a mixed breakfast cereal consisting of bran and fruits, and at other meals vegetables such as baked potatoes and beans are suggested. The diet is sound nutritionally, provides vitamins and minerals, and adopts a healthy and sensible approach to eating and drinking. The obvious problem with eating so much fiber is flatulence, diarrhea, and other associated disorders. Although fiber is good for you, too much of a good thing is not. Also, some fiber foods, such as beans and rice, are fairly high-calorie, so if quantities are not carefully watched, weight gain may result. Fiber has been proved of benefit from a health point of view but as a diet food it has no special value.

Combination Diets

Famous examples include the Beverly Hills, Enzyme Catalyst, and Lecithin, B_6, Apple-Cider Vinegar, and Kelp diets. These diets are based on the premise that if certain foods are eaten in combination, their magical fat-burning powers will be released. One is supposed to be particularly careful not to mix these foods with others because then their magical properties will be rendered ineffective. The gurus who promote these diets use the word "enzyme" very often, and make many fanciful claims.

A slight variation on this theme is the idea that we put on weight because we are allergic to certain foods either when eaten singly or in combination with others. The Mandels' It's Not Your Fault

You're Fat Diet presents this novel idea in a very convincing way. The point of the diet is to isolate the source of the allergy and learn to break free of it. While it has been proved that substances like caffeine are addictive and that people are allergic to certain foods, these are simply peripheral causes of overweight and not the central issue. Such diets usually seem to work because the allergy-causing foods almost always are fattening and unhealthful. So far I have heard of no theory about allergies to raw vegetables or clear soup!

There is no scientific evidence to support the contention that it is the *mixture* of foods we eat that puts on weight. It is not even the kind of foods we eat. What is of paramount importance in tipping the scales is the total amount of calories, no matter where these come from. Neither pineapple, wheat germ, vinegar, nor kelp are magic foods. They cannot help you burn off fat either alone or if you eat them before or after you eat anything else. The weight loss on combination diets results from boredom. You can get fed up with a certain food and you eat less, reducing caloric intake, something that most self-styled diet experts never seem to mention. Moreover, these miraculous nutrients rarely provide you with enough protein, calcium, vitamins, and minerals. Fruit diets are also high in acid and could lead to peptic ulcers and even worse gastrointestinal disorders. The Beverly Hills Diet may cause severe diarrhea in many cases. Beware of these diet myths and stay away.

High-Protein Liquid Diets

These diets are low in fat and carbohydrates. They are also *hypocaloric:* containing fewer calories than the average daily requirement. It has been calculated that around eight hundred to nine hundred calories is the limit, below which you break down lean body mass as well as fat. All that these diets consist of is a powdered protein formula. However, as we shall see, there are powders and powders.

Some Dangerous Examples

Let me start by saying that it is unwise to embark on any liquid protein diet without medical supervision. Seriously overweight people, under the constant supervision of skilled specialists, usually in a hospital, have undergone protein-sparing modified fasts, which are fasts supplemented by small quantities of high-grade protein (usually solid) and essential minerals and vitamins. The liquid protein diets widely available now, however, are not as safe as such a fast because they may not be as carefully composed of high-quality protein and almost all of the dieters using them are not under strict medical supervision.

A particularly dangerous, in fact fatal, example, is the Last Chance Diet invented by Dr. Robert Linn. This consists of a protein powder, Pro Linn. It is to be taken with vitamin and mineral supplements and two quarts of noncaloric fluids per day. Gradually a refeeding eating program is added to the fast, but some powder is still to be taken every day. By June 1978, fifty-eight deaths had resulted, probably from this kind of diet. The protein used in these diets is derived from gelatin, partially watered down and of low nutritive value. It is not adequate for optimal health. Many of the people who died on these diets had no other known health problems. They were still 7 percent above "ideal" weight and felt fine until they began to experience cardiac arrhythmias and died immediately. They had no warning symptoms and there was no time to treat them. Their deaths were caused by drastic weight loss and severe loss of body protein, as the diet is seriously deficient in high-quality protein.

This is the greatest danger of a liquid formula diet and of any hypocaloric diet. Under 800 or 900 calories the body cannot receive adequate sources of protein. As it only requires a deficit of 483 calories to lose a pound of body protein, this loss can and does happen rapidly and is especially dangerous over the long term. Another disadvantage of such diets is the occurrence of ketosis in the absence of carbohydrates. The wastage of lean body mass is also accompanied by severe dehydration and loss of essential vitamins and minerals, including electrolytes, which can disturb heart function.

To sum up, any low-grade protein powder, such as one derived from gelatin as opposed to natural, animal sources, should be strictly avoided. It is best to ask your doctor to prescribe a more reliable preparation, such as the ones described in the next section, but even then great care and medical supervision are advisable.

A Short History of Safe Low-Calorie Diets

Not every liquid formula diet need be fatal. Some can be safe and balanced. Take, for example, the very first formula diet to which we have all been introduced: the milk we swallowed as babies. Children are frequently given liquid substitute meals when they cannot eat solids because of pediatric allergies.

The first liquid protein diet was devised in 1944 specifically for allergic adults and for patients with intestinal disorders who could not consume solid food. The 1950s saw a further extension of the uses of the formula diet as a research tool. The logical step was then to apply these restricted diets to obese patients. There were many advantages. Doctors would know *exactly* how much and what their patients were eating. The contents thus could be manipulated and made more successful. The patient would find it much easier to follow a formula hypocaloric diet than one of ordinary food because it was easily measured, and overeating was much less likely.

Today the advanced knowledge of essential nutrients has enabled clinicians to invent complete liquid formulas containing high-grade protein from sources such as egg white and some carbohydrates. The inclusion of carbohydrates is a significant recent addition. It seems to spare the body's protein sources, reduces ketosis and high uric acid, prevents excess water and electrolyte losses, and prevents swelling upon refeeding, which happens after a noncarbohydrate diet. There are many low-calorie formula diets on the market today that offer a daily consumption of around three hundred calories. Despite their claims of being balanced, there is a risk of body protein loss. Also available on the diet food market are infinite varieties of mini-meals in the form of chocolate bars, cookies, etc., which have limited caloric value. These, although conveniently measured calorically, give you no long-term idea of how to enjoy real food in moderation. Dependence on any of these diet meals simply increases fear of eating in the real world.

However good a powder or a substitute meal may be, it cannot sustain you for long periods of time as a balanced diet can. Whenever you follow a diet, you should check with your doctor first and, in the case of the very low-calorie diets, keep on checking. It is essential to take daily vitamin and mineral supplements.

Fasting: A Preferable Alternative?

It is possible to eat nothing at all for quite some time and survive. Possible but not advisable. Fasting is the most extreme method of weight reduction and can be fatal. It should be approached with extreme caution, and I would not advise it at all. However, as a method of reduction, it has been included.

Fasting, either complete or partial, is advocated for spiritual reasons by most religions at certain times.

Because food and the toxic wastes it produces are regarded as a defilement of the body, starvation therefore represents purification. It is a widely held belief that when deprived of food, people have increased awareness of their spirituality and are close to God. Stylites, recluses who lived on top of stone pillars in the East (especially Syria, Palestine, and Greece) during the fourth through seventh centuries, exemplify this belief. The stylites believed that their severe asceticism, which included prolonged fasts, brought them nearer to God. Fasting may be an initial means of attaining greater spirituality along with many other techniques, such as different forms of yoga and meditation. In the most sensational case histories of saints and yogis, total abstention from food occurred.

Fasting must be medically supervised. The morbidly obese, who are usually the only ones for whom fasting is advised, are hospitalized and given ample liquids and vitamin and mineral supplements. Their blood and urine are checked regularly to monitor any serious chemical losses that may result from the severe metabolic changes that occur during fasting. Weight loss is usually very impressive and very rapid; at the same time hunger is minimal. This makes fasting look ideal, yet it has disadvantages. Not eating at all teaches nothing about eating less, which is eventually what every diet aims to do. Weight is regained rapidly, usually with stomach upsets. Another major danger is loss of body protein, especially muscle from the vital organs, and excessive nitrogen output that strains the kidneys. If all goes well, the body has a mechanism by which it switches off protein loss after so many days on a fast. On average this happens after about ten days and any further body protein is thus spared. Most deaths from starvation occur when the shift mechanism does not come into operation. Another major risk is ketosis. Fat loss occurs for only about a third of the weight loss in a fast; water loss accounts for well over another third. As the kidneys flush out

water, they also flush out electrolytes. Loss of these elements constitutes the greatest danger of fasting. Finally, a fast provides no vitamins and minerals.

Fasting is of great value only to extremely obese people but, in a
modified form, can be useful to cleanse and detoxify the system if
done, very carefully, one day a month or possibly one day a week.
At these times, try drinking only liquids and clear soups. Even if
you attempt this, use extreme caution at all times, especially while
driving or exercising.

Calorically Restricted Diets

These are the most effective diets for *permanent* weight loss. You
may not see immediate, dramatic differences, but over time reducing
your caloric intake enough will burn off body fat and burn it off
steadily. Because you are paying attention to calories, your choice
of types of foods is much freer and these diets tend to be healthily
balanced.

There are so many calorie-controlled diets that it is impossible
to include a whole range here. A good way of judging a calorically
restricted diet is to ask yourself the following questions:

1. Is the diet safe? Does it provide me with over 800 to 900
calories, giving me enough vitamins and minerals and other essential nutrients?

2. Is the diet balanced? Does it give me the flexibility to select
measured portions of *different* kinds of foods?

3. Is the diet flexible? Will it teach me how to compose my
own meals and learn about caloric values so that I can follow
the diet wherever I am and whatever I am doing?

4. Is the diet easy? Does it explain to me all I want to know
clearly and simply so that eventually I can memorize all I need
to know? Dieting can then become my way of life, and I can
adapt it to suit myself.

Do such diets exist? Let's find out.

6

The Only Diet for You

Out There on Your Own

If you attack your fat cells with shock tactics, such as fad diets, your cells will respond in an equally drastic way. They will resist. That's how you become locked in a lifetime struggle of weight loss and gain. The answer to successful, permanent weight loss must surely lie elsewhere.

The diet that really works is the one you design as part of you and your life. The only diet there is is one with which you do not have to be constantly obsessed. It should come naturally. People dislike dieting because they hate restriction and deprivation. Once I learned this, I really did begin to lose weight gradually and keep it off; I never *deny* myself any food. I may postpone eating the food for a few hours or days so that the craving sometimes subsides, but I never say, "I can't have this."

The only thing you have to give up on your diet is your own negative thinking about hunger, failure, and self-image. The things you should have every day in abundance are positive thinking, energy, enthusiasm, and the satisfaction of knowing that you are doing the best for yourself. When you have an off day, avoid punishing yourself and judging yourself as a failure by understanding that it takes several days to *really* gain a pound of fat and therefore will take several days to lose it. Dieting is not a contest; everyone loses at a different rate.

Eating for the good of our weight, shape, and life is a long-term commitment. It requires devotion, not just diet, courage instead of a carbohydrate counter. But as someone who hated herself until I started living what I wrote, and who now feels better and better with each day, you have my guarantee: it is worth it.

Setting Goals

When you are losing weight or improving shape, it is important to combine enthusiasm with realism. You *can* transform yourself but it will take time. I suggest that you keep accurate average records of your weight and measurements every week but that you also pay attention to the messages your body gives you. Tiredness, stress, and emotional trauma not only take their toll on the body but significantly affect the way we perceive and feel our bodies.

Because we cannot be sure from which part of the body we will lose fat or how many hours of exercise it takes to slim ourselves down, it is difficult to set an inches target. It is more fun to aim at fitting into a new dress or one that you already have that has not fitted for years. As far as a weight target is concerned, choose a weight that you feel would be right for you and that you are able to maintain.

How often should you weigh yourself? For many people, this becomes a mania: no matter how weak from hunger and exhausted after exercise, they leap onto the scale several times a day. I was one of them. As a teenager, I used to plunge into a boiling bathtub, emerge purple as a beetroot, and leap onto the scale (which nearly broke under the assault) to see how many pounds I'd sweated off! To obtain an accurate idea of fat gain or loss, and to allow water balance to stabilize, especially after a spicy or salty meal, a long flight, or a tiring day (all water retainers), I would advise that you weigh yourself every two days. Always use the same scale if possible; keep it in the same place and position, always on a hard floor and not a rug. Moving the scale may cause it to be inaccurate. It is preferable to weigh in before breakfast, but if this is not possible always choose the same time, wear the same clothes (weighing naked is preferable), and take off your shoes. Be honest with yourself; even if your weight is up, record it. More important, be kind to yourself; forgive yourself for gaining those pounds and let your next positive thought be to lose them.

Balancing the Diet: All You Need to Know

A balanced diet is one that includes adequate amounts of the following:

Macronutrients. "Macro" means large; this word indicates nutrients that we need in large quantities to support life—proteins, fats, and carbohydrates.

Micronutrients. "Micro" means small; this term thus covers all the essential nutrients we need in smaller amounts—vitamins and minerals.

When looking at nutrition or the art of eating well, we are faced with several forms of classification. Apart from the macronutrient-micronutrient division, a balanced diet is also characterized by having enough foods from each of the four basic food groups. Calorie-controlled diets normally allow a certain amount of servings per day from each of the following:

Meat Group. All meats, poultry, and fish, including smoked and dried varieties, cheeses (usually the hard ones), and eggs.

Bread Group. All types of bread, bakery items, all grains and cereals (wheat, bran, oats, etc.), all pasta. Potatoes and other starchy vegetables are sometimes included in this category instead of being considered root vegetables.

Vegetable Group and Fruit Group. These two groups are usually separated. The first includes all types of vegetables except starchy ones, which usually go into the bread group. The fruit group includes all fruits, fresh and canned.

Milk Group. Includes milk and milk products, such as yogurt, ice cream, cream, and cottage and other soft cheeses.

Even though there are four theoretical food groups, there are actually six: fruits and vegetables count as two and the sixth is the fats group, including butter, margarine, cooking fats, and all oils.

When you create your balanced diet, you have to be like a juggler and concentrate on several things at the same time. You must have just the right amounts of fats, proteins, and carbohydrates while still achieving the right mixture from the basic food groups. Meanwhile you must not forget to get all the essential vitamins and minerals. Remembering all this can be confusing. That's why I've tried to set out the information as simply as possible. Let us begin with the macronutrients, which foods contain them, how much we need, and what their functions are.

Proteins

The Greek root of the word "protein," signifying "first," indicates its importance. Protein is a priority, the most important macronutrient. Without protein our bodies could not repair and rebuild cells, nor form such essentials as the plasma proteins that transport nutrients to cells, hormones and enzymes, antibodies in the immune system, hair, skin, and nails. Protein is thus the very stuff of life. When we speak of protein we are not only speaking about the kind we eat. As we know, part of our body is protein. Therefore the protein we eat goes toward making that lean tissue. Proteins are constantly being synthesized and degraded in a dynamic cycle within our bodies.

Protein is made from chains of carbon, hydrogen, and oxygen and from amino acids that are really the building blocks of proteins. The body has the ability to produce almost all the amino acids necessary to make up protein except for eight or possibly nine of them. These essential amino acids can be found only in protein-rich foods, and if we do not eat enough of these, or do not get a complete combination of them, protein cannot be synthesized.

While the fuel from fats and carbohydrates can only be used for energy expenditure or for storage in the form of fat, the fuel from protein can be used either to make protein itself or for energy expenditure or storage. If a person is not obtaining enough energy from fats and carbohydrates (more likely to happen in underdeveloped countries or if a person is voluntarily fasting), his or her protein calories can be used to fuel the body. Protein therefore cannot be synthesized from the protein foods the person eats, and a protein deficiency may result.

In the West, we consume too much protein. Protein cannot be kept in reserve. Because we need a new supply of it every day, eating vast quantities of it does no good, and in fact can be very dangerous and unwise. A by-product of protein is nitrogen. In large amounts, nitrogen is toxic and has to be excreted in the form of urea in the urine, thus straining the kidneys. The liver also overworks in the attempt to process so much protein, which also harms the bones. In addition, the protein foods we know and love so well—meat, milk, cheese, etc.—are also very high in fats and in calories. The amounts we eat of them are vastly in excess of our daily requirement.

Not only are we ingesting too much protein, but along with it extra calories; they only turn into one thing—fat!

Reliable books on nutrition tell us that adults need 0.36 grams per every pound of our ideal body weight. You have to work out how much you *should* weigh and go from there. The basis of this formula is that protein allowances are estimated in accordance with the amount of lean tissue you have. When you are at your ideal weight, most of your body is lean tissue. Once you exceed this weight, you do so because of excess fat. Another guideline for establishing protein needs is to know that, on an ideal diet, protein should account for only 12 to 15 percent, maximum 20 percent, of your daily calories.

The difficulty is to eat foods that give maximum nutritional value as a protein source without adding too many calories. If you're really interested, the best way to obtain accurate information is through books of food composition tables, which will show protein content of foods. Here are some brief guidelines:

1. Complete proteins. To make protein, a certain amount and balance of the correct amino acids are essential. Animal proteins, meat, fish, poultry, dairy products, and eggs all contain adequate amino acids, including those that the body cannot produce. These foods are the best sources of protein, but always remember they are no better for you if eaten in quantities larger than necessary.

2. Partially complete proteins, such as those in some fish and in milk, do not contain all the essential amino acids and unless supplemented with foods from 1. cannot support continued growth.

3. Incomplete proteins are nuts, seeds, grains (rice, wheat, barley, oats, corn), and legumes (peanuts, soybeans, various kinds of beans and peas). These, if eaten separately, are incomplete proteins and must be supplemented by animal sources; however, if certain legumes and grains are eaten in combination, complete proteins can be synthesized.

Carbohydrates

Carbohydrates are high-energy foods. They are broken down into glucose, which is the body's most immediate source of fuel. Complex carbohydrates are the starches in vegetables, grains, and legumes.

Called polysaccharides because of their lengthier molecular structure, they take longer to be absorbed and have to be broken down into monosaccharides, or simple sugars. Simple carbohydrates are much more readily absorbed than starches. They are found naturally in milk, fruits, and vegetables, and in refined form in sugar.

The complex carbohydrates include foods such as baked potatoes, pasta, whole grains, breads made with unrefined flour, raw or partially cooked vegetables, and fibrous fruits such as bananas. Starches, previously considered the enemies of the dieter, are now recommended as our staple food, though we do still have to watch calories. Too much of any food can be fattening. However, the belief that starches in general are fattening is invalid. One gram of protein *has just as many calories* as a gram of carbohydrates—four—and the complex kind of carbohydrate can satisfy you more, both in the stomach and in the mind. Carbohydrates are filling foods, giving you more volume for your calories, and are soothing and satisfying. Why this is so is uncertain. There has been talk of a connection with endorphins, the brain's natural opiates, though nothing as yet has been proved. Nothing is certain except that warm, soothing feeling that carbohydrates produce.

Carbohydrates should constitute 55 to 60 percent of our caloric intake, fifty to one hundred grams per day minimum, and most of the carbohydrates you eat should be complex.

Sugar: The Controversial Cube

Simple sugars contain many fewer nutritional advantages than a complex carbohydrate such as brown rice, which has more fiber, vitamins, minerals. However, the body does need some sugar. All ingested sugar, whether fructose (fruit sugar), sucrose (table sugar), or any other kind, is eventually turned into glucose, a monosaccharide. When sugar enters the body, the pancreas secretes the hormone insulin, which removes sugar from the blood, allowing it to be burned up or stored as fat, depending on energy balance. When blood glucose levels drop and sugar is eaten, it seems to provide an instant pick-me-up. This "sugar high," to which millions are addicted, lasts all too briefly. As part of the body's attempt to maintain homeostasis (balance), insulin is pumped into the circulation to normalize blood sugar levels. Sometimes, however, things can go wrong.

Diabetes is the prime example. Insulin-dependent diabetics, who have been diabetic since childhood, fail to secrete enough insulin when they consume sugar. The body cannot handle the load of blood sugar, which is high because none can be absorbed. Noninsulin-dependent or adult-onset diabetics have a different problem. They secrete too much insulin, but because their cells are insensitive to insulin, their sugar level remains unaffected. The opposite of diabetes is hypoglycemia, a condition in which the large amount of insulin secreted is *too* efficient and blood sugar levels drop so much that they leave the sufferer feeling dizzy, nauseated, and faint. True hypoglycemia is a definite disease and can be accurately diagnosed by tests that measure the body's glucose tolerance. It is fairly common to feel faint, tense, and ravenously hungry a few hours after eating a lot of sugar. That does not mean you have true hypoglycemia. The process that your body goes through to handle excessive sugar intake may be similar to the process of hypoglycemia but the disease itself is a lot rarer than people think.

Sugar has been attacked by a crusading mob of "health" and nutrition writers. It has not been categorically proved that sugar consumption is one of the causes of diabetes. As to whether sugar makes you fat or not, the answer is not more so than any other food. Whatever you eat in large quantities puts on weight, be it carrots or carrot cake. Sugar is more fattening only in that it is more concentrated than some other foods, such as complex carbohydrates.

How do you decide whether sugar is bad for you? As with almost everything to do with diet: experiment. From personal experience, when I was cutting calories, it made sense to me to cut out desserts and eat fruit instead as I could have more fruit and more satisfaction for fewer calories. Some people crave sugar more than others. There were times when I would be desperate for it: other times I didn't care. By avoiding it or limiting myself to candy or ice cream once a week, I felt less of a "sugar swing" from high energy to low energy a few hours after eating it. As part of an effort to balance my diet, cutting sugar did help. I am not an antisugar fanatic. I keep sugar low in my diet but I don't eliminate it completely. Obviously how much you should abstain depends on the degree of your addiction.

Fats

The third macronutrient is fat. Whether it is fat from nuts or seeds, oils, dairy products, or animal sources, the fat we eat is identical in structure to our own adipose tissue. It is made up of triglycerides; three fatty acid molecules bound with one molecule of glycerol. It is sometimes wrongly believed that when we eat fat it turns into adipose tissue automatically, but dietary fat does not therefore become adipose tissue any more easily than protein or carbohydrates. Dietary fat has several unique functions. Adequate fat in the diet ensures the absorption of fat-soluble vitamins, the formation of certain vital secretions such as prostaglandins, which regulate cholesterol. It also helps keep the texture of your skin smooth.

We do not need to eat a lot of fat. Fifteen to thirty grams daily is adequate, and it should supply between 25 and 35 percent of our calories. In the West we exceed a healthy fat intake, which could be dangerous. The three fatty acid molecules in triglycerides come in three different degrees of saturation or density. The degree of saturation depends on how much space the fatty acid molecule has left along its chain for hydrogen atoms to fit in, which will reduce the density. A saturated fat is the most dense, having no room for hydrogen; a monounsaturated fat can take two hydrogen atoms; and a polyunsaturated fat four or more. An easy way to test the saturation of a fat is to see how hard it is at room temperature: the harder the fat the more saturated.

Fat is found in dairy products, egg yolks, coconuts, vegetable shortening, all meat, poultry, some fish (especially in the skin), avocados, nuts, and obviously all oils. From a caloric point of view all three kinds of fat are equal, but from a health point of view they are not.

The most threatening aspect of fat is cholesterol. The body makes more than enough of its own cholesterol in the liver and we really have no need of it in our diet. The more we eat, the higher our blood level seems to rise, even though our body tries partially to compensate for our intake by decreasing its own production. Cholesterol is measured in milligrams. It has been estimated that in the United States people eat six hundred milligrams a day. A more acceptable figure would be half that. High blood levels of cholesterol, which can be estimated with a blood test, are known to be caused partly by diet, but genetic factors also play an important role. Saturated fats, present in butter, milk, animal fats, and in some oils of palm and coconut, are known to raise blood cholesterol levels, while monounsaturated or polyunsaturated varieties, found in vegetables, nuts, and vegetable oils, are less risky.

As a fat, cholesterol is not water soluble and is carried around in the bloodstream by lipoproteins. There are three different kinds of lipoproteins: a safe kind—high-density lipoproteins—and two dangerous kinds—low- and very low-density lipoproteins. We all have a mixture, but your level of high-density lipoproteins can be increased by reducing the amount of saturated fat in the diet, losing weight, and exercising. On the cellular level, some people inherit an abnormality that prevents their liver cells from stopping cholesterol production once they are receiving cholesterol from the lipoproteins. They may have a higher risk of having a heart attack.

Obesity and abnormally high cholesterol levels do not necessarily go together. However, it is generally a good idea to keep saturated fats low in your diet (only 10 percent of your total fat calories) and divide the rest among monounsaturates and polyunsaturates, keeping in mind that some theories show polyunsaturated fats to be carcinogenic. That is even more reason to emphasize *balance* in a diet. If types of food are eaten in moderation, the risk of the ill effects that come from them will be reduced.

Let us now go on to the micronutrients.

Vitamins

Their most conservative claim is that they sustain life and make us healthier, their most extravagant that they can cure cancer, preserve or give us youth, cure depression, and make us energetic. What is the truth?

Micronutrients have no caloric value and are therefore not energy-giving, but certain amounts of them are essential. Vitamins help to process other nutrients and generally cooperate with enzymes. What we tend to forget and what the vitamin promoters encourage us to is that on an adequate and *balanced* diet, containing enough fresh and raw foods, and usually over 1,200 calories, we get all the vitamins we need.

There are two kinds of vitamins: fat- and water-soluble. Vitamins A, D, E, and K belong to the first category: they can be retained in the body and do not have to be ingested daily. Water-soluble vitamins are much more fragile. They are easily lost in cooking and cannot be stored. They include vitamin C and the enormous B group of vitamins: thiamine (B_1), riboflavin (B_2), niacin (B_3, otherwise known as nicotinamide or nicotinic acid), B_6 (which includes pyridoxine, pyridoxal, and pyridoxamine), B_{12} (cobalamin), folacin or folic acid, pantothenic acid, and finally biotin.

Vitamins are organic compounds, without which specific metabolic disorders may result. Vitamins have to be obtained from external sources, for even though the body can produce some of them, it sometimes cannot produce adequate amounts. For instance, vitamin D can be formed on the skin by sunlight, vitamin A can be synthesized from substances called carotenoids, niacin can be made from the amino acid tryptophan, and vitamin K and biotin are synthesized by the bacteria found in the gut. To have adequate amounts, however, it is best to ingest these vitamins through the foods you eat.

The main question that people want answered is, "Should I take a vitamin supplement?" The answer to this does to a large degree depend on what you eat, how old you are, and the type of life you lead. Only if your diet is perfectly balanced can you be sure that you are getting enough vitamins and minerals. This is rarely the case today, when our eating pattern consists of several sporadic, rushed meals based on convenience foods. In addition to not getting enough vitamins in your diet, if you smoke or drink you will destroy the vitamins you are ingesting. More important still is the case of the dieter. If you are on a regimen of 1,200 calories a day or less, you are probably deficient in some micronutrients. How are we measuring "adequate" and "deficient"? The usual guideline is the U.S. R.D.A. (Recommended Dietary Allowances), which establishes how much of each nutrient is necessary for "all healthy persons." The R.D.A. may be questionable in several ways. First, there is still a lot about nutrition that no one knows. Second, "all healthy persons" are not the same: nutrition varies from one individual to another, depending on genetic make-up, lifestyle, age, etc. And what about unhealthy persons? They will obviously require different nutritional strategies. It is claimed that certain vitamins, such as niacin, and other related compounds can aid metabolism and help you lose weight. This is a misinterpretation of the truth. As we know, lipolysis, or fat release, occurs through the stimulation of fat-mobilizing hormones. These hormones work through enzymes, which in turn work with coenzymes; for example, vitamins. This means that *indirectly* the presence of certain vitamins and trace elements can aid enzymes to aid hormones to mobilize fat.

Lecithin has a great claim to fame in this field. Like triglyceride, lecithin is composed of fatty acids and glycerol but with phosphoric acid and choline (a B vitamin) added, and is found throughout the body. It is actually *not* a fat mobilizer but an emulsifier that breaks down large fat droplets into smaller ones. In that sense, then, lecithin is not a pharmacological mobilizer, and even if it does contribute minimally to fat mobilization, which *could* lead to fat utilization if there is negative energy balance, our central nervous systems make enough of it and we do not need to take it in tablet form. By now we know that there is only one effective fat mobilizer and utilizer: caloric deficit.

Perhaps the long-term results of experiments being conducted now will show that megadosing can at best prevent and cure serious illness and at least contribute to greater well-being. If you do wish to embark on a megadosing experiment I suggest you look into the subject with the utmost care and caution. Megadosing can easily become overdosing. Excessive amounts of fat-soluble vitamins can be toxic because they are stored within your system. Excess amounts of water-soluble ones are simply excreted. The fantastic claims may be true but may also be attributable to psychological persuasion. In the field of nutrition or exercise, we should always be looking for results, and results that are facts.

My advice is if you are on a diet of fewer than 1,200 calories, take one multivitamin supplement daily, and if you are a woman take an iron supplement as well, as menstruation depletes iron levels. Also, when cooking and preparing foods, to retain vitamins use minimal liquids in cooking, especially when boiling vegetables, avoid removing skins whenever possible, and minimize cutting and shredding of vegetables.

Minerals

Minerals are also micronutrients. They are metallic elements that form enzymes and hormones and aid in metabolism. Minerals occur in the waters of rivers, lakes, and oceans and become incorporated into plants and then into animals. Certain concentrations of them within the body—for instance, sodium, chloride, and potassium, the electrolytes—are vitally important to the heart and to all metabolic activity. Minerals come in two categories, macrominerals, more of which are needed, and trace elements of microminerals, which are less important. Macrominerals include calcium, phosphorus, potassium, sulfur, sodium, chloride, and magnesium. Trace minerals are iron, zinc, fluoride, iodine, copper, selenium, manganese, molybdenum, and chromium. Certain other mineral substances are thought to be necessary, but nothing definite has been established about them. These are silicone, vanadium, tin, nickel, cobalt, arsenic, and cadmium.

As with vitamins, the only guideline to how much is necessary is provided by the R.D.A.s. The myth of megadosing prevails here also. Again the best advice seems to me to take a multivitamin supplement that includes minerals (they usually do).

Sodium

This previously innocent and historically precious (the word "salary" derives from it) mineral is now vehemently attacked. Sodium is an indisputably important mineral, without which we could not survive. It is already present in most of what we eat without our needing any extra. Unfortunately, because salt is used primarily to preserve and process food, foods such as luncheon meats, salami, and all types of sausages, bacon, smoked fish, smoked and processed cheeses, and all pickles and preserved food, such as canned vegetables, are full of it. According to the R.D.A. the requirement is 1,100 to 3,300 milligrams a day, but this is vastly exaggerated to cover circumstances such as water loss through sweating. Actually we need only 220 milligrams per day, though we are getting much more.

When the sodium level rises too high, more water is needed to dilute it; the body gives us the signal that we are thirsty. If we eat something salty, we almost immediately need to drink. Similarly, if we exercise and sweat profusely, we will also become thirsty because our dehydrated body has too much salt. Excess salt can actually dehydrate you; it draws fluid from the cells into the extracellular spaces between them, thus leaving wilted cells. No wonder that after a very salty meal or severe exercise with profuse sweating we feel rather weak and sometimes irritable. Swollen tissues, bloated with water, can make you feel very uncomfortable, and salt is primarily to blame for this swelling. There are other, more serious, health problems relating to the water retention caused by too much salt. Excess fluid increases the volume of blood, therefore blood pressure tends to go up. The kidneys are responsible for regulating the water-sodium balance in the body, but years of exposure to a high-salt diet can exhaust them and they may not do the job properly, thus water retention persists.

As far as your weight is concerned, salt should be avoided. Even though it is noncaloric, the fluid retention it causes can make an enormous difference, especially just before your period. Even though this weight is water weight and not fat gain, it can be very demoralizing and prevents you from seeing what your real weight is doing. There is a possibility that if the tissues are bathed in excessive salt, fat cells are more likely to absorb available glucose. Venus syndrome sufferers are well advised to limit salt intake, as fluid retention can cause puffy ankles, especially in bottom-heavy women.

The first way to reduce salt intake is to stop using it on your food, ask for your food to be prepared without it in restaurants, avoid salty foods, read labels, always remembering salt goes under many other names starting with "sodium," and flavor your food with herbs, spices, and, if needed, low-sodium soy sauce. Rich cheeses, potato chips, and oily, salted nuts should be especially avoided. You will often find that avoiding salty foods also means avoiding foods that are "wrong" in other ways, like being high in fats and calories. Your appetite may also decrease once you overcome cravings for salty snacks. The more salty foods you eat, the more difficult it becomes to appease the salt craving and the spicier the food has to be to impress the taste buds.

Water

Contained in everything we eat, water also constitutes between 40 and 60 percent of a person's body weight. To enumerate its functions within the body would be to mention almost every vital process. Apart from lubricating the eyes, the joints, and the spinal column and forming lymph and saliva, water bathes every living tissue, ensuring the transport of oxygen and nutrients. Water balance is intimately related to sodium levels, so how much water you need per day depends on your salt intake and your fluid losses, which occur basically through sweat and urine. They occur to a lesser degree through the lungs (our breath is moist) and in the feces, which are bound with water.

As far as dieting is concerned, drinking lots of water can flush out your system and actually help you lose weight, although not fat. If you are eating even remotely too much salt, drinking a lot of water will make you swollen and heavier. Most diets advise you to drink a minimum of eight glasses of water a day. Drinking water before meals helps to fill you up, and there is no evidence to suggest that drinking water with meals increases weight gain.

Natural Solution: The Truth About Health Food

Health food can be just as fattening as any other food if eaten in large enough quantities. Just because a loaf of bread has been made from "whole"—unprocessed and unrefined—ingredients does not mean that it is calorie-free. However, eating healthy, fresh food certainly can help you lose weight, for by avoiding high fats and high protein, sugar, and salt intakes, all rules of the health food game, you will automatically be cutting calories.

Health food can be as much of a gimmick as any fad diet; many foods fraudulently proclaim their "whole" contents. It's a good idea to read up on the subject and learn what to look for on labels. If you really believe in the idea, you will probably find yourself becoming a vegetarian. If you balance your diet correctly so as not to miss out on any essential nutrients, you will not be endangering your health but most likely enhancing it. However, the subject needs careful study, preparation, and commitment. Strict vegetarian diets using cereals alone as a protein source and not including legumes such as beans will be deficient in calcium, iron, zinc, and vitamin B_{12}.

Alcohol

Alcohol is the anonymous additive in many people's diets. Alcohol contains seven calories per gram, but they are empty calories in that they can only be used for fuel or be stored as fat. They have no nutritive value. The only exceptions are beers and wines, which do contain traces of vitamins and minerals. Actually, in moderate amounts alcohol is not as bad for you as some people think. Of course "moderate amounts" has to be defined. A "safe" amount from a health point of view would be either two ounces of hard liquor or two glasses (wine glasses, not tumblers) of wine. Such amounts can improve circulation by widening the arteries and pro- mote a general feeling of well-being.

Too much alcohol is not only dangerous but also fattening. Alcohol does not satisfy hunger, and it can often promote it. People with no appetite are often advised to have a glass of sweet sherry before meals. Alcohol relaxes you but it may also relax that dietary guardian angel, your willpower. It also progressively deadens the tastebuds and makes you crave salty, spicy foods. Any diet that is to be truly effective and nutritionally balanced will not include alcohol, at least not in the early stages of the diet. When you are maintaining your weight, you may include alcohol if you are careful. You could of course include it as part of your caloric allowance on any of the diets here, but it would mean less food and more appetite so I think it's best avoided at first.

For your information, one ounce* of whiskey has about 70 calories. One ounce of beer has 12.5 calories; light beer has approximately half that. One ounce of wine has 30-odd calories (light wine is just about half that). Keep in mind that even though beer and wine are calorically lower per ounce, you are more likely to drink more of them. A 12-ounce mug of beer has 150 calories; a 3-ounce glass of wine has 90. Of course, if hard liquor is mixed with tonic or ginger ale, the caloric value goes up accordingly.

---

* One ounce equals just under thirty milliliters.

Caffeine

Caffeine is a stimulating drug. It affects your nerves and makes you anxious; however, it does speed up metabolism. Therefore, if you are limiting caloric intake, caffeine can help you burn fat more quickly. Recent evidence suggests that caffeine speeds up the metabolic rate of sedentary people much more than people who exercise, so its effects may be more limited than previously supposed.

Beware of its harmful effects. The lethal dose is 10 grams a day, but even if your intake comes nowhere near that, which it probably doesn't (a cup of percolated coffee contains 110 milligrams), caffeine is known to raise blood pressure, increase risks of heart disease and certain forms of cancer, and to cause irritability, insomnia, and sometimes very unpleasant withdrawal symptoms. My advice, on which I am trying to act, is to limit your intake as much as you can, to one or two cups a day, preferably eliminating it completely.

I would like to mention cigarettes in connection with caffeine because people seem to have addictions for both simultaneously. Nicotine, like caffeine, accelerates metabolism; smoking twenty-four cigarettes a day can help you expend two hundred calories. However, the health risks of smoking far outweigh this benefit.

The Diet for You

A balanced diet is the one that works best. It must include a nutritional selection of foods from the basic groups. Contrary to the far-fetched beliefs of many diets "based" on enzyme and chemical reactions, there is no irrefutable evidence to prove that certain foods should be eaten in isolation or combination. Moreover, when you're losing weight on a proper diet, you burn fat, which is your desired result, and not lean tissue. From a psychological viewpoint, learning to balance your own diet will help reorganize your eating habits for life and give you the flexibility and power to design an eating plan that suits you best. However, balance need not mean rigidity. Though it is usual to eat three meals a day on a diet, you can easily divide the same amount of calories into three meals and three snacks. This is preferable, as eating one large meal a day may make you fatter. Even though there is no evidence to suggest that the metabolic rate tends to get lower at night, evening is the worst time to overeat, as you don't have that long to burn off what you ate before you go to sleep.

A reassuring thought is that what you are eating right now before you even start *could* be the basis of your diet, if you were to gradually reduce the quantities. Your present weight is probably not the result of *what* you are eating but of how much and when you are eating. Assess what you are eating right now from a balance standpoint and then almost imperceptibly over weeks and months cut the quantity. Make the approach a long-term one. This method will obviously take at least a few weeks to produce results but it may be psychologically less traumatic and more effective permanently than following a drastic diet alien to your eating habits.

An alternative approach to a conventionally balanced diet is offered in a fascinating book called *Food for Thought* by Saul Miller. He sees foods in terms of two extremes, expansive and contractive, and advocates that one stick to the "centered" foods in the middle of the spectrum: plant foods such as grains, nuts, beans, vegetables, and fruits. Expansive foods are those that give rise to erratic behavior and are derivatives of plants; sugar, tea, and coffee and all alcoholic drinks. Contractive foods are meat, fish, and all animal produce. These foods are dense because animals are, as a result of what they eat, concentrated vegetable energy. Salt is also a contractive substance. Contractive foods supposedly produce a rigid, "can't let go" type of behavior. I found it illuminating to know that if one eats too many contractive foods, such as cheese and eggs, one's body demands a lot of expansive foods, such as sweets and alcohol. Miller claims that if you are aware of this nutritional law of opposites and the nutritional conflict it produces, you can balance it out by selecting neutral foods.

Calculating Your Caloric Goals

Calories *count*—they are the only unit of energy measurement known. Even eating a few calories more or less in a day makes a considerable difference over a year. Let's say you eat one extra medium apple per day. That's 50 calories more per day, 350 more per week, and 18,250 more per year. One gram of the body fat you gain equals 9 calories, so if you divide 18,250 calories by 9, you have a weight gain of 2,027 grams, which is 2 kilograms or 4.4 pounds over the year and 44 pounds over ten years. And that's only from an extra apple a day. An extra 8-ounce portion of apple pie, on the other hand, can do a lot more damage: 620 extra calories eaten every day, 4,340 per week, and a staggering 226,300 per year. That tidy little sum means a weight gain of 25 kilograms or 55 pounds over the year!

What we all want to know is how many calories should we be eating if we want to lose weight? First you must decide how much weight you want to lose and how quickly you want to lose it. If you want to lose thirty pounds in six months, your calorie intake will have to be much lower than if you only want to lose ten pounds in that time. Here I must seriously advise you to be realistic in your goals. Many people who are not technically obese (roughly thirty pounds or more overweight) but more likely only ten to fifteen pounds heavier than they would like to be tend to exaggerate their problem. It is important to choose a weight target and stick to it. Making a chart or graph and tracking your progress sometimes helps. In deciding how long it will take, be generous with yourself and remember it's better to take your time. Weight lost very rapidly is just as rapidly regained.

To know how many calories you need to eat, you must try and guess how many you use up. Tables of caloric expenditure are available (see Chapter 7), but there may be great variations among individuals. The only way to find out accurately is to perform exercises in a doctor's office using an apparatus that collects expired air, calculates oxygen uptake, and from that energy expenditure. Activity is not the only way we burn calories; there's also our basal or resting metabolic rate, the energy we use to maintain our vital processes. It is very difficult to establish a common figure for basal metabolic rate, as it will not take variances into account.

A simpler way of establishing the ratio of output to input is to examine whether you are losing, gaining, or maintaining weight. Your answer is a guide to how many calories a day you must eat. If you want to lose two pounds a week (which is a very considerable weight loss that is unadvisable to attempt), you need a weekly caloric deficit of about 7,000 calories, remembering that you must create a deficit of 3,500 calories to lose a pound of fat.* ($3,500 \times 2 =$

7,000). Say that you are eating 2,500 calories a day and maintaining weight. Your weekly intake would be 17,500 calories. From these 17,500 subtract the deficit of 7,000: you would have to eat 10,500 calories a week or 1,500 a day to lose two pounds a week. This does sound like a lot because the figure of 2,500 calories daily maintenance is just an average figure. Many of us would gain on this amount and actually need far less to maintain. Therefore 1,500 calories a day would not be low enough to make us lose two pounds of fat a week.

Unfortunately, basal metabolic rate works against you the longer you diet. Some evidence suggests that it takes a progressively larger caloric deficit to lose one pound in weight the longer you diet. At the beginning it may mean only a few hundred calories less; after months that figure will be up in the thousands. That's because the longer you diet, provided you meet your protein needs, the more the body draws on its fat reserves, and it always takes 3,500 calories to lose one pound of fat.

Once you have decided how many calories you need on your diet, the next step is to compose it. Become familiar with the caloric values of food. Finding them out can be very interesting, and you will not always have to weigh and measure and arithmetically juggle what you're going to eat. Eating fewer calories will become a habit, but only if it is done gradually, almost imperceptibly, without your feeling denied. You are in control and can adapt all the nutrition and calorie information here to suit your own lifestyle. No one is forcing you.

How to Structure Your Own Diet

Nutrition and diet can be very complicated. Even though most foods in the United States are labeled, there's still so much to think about, take into consideration.

To avoid confusion I asked myself the following questions:

1. What was my main objective? The answer was to lose weight slowly and steadily, as I was fatter and heavier than I wanted to

---

* Remember, this is not pure fat, but about 85 percent fat.

be. I realized that even though I couldn't consciously guide my body to lose weight from selected areas, losing weight generally was a good beginning. Eventually, especially in combination with exercise, some fat would be lost from the hips and thighs.

2. Did I have any specific health problems to worry about in my diet? Not really. I was young and healthy and even though a tendency to high serum cholesterol existed on my mother's side of the family, my levels were still low to normal. My blood pressure was normal too. It is important to take your family history or any personal ailments into consideration when planning your diet, so that you avoid those foods that don't agree with you. A common example is poor digestion and tendency to become bloated. In this case it would be sensible to limit fiber and not eat too many irritating foods, such as onion and garlic.

3. Did I have to watch my sodium intake? I had normal blood pressure, but I didn't like salt and it always made me retain fluid. Because my legs were heavy, water retention in the calves and ankles made me look and feel worse. Also, swelling made me heavier on the scale. Cutting salt was a priority.

4. How was I going to balance my intake of fats, proteins, and carbohydrates without continuously having to think about it? Once again I reminded myself that my priority was weight loss. Thus from a caloric point of view, it made sense to keep fats low since they are so dense in calories. However, fats stay in the stomach longest, so it was important to have them from a satisfaction point of view. Cheeses and meats tend to be high in calories, so I chose instead fish and poultry for protein. Because unrefined carbohydrates gave me so much satisfaction for fewer calories, they were the obvious preference. If you think of the way you fuel your car to get maximum mileage to the gallon, it makes sense to do the same with your body.

Composition of Diets

There are four diets in this book. They have been medically approved and their emphasis is on balance. Before I list the foods you can select on your diet, let's have a brief closer look at the diets themselves. See Table 1. When one is creating diets it is impossible to obtain exactly correct caloric totals. Therefore, the diets that follow are either slightly under or over 800, 1,000, 1,200, or 1,500 calories. The variance is between 5 and 30 calories either way. As far as percentage of calories is concerned, the highest is that of carbohydrates. The percentage of calories derived from protein is proportionately higher than is otherwise advised by correct nutrition. When you are on an unrestricted-calorie diet, it is wise to limit your protein intake to 20 percent of total calories. When you are on a calorie-controlled diet, protein intake should form a greater proportion of total calories to ensure that protein demands are met and wastage of lean body mass does not occur.

Which Foods and How Much?

If you know the different types of food, what their nutritional and caloric values are, you can construct your diet from them. Table 2 lists the six different food categories and the selections of foods from every group that you can choose.* One choice from a certain group, such as a small apple from the fruit group, counts as one selection, or óne point if you like, from that category. If you are on a 1,000-calorie-a-day diet you would be allowed four points or selections from the fruit group. Table 2 also tells you how many selections from each group you are permitted on the 800-, 1,000-, 1,200-, or 1,500-calorie-per-day diets.

It is up to you to decide which diet you want to go on. The best thing to do is experiment. If you are happy on a certain diet and happy with your weight loss, stick to it. If you are not losing enough, decrease the calories. Timing is all-important, because we know that metabolic rate does go down in some people when they diet. When you reach a plateau, where your weight won't budge, don't panic and give up. I have found that if I stop the diet, slightly increase calories for a couple of days, and then go on a stricter

---

* All servings are in ounces. A one-cup serving equals approximately eight ounces, indicating a large tea or coffee cup but not a mug.

diet than the one I was on before, I usually see a result.

The food selections are listed in order of caloric value. Sometimes if a selection from one group contains some of the nutrient from another group, when you eat it you will have to omit one selection from that other group. For instance, when you eat certain meats that are not completely lean, you have to omit a half, one, or more fat exchanges.

Table 1
COMPOSITION OF DIETS

Caloric Amount	Protein	Carbohydrates	Fat
800	61 grams = 2.2 ounces	99 grams = 3.5 ounces	17 grams = 0.6 ounce
	1 gram protein = 4 calories	1 gram carbohydrate = 4 calories	1 gram fat = 9 calories
	Total protein calories = 244	Total carbohydrate calories = 396	Total fat calories = 153
	Percentage of total calories = 31%	Percentage of total calories = 50%	Percentage of total calories = 19%
1,000	69 grams = 2.5 ounces	139 grams = 5 ounces	22 grams = 0.8 ounce
	1 gram protein = 4 calories	1 gram carbohydrate = 4 calories	1 gram fat = 9 calories
	Total protein calories = 276	Total carbohydrate calories = 556	Total fat calories = 198
	Percentage of total calories = 27%	Percentage of total calories = 54%	Percentage of total calories = 19%
1,200	84 grams = 3 ounces	161 grams = 5.8 ounces	25 grams = 0.9 ounce
	1 gram protein = 4 calories	1 gram carbohydrate = 4 calories	1 gram fat = 9 calories
	Total protein calories = 336	Total carbohydrate calories = 644	Total fat calories = 225
	Percentage of total calories = 28%	Percentage of total calories = 53%	Percentage of total calories = 19%
1,500	86 grams = 3.1 ounces	196 grams = 7 ounces	40 grams = 1.4 ounces
	1 gram protein = 4 calories	1 gram carbohydrate = 4 calories	1 gram fat = 9 calories
	Total protein calories = 344	Total carbohydrate calories = 784	Total fat calories = 360
	Percentage of total calories = 23%	Percentage of total calories = 53%	Percentage of total calories = 24%

NOTE: 28 grams = 1 ouncee

Table 2
FOOD SELECTIONS PER FOOD GROUP AND NUMBER OF SELECTIONS ALLOWED ON 800-, 1,000-, 1,200-, AND 1,500-CALORIE DIETS

GROUP ONE: Vegetables	Selections	800	1,000	1,200	1,500
SERVING SIZE: ½ cup (approximately 4 ounces). Each selection contains about 5 grams carbohydrate, 2 grams protein, 0 fat. Energy value = 25 calories.	Asparagus	4	6	5	6
	Bean sprouts				
	Beans: wax, green, or string				
	Beets				
	Broccoli				
	Brussels sprouts				
	Cabbage: all varieties				
	Carrots				
	Cauliflower				
	Celery				
	Cress				
	Cucumbers				
	Eggplant				
	Escarole				
	Green Pepper				
	Greens: Beets, Chard, Dandelion, Kale, Mustard, Spinach, Turnip				
	Mushrooms				
	Okra				
	Onions				
	Radishes				
	Sauerkraut				
	Summer Squash				
	Tomatoes and Tomato Juice				
	Turnips				
	V-8 Juice (BEWARE high sodium)				
	Zucchini				

GROUP TWO: Fruits	Selections	800	1,000	1,200	1,500
SERVING SIZE VARIES (see specification). All varieties must be fresh or packed in water with	Apple–1 small	4	4	4	7
	Apple Juice–⅓ cup				
	Applesauce (unsweetened)–½ cup				

All servings are in ounces. A one-cup serving equals approximately eight ounces, indicating a large tea or coffee cup but not a mug.

artificial sweetener. No
ordinary canned fruits.
Each selection contains
10 grams carbohydrate, 0
protein and fat. Energy
value = 40 calories.

Apricots, dried–4 halves
Apricots, fresh–2 medium
Banana–½ small
Berries–½ cup of all except:
    Strawberries–¾ cup
Cherries–10 large
Cider–⅓ cup
Dates–2
Figs, fresh or dried–1
Grapefruit–½
Grapefruit Juice–½ cup
Grape Juice–¼ cup
Grapes–12
Mango–½ small
Melon:
    Cantaloupe–¼ small
    Honeydew–⅛ medium
    Watermelon–1 cup
Nectarine–1 small
Orange–1 small
Orange Juice–½ cup
Papaya–¾ cup
Peach–1 medium
Pear–1 small
Pineapple–½ cup
Pineapple Juice–⅓ cup
Plums–2 medium
Prune Juice–¼ cup
Prunes–2 medium
Raisins–2 tbs.
Tangerine–1 medium

GROUP THREE: Fats

SERVING SIZE VARIES
(see specifications). Each
selection contains 5
grams fat, 0 protein and
carbohydrate. Energy
value = 45 calories. If you
wish to limit intake of
saturated fats, select

Selection	800	1,000	1,200	1,500
AVOCADO (4″ diameter)–⅛	1	2	2	5 tsp.
MARGARINE 1 tsp.				
OIL: CORN, COTTONSEED, SAFFLOWER, SOY, SUNFLOWER–1 tsp.				
OIL, OLIVE–1 tsp.				
OIL, PEANUT–1 tsp.				
OLIVES–5 small				

items that are in capital letters, which are mostly POLYUNSATURATED, although some are MONOSATURATED.

NUTS: ALMONDS–10 whole,
   PECANS–2 large whole,
   PEANUTS–15 whole,
   WALNUTS–6 small,
   OTHER–6 small
Butter–1 tsp.
Bacon, crisp–1 strip
Bacon Fat–1 tsp.
Cream Cheese–1 tbs.
Cream, heavy–1 tbs.
Cream, light–2 tbs.
Cream, sour–2 tbs.
French Dressing–1 tbs.
Italian Dressing–1 tbs.
Lard–1 tsp.
Mayonnaise–1 tsp.
Salad Dressing, mayonnaise
   type–2 tsps.

GROUP FOUR: Meat

SERVINGS ARE ONE OUNCE unless otherwise specified. Each selection contains 7 grams protein, 3 grams fat, 0 carbohydrate. Energy value = 55 calories. Cheeses and other selections featured *per category* are equal in value to the meat selections in that category and may be substituted. *DO NOT SUBSTITUTE A SELECTION FROM LISTS B OR C WITH A SELECTION FROM LIST A.*

Selections

A. LEAN MEAT
Beef: Baby (very lean), Chipped, Flank Steak, Plate Ribs, Plate Skirt Steak, all cuts Rump, Spare Ribs and Tripe Tenderloin
Lamb: all cuts except Breast
Pork: Ham, Leg, Smoked
Veal: all cuts except Breast
Poultry: Chicken, Cornish Hen, Guinea Hen, Pheasant, Turkey (all without skin)
Fish: any fresh or frozen fish. Crab, Lobster, Mackerel, Canned Salmon, and Tuna–¼ cup (water-packed only, or if in oil, drain); Clams, Oysters, Scallops–5; Sardines (drained)–3
Cheeses: Containing less than 5% butterfat.

800	1,000	1,200	1,500
5	5	6	6

(of which ONE must be an egg white selection)

Cottage Cheese: up to 2%
butterfat–¼ cup
Dried Beans and Peas *(OMIT
one bread selection)*–½ cup

Separate Item: Contains
7 grams protein, 0
carbohydrate, 0 fat.
Energy value = 28
calories.

2 egg whites count as 1 egg
white selection. On all diets the
egg whites are a compulsory
selection as *ONE* of your lean
meat selections.

Meats in Lists B and C
are higher in fats.
Therefore, to keep the
energy value of each at 55
calories, for each of these
selections *OMIT* ½ fat
selection, plus any
additional ones specified
below.

B. MEDIUM-FAT MEAT
Beef: Corned (canned), Ground
(15% fat), Rib Eye, Round
Pork: Boiled Ham, Canadian
Bacon, Loin, Shoulder
Organ Meats: Heart, Kidney,
Liver, and Sweetbreads
(BEWARE high cholesterol)
Cheeses: Cottage (creamed)–¼
cup; Mozzarella, Neufchatel,
Parmesan, Ricotta–3 tbs.
Whole Egg (white and yolk,
*BEWARE high cholesterol in
yolk)*–1
Peanut Butter (OMIT 2 fat
selections)–2 tbs.

For each of these
selections, *OMIT* 1 fat
selection.

C. HIGH-FAT MEAT
Beef: Brisket, Corned, Ground
(more than 20% fat), Chuck,
Hamburger (commercial),
Roasts (Rib), Steaks (Club
and Rib)
Lamb: Breast
Pork: Country-Style Ham,
Deviled Ham, Ground, Loin
(back ribs), Spare Ribs
Veal: Breast
Poultry: Capon, Duck
(domestic), Goose

Cheeses: Cheddar and other
    hard cheese
Cold Cuts–4½" by ⅛" slice
Frankfurter–1 small

GROUP FIVE: Bread	*Selections*	800	1,000	1,200	1,500
SERVING SIZE VARIES	*Bread*	1	3	4	4

SERVING SIZE VARIES (see specifications). Each selection contains 15 grams carbohydrate, 2 grams protein, 0 fat. Energy value = 70 calories. Cereals, crackers, dried beans, etc. and starchy vegetables all have the same values as bread selections and may be substituted.

Bread
Bagel, small–½
Bread Crumbs–3 tbs.
English Muffin, small–½
Frankfurter Roll–½
Hamburger Bun–½
Plain Roll–1
Raisin–1 slice
Rye or Pumpernickel–1 slice
Tortilla, 6"–1
White–1 slice
Whole Wheat–1 slice

Cereal
Bran Flakes–½ cup
Cereal (cooked)–½ cup
Cornmeal (dry)–2 tbs.
Flour–2½ tbs.
Grits (cooked)–½ cup
Other ready-to-eat sweetened
    Cereal–¾ cup
Pasta (cooked): Spaghetti,
    Noodles, Macaroni–½ cup
Popcorn (popped, no fat
    added)–3 cups
Puffed Cereal (unfrosted)–1 cup
Rice or Barley (cooked)–½ cup
Wheat Germ–¼ cup

Crackers
Arrowroot–3
Graham, 2½" square–2
Matzoh, 4" × 6"–½
Oyster–20
Pretzels, 3⅛" long × ⅛"
    diameter–25
Rye Wafer–2" × 3½"–3

Saltines–6
Soda, 2½" square–4

Dried Beans, Peas, and Lentils
Beans, Peas, Lentils (dried and
  cooked)–½ cup
Baked Beans, no pork
  (canned)–¼ cup

Starchy Vegetables
Corn–⅓ cup
Corn on Cob–1 small
Lima Beans–½ cup
Parsnips–⅔ cup
Peas, green (canned or
  frozen)–½ cup
Potato, white–1 small
Potato, mashed–½ cup
  (nothing added)
Pumpkin–¾ cup
Winter Squash, Acorn or
  Butternut–½ cup
Yam or Sweet Potato–¼ cup

Prepared Foods
Biscuit, 2" diameter–1
Corn Bread, 2" × 2" × 1"–1
Corn Muffin, 2" diameter–1
Crackers, round butter type–5
Muffin, plain small–1
Pancake, 5" × ½"–1
Potato or Corn Chips *(OMIT* 2
  fat selections)–15
Potatoes, french-fried, length 2"
  to 3½"–8
Waffle, 5" × ½"–1

GROUP SIX: Milk	*Selections*	800	1,000	1,200	1,500
ERVING SIZE 1 CUP		2	2	3	3
approximately 8 ounces)			from list A only		
unless otherwise					
specified. PLEASE					
NOTE THE					

DIFFERENT CATEGORIES.

Each selection contains 12 grams carbohydrate, 8 grams protein, negligible fat. Energy value = 80 calories.

A. Nonfat

Buttermilk (from skim milk)
Canned, evaporated skim milk–½ cup
Powdered (nonfat, before adding liquid)–⅓ cup
Skim or nonfat milk
Yogurt (from skim milk, plain)

Each selection contains 12 grams carbohydrate, 8 grams protein, and 2.5 grams fat (which is equivalent to ½ fat selection or 22 calories). Energy value = 102 calories.

B. Low Fat

B1. 1% fat fortified milk (*OMIT* ½ fat selection)

Each selection contains 12 grams carbohydrate, 8 grams protein, and 5 grams fat (which is equivalent to 1 fat selection or 45 calories). Energy value = 125 calories.

B2. 2% fat fortified milk (*OMIT* 1 fat selection)
Yogurt made from 2% fat fortified milk, plain (*OMIT* 1 fat selection)

Each selection contains 12 grams carbohydrate, 8 grams protein, and 10 grams fat. Energy value = 170 calories.

C. Whole Milk

Whole milk (*OMIT* 2 fat selections)
Canned, evaporated (*OMIT* 2 fat selections)

Diets adapted from Diet Manual of St. Luke's Hospital Center, New York City.

Table 3
SUMMARY OF SELECTION CHOICE AND
COMPOSITION OF DIETS

800-CALORIE DIET

Selections		Protein Grams	Carbohydrate Grams	Fat Grams	Calories
Vegetable	4	$4 \times 2 = 8$	$4 \times 5 = 20$		112
Fruit	4		$4 \times 10 = 40$		160
Fat	1			$1 \times 5 = 5$	45
Meat	4	$4 \times 7 = 28$		$4 \times 3 = 12$	220
Egg White	1	$1 \times 7 = 7$			28
Bread	1	$1 \times 2 = 2$	$1 \times 15 = 15$		68
Skim Milk	2	$2 \times 8 = 16$	$2 \times 12 = 24$		160
Grams		61×4	99×4	17×9	
		1 gram protein = 4 calories	1 gram carbohydrates = 4 calories	1 gram fat = 9 calories	
Calories		244	396	153	793
%		31	50	19	100

1,000-CALORIE DIET

Selections		Protein Grams	Carbohydrate Grams	Fat Grams	Calories
Vegetable	6	$6 \times 2 = 12$	$6 \times 5 = 30$		168
Fruit	4		$4 \times 10 = 40$		160
Fat	2			$2 \times 5 = 10$	90
Meat	4	$4 \times 7 = 28$		$4 \times 3 = 12$	220
Egg White	1	$1 \times 7 = 7$			28
Bread	3	$3 \times 2 = 6$	$3 \times 15 = 45$		204
Skim Milk	2	$2 \times 8 = 16$	$2 \times 12 = 24$		160
Grams		69×4	139×4	22×9	
		1 gram protein = 4 calories	1 gram carbohydrates = 4 calories	1 gram fat = 9 calories	
Calories		276	556	198	1,030
%		27	54	19	100

1,200-CALORIE DIET

Selections		Protein Grams	Carbohydrate Grams	Fat Grams	Calories
Vegetable	5	5 × 2 = 10	5 × 5 = 25		140
Fruit	4		4 × 10 = 40		160
Fat	2			2 × 5 = 10	90
Meat	5	5 × 7 = 35		5 × 3 = 15	275
Egg White	1	1 × 7 = 7			28
Bread	4	4 × 2 = 8	4 × 15 = 60		272
Skim Milk	3	3 × 8 = 24	3 × 12 = 36		240
Grams		84 × 4	161 × 4	25 × 9	
		1 gram protein = 4 calories	1 gram carbohydrates = 4 calories	1 gram fat = 9 calories	
Calories		336	644	225	1,205
%		28	53	19	100

1,500-CALORIE DIET

Selections		Protein Grams	Carbohydrate Grams	Fat Grams	Calories
Vegetable	6	6 × 2 = 12	6 × 5 = 30		168
Fruit	7		7 × 10 = 70		280
Fat	5			5 × 5 = 25	225
Meat	5	5 × 7 = 35		5 × 3 = 15	275
Egg White	1	1 × 7 = 7			28
Bread	4	4 × 2 = 8	4 × 15 = 60		272
Skim Milk	3	3 × 8 = 24	3 × 12 = 36		240
Grams		86 × 4	196 × 4	40 × 9	
		1 gram protein = 4 calories	1 gram carbohydrates = 4 calories	1 gram fat = 9 calories	
Calories		344	784	360	1,488
%		23	53	24	100

How to Put It All Together

Now you know what you are allowed on each diet. Because both the 800- and the 1,000-calorie diets are inadequate in vitamins and minerals, take daily:

> 1 Multivitamin pill
> 400 milligrams calcium
> 2.4 grams potassium
> 30–60 milligrams iron (especially for women)

You may be wondering how to combine the food selections on your diet. Here are some basic guidelines and some sample selections. For example, on the 800-calorie diet:

800-Calorie Diet

Breakfast Selections	Examples
1 fruit	½ grapefruit
2 meat (compulsory egg white selection and 1 lean meat)	2 hard-boiled egg whites diced with 1 ounce of low-fat cheese (less than 5% butterfat)
1 bread	½ toasted muffin
1 fat	1 teaspoon butter or margarine (if desired, use your 1 fat selection in the evening on your vegetables or use it to cook with)
Unlimited	Tea or coffee. If you take them with skim milk, you must subtract it from your skim milk selections.
	Tea or coffee must be sweetened with artificial sweeteners

Mid-Morning Snack	
1 skim milk	1 cup yogurt (plain) from skim milk
1 fruit	½ small banana diced and mixed with yogurt

Lunch Selections	
1 meat	1 ounce cold roast chicken (no skin)
1 vegetable	Lettuce (unlimited) and tomato and radish; season with lemon juice and pepper
1 fruit	2 water-packed peach halves
Unlimited	Tea or coffee with milk subtracted from your skim milk selections. Artificial sweetener.

Dinner Selections	
2 meat	2 ounces lamb chop (careful to have it very lean and to subtract weight of bone)

2 vegetables	Boiled zucchini and carrots mixed
1 (salad) vegetable	Shredded red and white cabbage with vinegar and a little mustard
1 fruit	1 small apple
1 skim milk	8 ounces skim milk (you can save this up and drink it hot just before sleeping)

Anytime, Unlimited Foods

These can be munched or nibbled whenever you feel the need to eat. Especially useful between meals, these snacks will persuade your stomach you have eaten something and can be very helpful when you eat out, especially if you eat them at home an hour beforehand. You can eat and drink as much as you like of the following:

Bouillon or clear broth (watch salt content)
Chicory, endive, escarole, radishes, parsley, and cress
Gelatin (unsweetened)
Pickles (unsweetened)
Coffee or Tea—CAUTION: if either of these, especially coffee, makes you nervous and jittery, either stop them completely or limit intake to one cup daily.
Water—from the tap or bottled.
Mineral Water—some sparkling mineral waters have a high salt content, and still water may be better for your digestion.
Carbonated Beverages—when I advise you to drink as much as you like, I do not mean diet soda. Diet soda may have "just one calorie" but they have an awful lot more besides, particularly a high sodium content. Club soda is also high in salt, and carbonated drinks in general may upset digestion.

Just because you choose to give up calories doesn't mean you have to give up imagination or good cooking. If you use herbs, spices, and low-sodium soy sauce correctly you can flavor your foods far more subtly than with salt and heavy fats.

Some useful tips to remember are:

1. Obviously avoid all oil- and sugar-packed canned foods. If this is impossible, drain them thoroughly and rinse with water.

2. Avoid fat in meat. Even when you have trimmed off all visible fat, a lot of meats (depending on the cut) are still marbled with fat. It's best to consult the three categories of meat selections and remember you get more for your calories the leaner the meat. When cooking, use nonfat sprays or better still nothing at all. Just broil, bake, roast, or boil, whenever possible using a rack so fat can drain off.

3. Don't eat too many eggs; no more than three or four per week. Eggs are not only high in cholesterol but may also tend to make you bilious or constipated.

4. Avoid salty foods.

5. Break down your calories into as many meals as possible. Experiments conducted in a shoe factory showed that workers' productivity increased when they ate five meals a day instead of three. These were extra meals (the workers were not on diets), but the important result is that *it seems* that if people eat more frequently, they perform better. Morale may have something to do with this, but I found that on a diet, if I saved some of my calories for midmorning, midafternoon, and before bed, I was less hungry. That is why I recommend saving one of your milk allowances and having a hot drink of milk before sleeping. Often one of the problems with dieting is insomnia caused by a rumbling stomach, and this can help.

6. Plan your shopping. Before you go out make a list of what you need. Be strict with yourself, and if you deviate from the list make sure it's to buy some exotic fruit or vegetable rather than cake. Take time to choose the best meat, cheese, or whatever but don't take too long over it; otherwise your resolve may weaken. Keep away from temptation and never go shopping on an empty stomach.

7. Make *small* savings: skim milk instead of whole milk, yogurt instead of sour cream, a baked potato instead of fried, chicken instead of steak, and you will find you save calories without even thinking about it.

8. Drink plenty of water, at least eight glasses a day.

Eating Behavior

How you eat is as important as what and how much. Obese people have been shown to eat faster, not chew as thoroughly, and to drink more water than normal-weight people. The secret is to eat very slowly and chew very thoroughly. You have to reeducate yourself to concentrate on the act of eating, without distracting yourself with conversation, reading, or watching television. Mealtimes should not be rushed. To prolong them learn to put down your knife and fork between mouthfuls. Really devious eaters (I'm one) tend to discount the calories consumed during "informal" eating, so make every time you eat an occasion by serving food on plates with cutlery. Both plates and knives and forks should be as small and as attractive as possible. This makes portions look bigger and makes you eat more slowly.

Eating slowly and chewing thoroughly not only means you eat less because you are taking longer to do so, it also means that the food you are eating is more efficiently broken down in the mouth, where digestive enzymes begin their work on starches. Well-chewed food is better digested and chewing itself is a meditative activity. It also allows your brain to register that food is being ingested. An average time for that is twenty minutes, but if you have previously conditioned yourself to ignore or disobey the signal, becoming aware of it again is hard. There is also a possibility that fat people do not receive the signal as promptly or strongly as slimmer ones. It is therefore best to stop eating when you feel even slightly full.

Eating Out

With careful planning ahead, you can go out to restaurants and not break your good habits. In the first stages of a diet, it is not such a good idea because it's more advisable to become familiar with weights and portions of food in your own kitchen. After a few weeks, though, you will have become used to calculating and can safely eat out. Plan what you're going to eat (have alternative choices ready) before you go, and have a low calorie snack (bouillon or raw vegetables) half an hour before going out. Appetizers should be consommé or another clear soup, half a grapefruit, raw vegetables (crudités) without dip but sprinkled with lemon juice, or melon (that means you can't have fruit for dessert if you are dieting strictly) or a salad without heavy dressing. If you are not dieting that strictly, seafood cocktail without sauce is a sensible choice. The main course can be any meat, fish, or poultry if it's lean and not cooked in any fat. Season it with pepper, mustard, and lemon juice. Ask for your vegetables not to have butter or oil added and for salt not to be used. Avoid desserts; have fruit (if not eaten as an appetizer) and/ or coffee. You should also avoid bread and butter. Instead ask for a baked potato without butter or sour cream, and eat the skin (very good when crisp). Occasionally you can have a glass or two of dry white wine.

Breakfast: Great Start or Bad Beginning

Medical evidence suggests that if you eat breakfast you respond better mentally for the rest of the day. This has not been confirmed, and many people claim that if they eat in the morning they go on eating all day long. There is some evidence to suggest that fat people skip breakfast and start eating around midmorning. Personally, I think it is wrong to characterize obese people's eating habits. In my experience, when I have had breakfast I can easily make it through until lunch without feeling ravenous. Leaving your stomach empty after an overnight fast may make you feel irritable and weak and give you a headache. You may also overeat later in the day to compensate for not having breakfast.

How to Keep Going

Even your very own diet can sometimes go wrong. Your weight loss may also come to a standstill or you may even gain a couple of pounds. Don't panic. The rate of loss slows down physiologically; your body fights to conserve its fat stores, interpreting a diet as a threat to its well-being and even its existence. Here are some ways of curing "dieter's block."

1. Make sure your plateau or even slight weight gain is not due to water retention. Cut down even more on table and cooking salt and drink *at least* eight glasses of water a day. This will flush out your system.

2. If you feel you can do it *and have checked with your doctor beforehand,* take time to create a peaceful weekend fast. Eat nothing and sip fruit and vegetable juices and drink plenty of water. Take a complete multivitamin pill and the essential mineral supplements, especially calcium, potassium, and iron, and get plenty of rest. Be careful if you exercise, even mildly, and avoid driving. Upon refeeding start by eating many small portions of raw foods.

3. Treat yourself to a weekend at a health spa. It is worth the expense to pamper yourself and give yourself a sense of increased self-esteem, which will fuel you with motivation.

4. If this is not possible, create for yourself a spa weekend, maybe with some friends. Book yourself a facial, massage, hair treatment, and do whichever exercise pleases and relaxes you most—yoga, swimming, stretching, long walks. Make sure your meals are low calorie, eat as early as possible, and get plenty of sleep. Take time for yourself, reading a good book or doing some handicraft. Very often lack of time, stress, anxiety, guilt, and lots of heavy emotions can make us gain weight. Taking some time to devote our energies to ourselves is the best cure.

5. Replan your diet. Boredom may be the cause of the problem. Decide whether you want to increase or decrease your amount of calories in this next phase of your diet. Giving yourself more can sometimes be a more efficient *long-term* way of losing those last ten pounds. As metabolic rate falls as a result of dieting, eating less and less may not be the most practical or pleasurable way of dealing with it. Giving yourself two hundred or three hundred more calories a day may give you an added incentive to go on dieting for some more months, may give you more energy for exercise, and make you feel happier. It's worth it!

6. Exercise. What may be missing from your life is an exercise program. When you are eating right, what can help you additionally to lose weight steadily and safely over the years is exercise. Now I'm going to show you why.

7

Exercise: The Shape and Weight Solution

Even though the decision to follow my own eating plan was a revelation, exercise was the greatest discovery I made about treating my body. Movement made me feel better about myself than ever before. I was finally convinced that both my body and my attitude to it could change. I was kind enough to myself to realize this could not happen overnight. No matter what lies you may read in beauty books, there is no way of actually changing your body's configuration: it is the plan on which nature built you. Instead of fighting your natural shape it is better to accept it. After that is done, you can take action. It is within your power to reform the bottom-heavy body. Some ways of doing that, like plastic surgery, are drastic; others, like following the correct diet, are more gradual. In the long term, the results of exercise may even exceed those of surgery, and it is within your control to make those results *last*. Unlike dieting, which can often seem a passive means of reduction, exercise is lively, dynamic. It can also be fun.

If you find it hard to believe that activity can do more to remodel your shape than any amount of dietary discipline or clever definitions of the plastic surgeon's knife, you are not alone. I tried both diet and surgery without seriously exercising, because I didn't believe in it either. The effects of what could have been otherwise successful attempts at reducing were almost entirely wasted as a result. To lose weight and inches, a combination of diet and exercise is necessary. I am not advising you to stop reducing your food intake, I'm simply saying that getting physically fit is the most exhilarating way of feeling trimmer, firmer, and better. Since I began my fitness program, I have felt more energy, more determination, and more assurance. I know now that even if I have a bottom-heavy figure, it can still be well-toned and attractive. Exercise also gave me an inner energy. I promised myself never again to allow my negative image of myself to dominate my thinking. Moving my body freed my mind.

As there are few things more infuriating than the exhortations of an exercise enthusiast, let me hasten to assure you I was not always this way. Before I started exercising, I was bewildered and unconvinced. I viewed exercise videos with venom. I kept telling myself that I really didn't want thin thighs in thirty days or to find forty ways to a better bottom: I didn't even want to try because I was sure I wouldn't like exercise and worse still, couldn't do it. Where, after all, was I going to find all that energy? Inside is where I discovered it, which is where you will discover it also, along with strength of mind and inner peace you never thought existed.

Questions to Ask

Physical activity does not simply involve the body, you have to use the mind to understand its benefits, how it works, and most important, how to incorporate it into your life. The increasing popularity of physical fitness means that a great variety of exercise programs is available. Not all of them are effective, reliable, and above all safe. Having to choose, you may become too exhausted and confused to start. Selecting type, frequency, and duration of exercise is vitally important. A random choice will not only *not* give optimum results, it may well damage your health. It is therefore worth asking the following questions:

1. How do I start exercising? I hope that after you read this chapter you will realize how great the benefits of exercise are. I am the first to admit that it requires energy, courage, and determination to start and to continue exercising. As with anything, once the decision is made the worst part is over. Here are a few suggestions on how to reach that decision.

  a. Go to a health spa. Although this is an expensive way of going about it, a visit to a spa immediately involves you in an exercise program that's supervised, devised for your personal needs, and carried out with other people around for motivation. If the spa's fitness staff is good, you can greatly benefit from their advice, not only on your progress but on how to continue once you're home. The results you obtain during your time there should be

encouraging evidence of your capabilities and enable you to continue. All of this depends on how professional the spa is and on
your own motivation once you leave. It can be a good way to
get started, especially as a week away from home gives you time
to look at life in a different way and can make room for a change
in habits.

b. Enroll at a health club. This is another way to get you started
if you lack the inner conviction and knowledge to devise your
own program (like 99 percent of us). Clubs do tend to be costly
but, as at a spa, you have the benefit of guidance from professional
staff who should be qualified to assess your fitness needs and abilities and fashion a program accordingly. Your progress can be
supervised and monitored, and exercising in class or with a trainer
should motivate your attendance and performance. You create
an environment away from the stressful demands of home or office
that gives you time to do what's best for you.

c. Make a pact with a friend or family member. Often it's easier
for two to make a commitment. Make a promise with the other
person to encourage and help each other attain your fitness goals.
The disadvantage of this method is that you don't have professional
advice or warnings. If you read this book carefully, especially
the "caution" sections, use your common sense, and *listen to your
body,* you shouldn't do yourselves any harm. The pact made between the two of you is what is important: that will be your motivating factor.

Let's assume that highest hurdle, the decision, has been crossed.
Now what?

2. What result am I looking for from my program? First you
must decide *why* you want to exercise. Is it primarily to reduce
your weight and your body fat? Is it to trim up a flabby area of
your body or to improve muscle strength and flexibility and general
health? Your desired results will determine what kind of exercise
you do and how you do it. For instance, if you are overweight as
well as bottom-heavy, you have two objectives: to lose pounds *and*
inches. Your exercises will be designed to burn calories and to tone
your muscles.

3. Is it safe for me to exercise? Generally speaking, any healthy
person can safely exercise. However, if you have any cause for worry
about your health or you have a history of heart disease in your

family or have found exercising difficult and actually painful, go and consult a doctor immediately. Even when you have had a professional go-ahead, always listen to your body and if in doubt, either slow down, modify your program, or get medical advice.

4. How will I know which exercise is good for me? You'll find out in this chapter. Usually an exercise that is good for you is one that is not too hard or too easy, that you like doing but that is also a challenge, and that you want to perform well. Enjoyment is the key, because if you like exercise, you'll go on doing it for a lifetime.

5. How frequently do I exercise? The whole point of exercise is results, and the sooner you want these, the longer and more frequently you will have to exercise. I recommend some exercise daily for several reasons. It will become a habit and, psychologically, it gives you a feeling of continuity. Your body will be accustomed to stretching and movement, so that if you are sore you will stretch out the muscles instead of letting them seize up. I am not advising that you exercise very strenuously every single day. When you perform certain exercises, especially with weights of any kind, it is best to exercise on alternate days. This allows the muscles to rest and replenish their energy store. For psychological as well as physical reasons, you should take off one day a week, although you can engage in easy stretches and a form of exercise that is entirely stress-free, such as swimming. Duration of the workout will be discussed later, as it depends on the type of exercise.

6. If I want to go to exercise class, what do I look for? Sadly, not every exercise class is taught or choreographed by professionals. Usually just by using your own instinct you can tell if the class is going to be good, if the teacher's personality is pleasant, and if, according to the fitness level of the others in the class, you are going to be able to keep up fairly well (being with people better than you makes you try harder). More specific points to look for that *are* important to your health are:

a. Does the class have an adequate warm-up and cool-down? Ideally, these two periods should each last about ten minutes.

b. Does the teacher give warnings to those with joint or lower back problems?

c. Is the teacher careful to show how each exercise should be done correctly?

d. Are instructions clear and easy to follow?

e. Is the routine interesting and lively, with good music?

f. Does the routine change slightly every lesson to avoid monotony?

Most programs or classes offer various combinations of similar standard exercises for each particular part of the body. There are only so many different ways to stretch and tone your muscles, so many programs follow the same or similar exercises. Two features can differentiate one program from another. The first is the *routine:* not so much the types of exercises as the combination and order in which they are performed. The routine should be simple and offer maximum effort for minimum time. It should also be logical in its progression, which is another time-saving factor as it's much quicker to work on your back, sides, and front consecutively than have to keep getting up to do standing work in between. The second is the program's *flexibility,* the extent to which it can lend itself to your adaption. In designing the workout in Chapter 8 and making other exercise recommendations, I have tried to keep in mind these two elements.

Work at your own pace—no one is dictating to you, no one is pushing you. You are in control. Competitive exercising and sports can be fun later on, when you have achieved a certain grade of fitness and self-assurance. Until then, work in isolation. By that I mean do not be concerned with others but only with your own progress and development. Listen to your body and observe the limits it sets. Do not abuse it or ignore them. Don't buy an exercise book because you want to look like the woman on the cover. There's always the possibility that she was born with pencil-thin thighs! Let your ideal be you, but with a few adjustments. If you can be positive and appreciate yourself now, you can start to work on the person you want to be later. Your target should be achievable.

Are There Reasons Why You Shouldn't Exercise?

Unless your doctor forbids it or you genuinely have cause for concern, there is no good reason not to. There are plenty of good excuses, though. If you are fat, especially with Venus syndrome tendencies, you may feel you are too heavy to move. I too felt that way, but what I honestly felt was that I was too awkward, self-conscious, and tired to move properly. The truth is that you are never too big or too heavy to move. Once you start, confidence will grow, so will flexibility, and you will feel lighter. Stretches, important for everyone, are especially important for heavy people. As your body has to support a fair amount of weight, stretching your body will keep it strong and flexible. Activities to start off with are swimming and walking, where there is minimum stress on the knees and ankles and where fat legs will not be an encumbrance. This type of exercise, especially if started slowly, will not make you panicky and breathless, and you can feel graceful right away. After a few weeks you will feel ready to be more adventurous, step up the pace, and try other things. I speak from experience; because of my bottom-heaviness I was always too self-conscious to exercise. At first I started in private; only after several months was I ready to appear in class. Concentrating on my own progress and feeling proud of myself instead of making negative comparisons with others was what helped.

Another favorite excuse is that if you exercise, fat will turn into muscle. This idea is NONSENSE. Muscle and fat are distinctly different. Fat cannot become muscle and muscle cannot become fat. What will happen with exercise is that body fat will decrease and lean body mass, including muscle, will increase. What happens when you stop exercising and keep eating the same amount or even more is that you will gain weight because you decrease energy expenditure. You gain fat and there is also some wastage of muscle. The flab you see isn't muscle turning to fat—it is simply the return or the increase of fat. What is true is that some exercises build more muscle than others. It is essential always to stretch out after exercising to avoid bulky muscles and maintain suppleness.

The Physical Reasons for Exercising

Fitness is addictive. The more you do, the more you want to do and the more you can. It can not only make you healthier but can make you feel better about yourself and your life. This psychological plus may be attributable to the healthy glow and feeling of energy after exercise, also by the "good" tiredness that follows, but it could also be founded in physiological fact. Exercise improves circulation, which might otherwise be sluggish. There is also a popular theory that even mild exercise stimulates endorphin production, and as we know endorphins are the body's pleasure opiates. Even though this has yet to be proved, there are other sound reasons why continued exercise is beneficial.

The main one is the cardiovascular benefit of exercise. Like any other muscle during exercise, the heart benefits from increased circulation. When you are fit, the heart can pump more blood with each stroke. It is thus under less strain, as it gets a longer rest between beats. During stress and activity the heart does not have to work as hard, which means that the more you exercise, the stronger your heart and the more exercise you can do. When the heart is healthier, there is less risk of heart disease and high blood pressure. Exercise also lowers your uric acid and triglyceride levels and gives your joints increased flexibility and a fuller range of movement. Because of improved circulation, an increased supply of nutrients to the skeleton may cause the bones to grow and strengthen. There are also benefits to your respiratory system and you can inhale more oxygen.

What Can Exercise Do for Weight?

It had long been supposed that fat people were fat because they ate too much, but increasingly studies have shown that the obese eat the same or less than lean people. It was then assumed that the secret of their obesity had something to do with the fact that fat adults, but not children, were less active than thin ones. Although there are, as usual, contradictory studies on this, it does seem to be true in most cases. For instance, two studies that observed fifty thousand people in a public place noticed that significantly more obese people used the elevators. But it is important to keep several qualifications in mind. Less activity does not necessarily mean less energy expenditure, for the fat person will use up more calories than the lean person with every movement. Also, that fat children are no less active than thin children indicates that inactivity may be not the cause but the consequence of an unhealthy body image and being fat for a long time.

If inactivity is not definitely a cause of obesity, is exercise a suitable treatment for overweight? For far too long, both doctors and dieters had been ignoring caloric output in favor of input. Wiring up your jaws was thought to be more important than zipping up your track suit. Exercise has been popular in the United States for some time, but usually as a health measure, not primarily as a means of reducing.

One of the aims of this chapter was to show just how effective exercise can be in reducing weight and body fat. In the course of my research however, I discovered that the picture wasn't that simple. Some studies supported what I had actually experienced firsthand: that by exercising, over time one can lose weight without necessarily dieting. Even though most of these studies have been done on very obese people who had not previously exercised, the evidence is still strong. Other studies seem to be in absolute contradiction, showing that even with diet, exercise does not significantly reduce weight. Faced with such a battery of inconclusive results, I had to keep reminding myself that the answers to the problem of overweight are always tentative and that each study must be interpreted within its own context. A comparatively clear way of approaching the results is to look at the different ways exercise affects weight loss.

Exercise and Appetite
At first it was thought that exercise actually increased appetite. Then studies began to appear suggesting that this was incorrect and that exercise can depress appetite. However, most of these studies have been performed on animals and human confirmation is still needed. Some proof does exist. In an often-quoted study performed on Indian bazaar workers, the obesity specialist Jean Mayer found that the sedentary workers actually ate more than other more active workers and were heavier. The physiological reasons why appetite is reduced by exercise have not been established, and even the degree to which appetite is decreased depends on the degree of obesity. The more obese and sedentary a person is, the more his or her appetite will decrease with activity. The decrease also depends on the severity of the exercise. Moderate exercise *does* decrease appetite, but obviously marathon runners are not going to become progressively less hungry the longer they ru. Very strenuous exercise causes a rise in appetite, but the resultant increase in food intake is not proportionate to the output of the exercise.

Exercise and Metabolic Rate

While other effects of exercise still remain somewhat inconclusive, it is undeniably agreed that exercise accelerates metabolic rate. This is the secret of its success. Yet even this statement must be qualified: does this happen in all forms of exercise and in all people? Some kinds of exercise can accelerate metabolism more than others, and some people have higher metabolic rates than other people.

The rate at which our body burns fuel for energy increases with exercise for the simple reason that the body uses more oxygen. Oxygen uptake is the determining factor of metabolic rate: the more liters of oxygen we use, the more calories we burn, approximately five calories per liter of oxygen. Metabolic rate goes on increasing as exercise becomes more strenuous.

After we stop exercising the metabolic rate *may* remain elevated. The main reason for this is that when we exercise, we incur an oxygen debt in the recovery period. If exercise is strenuous enough, our muscles use up oxygen faster than we can inhale it. The body does not have enough oxygen. As soon as we stop, we breathe faster and deeper to "recover" that oxygen for the body. When we rest after exercise we are consuming the certain amount of oxygen that we would have done anyway in a resting state but we are also breathing "extra" to make up for the oxygen cost of exercising. The body is striving to return to its preexercise levels of oxygen consumption. Because there is a lot we still don't know about this we cannot definitely quantify the oxygen debt. For instance, the body's resting oxygen consumption after exercise might not be the same as before, which would spoil the calculations of the debt.

This elevation of metabolic rate, which could last for as long as twenty-four hours after exercise, is one of the greatest claims that exercise helps you lose weight. However, the degree of the oxygen debt after recovery depends on how much oxygen you need to recover. Athletes' recovery time would be less, since their capacity for oxygen uptake would be greater because their heart was fitter. Untrained obese people, whose oxygen uptake during exercise would be less because their heart is not as fit, would need a longer recovery period; therefore their metabolic rate would stay more elevated for longer. It has not been categorically proved that exercise *always* increases energy expenditure for a long time after activity, but it is a distinct possibility.

Exercise as a metabolic accelerator actually counteracts that metabolic brake: diet. As we know, dieting lowers our metabolism. It's the body's way of signaling that inactivity means survival, which was demonstrated in concentration camps, where the most inactive survived. Exercise can of course help this situation of minimized expenditure, but to what degree can it fight a diet-reduced metabolism?

Exercise Versus Diet

To assess this, let's look at some studies done on some different groups of people. A group of obese women was studied while they pursued an arduous ten-hour-a-day exercise program. Even though they ate an unrestricted diet, their weight decreased significantly. On such a strenuous program it would be hard not to lose weight, but one wonders if perhaps the success of these women was also attributable to the fact that they were eating "normally," over two thousand calories a day. Their success is in marked contrast to groups of *dieters* who were made to exercise for certain periods but who lost no more weight when exercising than when not. There is always the possibility that the dieters were not exercising as arduously as the group of women eating normally, and this, combined with their dietetically reduced metabolic rates, explains their failure to lose more weight with exercise.

The impression does emerge that over time, even without dieting, exercise reduces weight. People in a group ran thirty-five miles per week for five years and lost an average of seventeen pounds. Admittedly, weight loss by exercise is much slower than loss achieved through dieting, but it is much more likely to involve loss of body fat. Finally, the effectiveness of an exercise program for the obese depends on their degree of obesity at the start.

Exercise and Body Composition

With frequency, probably three times a week, exercise can change body composition. Weight loss achieved through diet and exercise combined or through exercise alone is the safest and most permanent because it is owing to *reduction of body fat*. While exercise does not seem to reduce size of the fat cells, it may affect production and number. Weight loss through exercise is not caused by loss of water or body protein. Actually, lean body mass percentage increases because you are reducing fat and increasing muscle.

The increase or sometimes just maintenance of lean mass with exercise occurs for several reasons. Very vigorous exercise, such as aerobics, which we shall discuss presently, actually enhances the burning of fat. Exercise also increases the amount of protein in the muscles and decreases its breakdown. Prevented from using muscle protein for fuel, the body has to draw on its fat reserves. When you are dieting and not exercising, the protein in the muscles is an available source of fuel and will be drawn on.

In some cases, if muscle mass increases too much weight will not be lost and may even be gained, but this depends very much on the individual. Women do not produce enough of the male hormone testosterone to develop very bulky muscles, and unless they undertake the very vigorous training of female bodybuilders, they are not in danger of becoming overly muscular.

Energy Output

Energy intake minus energy output equals energy stored. The factors look simple enough, but whereas the first and last are relatively uncomplicated, energy output happens at several levels.

Basal Metabolic Rate or BMR

No matter what we do we expend energy just staying alive. When you are ill, you may need twice as many calories to account for the destruction and replacement of tissue that occurs in acute infection. Tetanus convulsions have been estimated to consume as many as nine thousand calories a day!

Specific Dynamic Action

This is the energy cost of digesting and assimilating food. It used to be believed that the caloric cost of digesting protein was greater than that of digesting fats or carbohydrates. Hence all sorts of theories arose, such as that hard-boiled eggs were perfect foods that paid their caloric content by their digestive cost. This is no longer recognized as true.

These two factors apply to everyone. The next three vary in different people.

Cold-induced Nonshivering Thermogenesis

As we saw in Chapter 3, some rats expend more than others to keep warm. The same may be true in people.

Diet-induced Thermogenesis

Similarly, it is suspected that in some people (as is the case with some rats) overeating causes an increase in energy expenditure.

Physical Activity

Caloric expenditure in this case depends very much on the weight of the person (heavier people burn more), the temperature you exercise in (energy expenditure is greater in the cold but exercising in the heat makes you sweat more), and the speed and intensity of the activity itself. Exercises that involve big muscle groups and total body movement like running and swimming can raise almost everyone's BMR by as much as ten times. If one is very physically active, this component of energy expenditure takes over from BMR as being the major one. Whereas in the resting state muscles account for only 20 percent of our oxygen consumption, in strenuous exercise they use 35 percent or more.

Calculating BMR

Unless BMR is measured by laboratory techniques, it is useless to try to calculate it. BMR can be estimated accurately only in a specially sealed chamber called a calorimeter, where oxygen uptake and carbon dioxide and heat production can be measured effectively; with these values, BMR can be calculated. Another way is to use a special ventilated hood over the head that measures oxygen consumption.

Calculating Energy Output

It is much more meaningful and indeed more possible to calculate total energy expenditure; that is, BMR and physical activity. It is easier to assess this during a steady weight phase. When you see that your weight is stable for a few weeks and you are doing an average amount of physical activity, you can calculate your average daily intake and estimate that this is also your output. This is a much more useful and relevant calculation than just BMR.

As far as exercise is concerned, it is often easy to either over- or underestimate the energy cost of sports and activities. It would be unrealistic to think that because you go to an exercise class daily you can overeat afterward daily. It supposedly takes one and a half hours of running or brisk walking for the average person to burn off one chocolate milkshake and no more than a minute or so to drink it. On the other hand, some people take the pessimistic view that exercise must be performed for great lengths of time and for interminable duration to burn off any calories at all. This thought is a defeatist one. Exercise must be viewed over time for the benefits to become evident.

Take a simple example. If you weigh 150 pounds, you burn 240 calories per hour playing golf. You reason miserably with yourself that you would have to play for approximately fifteen hours to burn the 3,500 calories needed to lose a pound of fat. However, you can look at it another way. If you played golf for two hours per day, two days per week, you would burn 960 calories per week and would only need to play for 3.6 weeks to lose a pound of fat. This is an admittedly slow but nevertheless sure way. You could actually lose 14.4 pounds of fat in a year if you played two days every week, and all without dieting!

Table 1 shows the caloric cost of certain activities. These figures are *gross* and not *net*—they incorporate the calories expended during the exercise period plus the calories the person would have expended anyway just by staying alive; they represent total expenditure. The figures in Table 1 are based on averages. Obviously the amount of calories expended is going to depend on your general rate of metabolism (probably only responsible for a small difference), weight (could be a considerable difference), and the vigor with which you exercise. As a guideline this table should help you select maximum calorie-burning activities that will help you arrive at your weight goal. I do advise that you use the steady weight phase method previously described to calculate your energy expenditure rather than calculate only from this table.

Table 1
CALORIES EXPENDED FOR 10 MINUTES
OF PHYSICAL ACTIVITY

Activity	Body Weight				
	125 Pounds	150 Pounds	175 Pounds	200 Pounds	250 Pounds
Personal					
Sleeping	10	12	14	16	20
Sitting (reading or watching TV)	10	12	14	16	18
Sitting (talking)	15	18	21	24	30
Dressing or washing	26	32	37	42	53
Standing	12	14	16	19	24
Movement					
Walking downstairs	56	67	78	88	111
Walking upstairs	146	175	202	229	288
Walking—2 mph	29	35	40	46	58
Running—5.5 mph	90	108	125	142	178
Cycling—5.5 mph	42	50	58	67	83
Housework					
Making beds	32	39	46	52	65
Washing floors	38	46	53	60	75
Dusting	22	27	31	35	44
Preparing a meal	32	39	46	52	65
Weeding garden	49	59	68	78	98
Sedentary Occupation					
Sitting writing	15	18	21	24	30
Typing 40 words/min (electric)	19	23	27	31	39
Sport					
Dancing (moderate)	35	42	48	55	69
Dancing (vigorous)	48	57	66	75	94
Golfing	33	40	48	55	68
Horseback riding	56	67	78	90	112
Ping-Pong	32	38	45	52	64
Skiing (Alpine)	80	96	112	128	160
Skiing (water)	60	73	88	104	130
Skiing (cross-country)	98	117	138	158	194
Swimming (backstroke—20 yd/min)	32	38	45	52	64
Swimming (crawl—20 yd/min)	40	48	56	63	80
Tennis	56	67	80	92	115

Chart adapted from: Brownell, K. D. The Partnership Diet Program. New York: Rawson-Wade, 1980.

To give you an idea of *average* caloric expenditure during a twenty-four-hour period, the leading studies show that usually 34 percent of the day (almost eight hours) is spent in bed, accounting for 17 percent to 22 percent of total energy costs. It is impossible to say on average whether more calories are consumed during work or leisure because it depends on the nature of the occupation and on the tasks engaged in during free time. Sitting is a prime contender in the energy stakes, unfortunately from an expenditure point of view, and can account for from 15 percent to 37 percent of output. Men tend to have higher energy outputs than women, because they are generally heavier and expend more energy and because they tend to have higher metabolic rates. Men's average (I use this term with trepidation) expenditures are around the 2,700-calorie mark; women are lower, probably at around 2,000 to 2,400.

How to Maximize Energy Expenditure

Because energy cost figures are based on averages, it is difficult to assess precisely how many calories should be burned per exercise session for there to be some effect on weight and body fat reduction. Of course it depends on the person's weight and the strenuousness of the activity, but a reasonably accurate figure would be three hundred calories per workout if the workout lasts for about an hour. With this amount of expenditure you can be sure you are getting a good workout without getting so exhausted that it will be counter-productive.

As we shall soon see, exercises that require whole body movement are the best calorie burners, for they require that you transport your whole body weight rather than resting part of it and moving one part of the body. Surprisingly, therefore, walking is better than bicycling. Another important fact of which many people are ignorant is that with certain exercises, such as walking and jogging, your body weight and the distance you cover, not the speed or the time it takes to perform the activity, determine the calories you burn (although speed and time do affect cardiovascular fitness).

This statement does not apply to all sports. For instance, if you cycle fast uphill against a strong wind, you burn more calories than if you cycle slowly on level ground with no wind resistance. Also, swimming is more efficient for calorie-burning if you swim fast, but other considerations are the drag effect of the water and your body weight. Swimming expends about *four times* the calories of running an equal distance. Even walking is made more calorically cost-efficient by including an element of resistance: walking on a beach burns more calories than along a sidewalk.

Exercise and Shape

For many years now the popular solution employed by health spas and exercise programs has been "spot reduction." The belief was that spot exercises burned off fat locally. It is about time this myth was exploded. If spot reduction really worked, all the world's tennis champions, with one lean arm and one plump one, would look most peculiar!

When you burn calories, some are obtained from glycogen, and gradually more and more are taken from fat deposits all over the body. Selective fat loss is a mechanism about which we know little. One would expect that the fattest areas would be those that are mobilized first; however, most often this is not the case. No wonder, then, that the complaint most women have is that they can't shift any weight from the lower half. You would think that if your thighs were your fattest part, you would lose from there first. There may be several reasons why this doesn't happen. There may be strong hormonal influences that inhibit fat release from this area at most times in a woman's life. In addition, we may lose fat from internal depots first: the subcutaneous and visible fat stores may give up fat later. If there is plentiful fat in the deeper depots, the body could always mobilize that first.

No particular type of exercise can possibly move fat from a specific area. Doing one hundred sit-ups will not reduce the girth of your abdomen anymore than swimming briskly for half an hour; actually, the caloric cost of the swim would far exceed that of the sit-ups. One study, reported in a popular women's magazine, observed fifteen men on an intense four-week exercise program consisting of hundreds of sit-ups a day. Fat cells were measured in several areas of the body before and after the program. If spot reduction really did work, there should have been a significant decrease in the total amount of abdominal fat, as the abdomen was the area being worked. In fact, the abdominal fat cells had decreased neither in size nor in number. Another experiment shows the same result more clearly. Ten middle-aged women performed a five-week one-leg exercising program. The differences observable in the exercised leg were increased thickness of muscle tissue and decreased thickness of subcutaneous fat tissue. This decreased thickness did not represent fat loss from the depot over the exercising muscle, for there was no actual decrease in fat cell size or number there. What had happened was that the thickened muscle, which had expanded with exercise, had pushed the fat cells more tightly together, thus reducing fat *volume*.

By exercising a particular muscle group you cannot lose fat, but you do work and consequently tone the muscles in that localized spot. As muscle condition improves, it starts to hypertrophy, grow larger and thicker. As it expands, the fat above is increasingly squashed into a tighter, more compressed space, giving the *impression* that exercising a certain spot reduces it.

The more defined your leg and buttock muscles are, the more your body will be contoured. Gradually, with hard work, *correctly* done, you will achieve a sculptured look and the flesh will be more compressed and therefore tighter and less apparent. Don't make the mistake, however, of thinking that muscle-toning exercises alone will help you lose a lot of weight. The exercises that move the *whole* body, aerobics, burn most calories.

Beware of Gadgets

There is no effective substitute for sweat and hard work. The advertisements you see in magazines recommending these electric miracles *do* sound very tempting. All you have to do is apply pads to the areas where you want to work your muscles and plug in. Electrical impulses cause the muscle fibers to contract just as they would if you were doing spot exercises.

Even though this may sound like the perfect solution, it isn't. What the advertisements don't tell you is that the energy you expend contracting your muscles is less than that expended on a short walk. The only value these machines have is for paralyzed people, who cannot exercise. Also popular but ultimately ineffective are machine-operated vibrator belts. You step into them, wrapping them around your hips and buttocks, and they vibrate, supposedly spot reducing you. Studies show that when people were asked to use the machine on one side of their hips or on one leg, that area did *not* become smaller.

There is a widespread fallacy that fat can be broken down or melted away by external means, by thumping it or bumping it or pummeling it. THIS IS NOT TRUE. Fat is inaccessible to such surface assaults, it is stored in cells, each with a cell wall. These do not get broken like eggshells. Fat is soft and globular and safely cushioned under the skin. It can only be melted away internally by the tedious but proven method of eating less and moving more. Gadgets and aids are designed to make money for their marketeers and to confuse and distract you from the ultimate exercise machine for which none of us thankfully has to pay a penny: your very own body.

Shaping Up Your Attitude

Before you limber up your body, you have to work on your mind. As you physically prepare your body for exercises, you should also be doing psychological warm-ups. No bodily change will occur unless it is preceded by a change of thought. Once this is accomplished, tasks previously thought impossible will now seem a challenge, and an achievable one. If you get your attitude in shape, the rest of you will follow.

It seems to me that one of the reasons why exercise seems so threatening is that it is nonverbal: it exposes our physical being. In our society we are safe behind various facades. Suddenly we are stripped of all these distractions. It is perhaps natural that all we most hate and fear about ourselves will have a chance to surface when we are faced with the prospect of using our bodies and nothing else. Exercises can be a key to unlocking many anxieties. Euphoria, bliss, and rediscovered energy are freely made available to those who have learned the secret of movement. All you have to do is be willing to lose your mind in your body and be aware of your physical power and beauty. To do this you must have a positive approach.

Before You Start

When you start to exercise, you want to be able to continue to do so forever. Many people spontaneously decide to begin. They rush into it, feverishly enthusiastic for the first few days. Their mind is ready but their body is not. It is untrained. Without the correct preventive measures they get hurt. In your mind, exercise must be positive and pleasurable. It must not have a connection with pain and injury. A prepared, warmed-up body is a safer body. That's what precautionary measures are all about.

Organization

Work out an exercise timetable, realistically calculating how much time a day you can spare, how you can gradually increase that, and what your fitness goals are. Set aside your exercise time and treat it with respect. Don't allow yourself to be disturbed by others and don't give up that for anyone. You are obligated to your own health and well-being first: you deserve time to take care of yourself.

Know Your Limitations

As with everything in life, pacing is essential. Strong and healthy muscles do not appear overnight. Before you begin any sort of exercise program I strongly urge you to check with your doctor first. He or she will be able to tell you if you have a heart or blood pressure problem and will test the strength in your joints and spine. Once you start, be aware of your weak spots and do preventive exercises for them. Warm up and cool down before and after every time you exercise, even if you do it more than once a day. Start out slowly, and always listen to your body. If you can't stand the intensity of some exercise at first, choose something you can do that's easier and do it for longer. If you push yourself to the point of exhaustion it would be counterproductive, as you'll have to stop exercising for a few days to let your muscles recover and recoup their energy stores. Regular exercise with a steadily increasing workload is best.

We all have our off days, and we should respect them. Lack of sleep, hang-overs, emotional disturbances, menstrual periods, and stomach cramps all weaken the body, so be kind and don't bully yourself. Beware of fatigue. Exercise can actually relieve mental tiredness, but physical fatigue as a condition does exist. You may feel nauseated and giddy after exercise. This is the result of a lowered blood sugar level, as your immediate energy reserves have been drawn on faster than they can be replenished. The condition disappears after resting.

Fatigue also manifests itself in muscle stiffness. This can occur while and shortly after exercising because of the buildup of the waste product lactic acid, which we shall discuss shortly. Pain that appears a day or so after exercise may be caused by minute tears in the muscle fiber that happened during exercise, or by water retention in the surrounding tissues, muscle spasms, or overstretching of the muscle's overlying connective tissue. Treat yourself well after exercise. Stretch out the muscles with some yoga, soak in a hot tub, or take a sauna for five or ten minutes. Again, check with your doctor before you start using a sauna and never enter it just after a very strenuous workout.

Learning How to Breathe

Correct breathing is the origin of correct exercising. Breath will bring you energy. Yoga, the most complete form of exercise in that it integrates body, mind, and soul, concentrates primarily on the breath, on the visualization of its reaching different parts of the body. Considering how fundamental a reflex action breathing is, it is surprising how much we inhibit it. Restricted, shallow breathing is most often the result of tension, stress, and inhibition. We unconsciously reduce the flow of air in and out of our lungs and thus resist the life-force. When we move, this life-force is even more essential, as it is the means by which our body makes energy over time. After all, oxygen uptake burns calories. Freeing your breath during exercise is vital. You supply your muscles with fuel quicker, get rid of waste products faster, and thus have more energy and are less likely to suffer from cramps. When most of us exercise, we tend to tense up and hold our breath in the effort to concentrate on the movement. We may do this without realizing it, so make a conscious effort to breathe deeply and regularly.

Always exhale on a stretch or on the part of the exercise that exerts you. For instance, during a leg raise or sit-up, breathe *out* when you raise your leg or sit up. That way you will be helping your body and your mind, which could easily be sabotaging your efforts by telling you you're not going to make it. Deep rhythmic breathing while exercising will convince you otherwise. Hyperventilation is not what I am advising. Never force the breath but rather encourage it and get your movements to blend into the breath's rhythm. Inhale through your nose and exhale through your mouth.

The Inch Initiative

Dieting is all about losing pounds and inches. We tend to give undue importance to the former when it is the latter that really shows. The most noticeable effect of exercise is that of reducing measurements. Inches are usually lost more rapidly than pounds, but neither disappears overnight. Especially after heavy exercise, the muscles will feel bulky from overcontraction and certain areas of your body may be holding fluid. Another possible risk is that to lose inches from where you want, you may also have to lose them from elsewhere. As there is no such thing as spot reduction, this is unavoidable; however, if you tone the muscles in a certain area for a long period of time, some local difference will certainly be noticeable. Measuring yourself and recording the figures on a chart or graph is a good way of checking your progress. In your enthusiasm, however, don't measure yourself too often. Thin thighs do not happen in thirty minutes! Just as hopping onto the scale twice a day or even every day is not advisable, so you should also be patient with the inch loss and measure yourself every month to six weeks.

Measurements are going to be useless unless you have standard measurement points. To help you standardize the points on your body where you measure yourself, here is a list of them and an illustration of their positions. Do not flex the muscles or hold your breath when you measure. Just stand straight with legs straight and relax. It's easier to get an accurate measurement this way; if you tense the body more one time than another, you'll produce a false result.

Bust	Measure around the largest part, resting the tape measure on the tips of the breasts.
Upper Arm	Flex your biceps muscle to find its middle. Then relax muscle and measure. Always measure same arm.
Diaphragm (Upper Waist)	Halfway between the place you measured your bust and your natural waistline. Around the largest part of the ribs.
Waist	Your natural waistline. Usually two inches above the navel.
Hips	Around the lower abdomen, approximately two inches below the navel.
Legs	Always measure the same leg.
Upper Thigh	Largest part, which tends to bulge out. Usually where the buttocks join the thigh.
Lower Thigh	Three inches above the knee.
Knee	Directly over knee cap.
Calf	Midcalf. Approximately four inches below knee.
Ankle	Measure slightly above joint.

Exercise Clothes

One of the best things exercise did for me was to make me aware of my body and the clothes in which I dressed it. Soon I didn't want to wear clothing that restricted or camouflaged me. I wanted clothes that gave my body definition. You'll notice that more and more people are wearing exercise clothes even when not working out. That's because those clothes are comfortable; the body can stretch and move. They also tend to fit well and mold their shape to yours, not try and disguise it. Mistakenly, I used to think that if I wore loose clothes, I would look thin. Now I find that a bolder approach to dressing, choosing clothes that make me aware of what's underneath, gives me more confidence. It is worth investing in exercise clothing for class. Leotards and tights make you feel thinner and help you look at your body in the mirror and actually *see* it. Hiding under loose, bulky clothes only draws attention to what you are trying to hide. There are subtle ways to bring a bottom-heavy figure body into proportion. For instance, jeans or slacks, which are more flattering if firm but not too tight, should be worn with

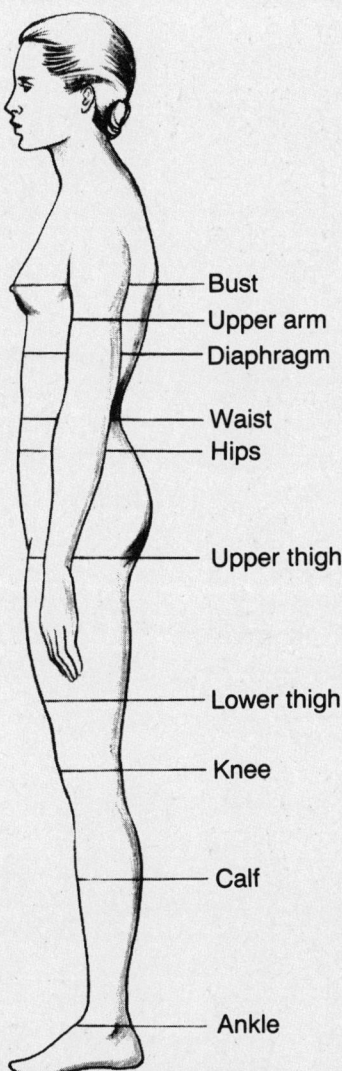

— Bust
— Upper arm
— Diaphragm
— Waist
— Hips
— Upper thigh
— Lower thigh
— Knee
— Calf
— Ankle

Figure 9 STANDARD MEASUREMENT POINTS ON THE FEMALE BODY

The reader should be aware that it is impossible always to obtain perfectly accurate measurements. These points are intended as guidelines.

full sweatshirts or sweaters. When you are exercising, leg warmers not only help you look the part but keep your lower leg muscles warm and help balance out heavy thighs.

The main thing is to believe in yourself. If you hold yourself tall, feel firm and sleek with every workout you do, no one will notice your thighs. The physical impression we make is *our* responsibility, so commit yourself to creating the one you deserve.

Types of Exercise

While the most important thing about exercise is actually to get out there and do it, it is vitally important to remember:

1. *Every time* you exercise, even if it's twice a day, be sure to do a few minutes of prevention stretches if you have problem areas. These can save you hours of inactivity due to injury.

2. *Every time* you exercise, even if it's twice a day, always warm up and cool down.

3. When doing any kind of stretch, do not bounce. Holding the stretch (the technique is fully described in Chapter 8) is much more effective than bouncing and tugging at your muscles. The point of stretching is gradually to persuade the muscle to lengthen and increase elasticity.

4. When doing any exercise that involves lifting the limbs or drawing up the upper body, such as a sit-up, be very honest with yourself and do not use *momentum.* If you fling your body, the exercise will be that much easier because the swing of your body weight will be generating the strength behind the movement. You will not be strengthening your muscles, however; that comes only from controlling your movements. You are aiming for flexibility and muscle strength, which can come only with the building up of strength, control, and endurance. Be patient. Do the movements slowly, and never stretch beyond your limit but really feel the muscles as they work.

5. The first thing to learn is the pelvic tilt. I shall emphasize this constantly because it helps relieve pressure on the lower back, prevents injury, improves posture, and ensures you work your mus-

cles more during standing and lying down movements. When you are standing, the pelvic tilt involves the following:

    a. Stand tall, legs either straight or slightly bent at the knees if you have lower back problems.

    b. Pull your stomach in.

    c. Tuck your buttocks underneath you.

    d. Tilt the pelvis forward.

When doing floor work, you can still tilt the pelvis by pushing the lower back into the floor. This is a very basic position; once you learn it, it will come automatically.

To ensure you work your body completely there are five different types of exercise: prevention stretches, warm-up stretches, aerobic or cardiovascular exercises, muscle-strengthening exercises, and recovery stretches.

Prevention Stretches

If you have any troublesome area of the body, such as knees, lower back, neck, or shoulders, you should stretch and strengthen them regularly to prevent them from becoming injured during exercise. If you have not exercised before, it is a good idea to do these exercises for a week before beginning an activity program.

Another way of not hurting yourself is to do exercises *properly*. If you are following exercises out of a book or from a cassette or videotape, learn the exercise first and then do it. When you go to exercise class, always pay special attention to how the teacher is doing the exercise and copy him or her, not the person nearest you. Often we engage in a movement thinking we are doing it right, not being able to visualize our body. It is vital to look in a mirror when you move, however much you dislike doing that.

Here are some tips about special problem areas.

The Neck

This is my problem area, where I experience a lot of soreness, stiffness, and tension. Floating in the water on your back or swimming backstroke can ease the neck muscles, and a neck massage can be very relaxing.

The Knee

Always a weak joint, the knee is particularly sensitive to strain in people who have heavy legs or who are heavy generally, as the knees have to support so much weight. What tends to occur, especially if you are also flat-footed, is a process known as femoral rotation. If you have fallen arches, your feet tend to roll out sideways when you walk. If you have a lot of fat distributed in your inner thighs around the knee, the whole leg tends to rotate outward and puts a strain on the knee, twisting it slightly. With all this pressure, the joint can become painful and flexibility is reduced. Any activities that involve running and jumping for any length of time can cause discomfort, so also can any exercises including deep knee bends, lunges, or bounces in a squatting position. If you have pain in this joint minimize such exercises; do them only as much as you can. To help the knees, you should gently bend them and stretch them to improve flexibility. When you do stretch the knee, try and do it in a hot bathtub or in a whirlpool. After injury apply icepacks: they are very effective at improving circulation, relieving pain, and reducing fluid buildup.

Shinsplints

When you are doing any kind of exercise that involves jarring, when your feet land on the ground with impact—for example, jogging, aerobic dance, or skipping rope—one of the problems is a burning in the shins, up the inside of the calves. The dull, cramplike pain that occurs in the shin can be agonizing, and is caused by the separation and *tearing* of the calf muscle from the fibula in the lower leg. To avoid shinsplints, whenever you do any jumping exercises wear sneakers and when you jump, land on your heels, *not* on your toes. Any calf-developing exercises that work the calves and feet are good for shinsplints. If you persevere, the pain should gradually ease. Again, applying ice is particularly helpful for shinsplints. As with any area of the body, if the pain doesn't go away, it's best to see a doctor.

The Lower Back

Pain in this area, or fear of it, discourages most people from exercising. Lower back problems are very common in women, especially in those of us who are bottom-heavy, as there is a lot of weight pressing on the sacral vertebrac. All abdominal exercises, especially any type of sit-up, and any exercise done on all fours can hurt the lower back if done too strenuously without the proper precautions. When you are in class or exercising at home, six things to remember are:

1. Whether doing floor work or standing exercises, always hold a pelvic tilt. When you are on the floor, check whether your lower back is pressed down onto the floor.

2. Keep one or both knees bent when you are lying on your back. That avoids straining it.

3. If performing exercises that involve lifting and lowering both legs while on your back, place your hands under your buttocks for support so that your lower back is *flat* on the floor.

4. Whenever you do any exercise involving bending from a standing position or twisting from the waist, bend the knees slightly, tuck in the tummy and the behind, and hold the pelvic tilt. Unless otherwise specified in an exercise, it is always best to stand in this position. If your back is strong, you can straighten your knees.

5. When lying on your side to do leg lifts, always make sure your legs are in line with your spine, not pointing either forward or back, which could injure the lower back. Don't let your back curl. *Keep in alignment.*

6. When lifting the leg behind you from an all-fours position, do not lift too high and do not arch the back too radically.

Stretch Versus Stress

Warming up is as important as the activity that comes after it. Without preparation, the shock of a sudden, strenuous workout may upset your whole body. The heart and other muscles need to be warmed, coaxed, and eased into a workout. However, unless these stretches are done properly, they may cause the injuries you are trying to prevent. Be careful not to overstretch, as you will tear the muscles. Generally speaking, your movements must be elongated; think of an elastic body extending its natural stretch; imagine the limbs of a cat, which seem to extend without limit. Keep the movement fluid and velvety smooth.

The warm-up also prepares you psychologically. It is time during which your mind switches from the cares and concerns of the day to thinking about movement or preferably to not thinking of anything at all. Your body can now take over.

Dress warmly. The exercise studio or the room you use might be chilly and your muscles need heat to help them stretch. It's always worth putting on leg warmers or, even better, those all-in-one wool jumpsuits. In any case, wear a cardigan or sweatshirt over your leotard until you warm up.

Aerobics or Cardiovascular Exercise

Recently there has been more talk about aerobics than any other type of exercise. Not only in fitness-crazed America but all over the world aerobic programs have multiplied. It is encouraging to see that the kind of fitness that burns most calories is being made so available, but there are disadvantages. First of all, very few books, cassettes, videos, or instructors bother to tell you what aerobics are, what the body does while you are doing them, how to do them safely and correctly, and how to monitor your progress. Rarely is enough importance ever given to preparatory warm-up or to recovery. *Lack of instruction and inadequate information about aerobics can lead to serious health problems and even fatal accidents.* The aim of this section is to provide you with the information you need to make aerobics safe and effective.

There is a great deal of misconception surrounding the term "aerobic." Not all exercises advertised as such are actually aerobic. What does the term *really* mean? Aerobic describes activity that uses oxygen. Aerobic exercise does not push you to the point of exhaustion. When you perform an activity aerobically, your muscles follow aerobic pathways; that is, they work in the presence of oxygen. Their primary source of energy is fat. This definition can help us to understand that aerobic refers to the *energy system* used by the body. It therefore indicates *how* the body behaves when the exercise is performed and does not technically refer to a certain exercise, although some aerobic exercises, when performed by the average person, use the body's aerobic system. Examples would be running or jogging, walking briskly either out in the open or on a treadmill, swimming with vigor, skipping rope, cross-country skiing, and dancing with jumping and expansive arm movements. As we can see, all these exercises are done in an upright position and with the large muscle groups of the lower body, using total body movements. The one exception is swimming, but even though the movements there are horizontal, the whole body is once again used. Aerobic exercise is characterized by whole body movement because:

1. Moving the large muscle groups in the body causes increased blood flow to the heart, more heartbeats per minute, and thus increased oxygen uptake (the aerobic energy system).

2. As these large muscle groups pump more blood to the heart, the heart becomes more efficient.

3. With the increased uptake of oxygen, which determines the rate of caloric expenditure, more calories are burned.

As aerobic therefore refers to the physiological way the activity is carried out, *theoretically* any exercise could be done aerobically. Even muscle-toning exercises performed on the floor, which are not whole body movements because the floor is supporting your weight, or exercises performed on machines, which again use only isolated areas, could be done aerobically. For this to happen, though, they would have to be sustained for an extensive time period. Therefore, when you see an exercise program that is labeled aerobic that does not consist of whole body exercises, you know that it is not really aerobic.

Immediate Energy System

Because aerobic exercises are done in the presence of oxygen, they can be sustained for some time. Exhaustive exercise taxes the body to such an extent in such a short time that the body does not have time for oxygen uptake. Such exercises are *anaerobic*. Activities that require a very short but very intense energy bout are weight lifting, a short sprint, or a twenty-five-yard swim. For these exercises the body uses high-energy phosphates, which are stored within the activated muscles. This source of energy is so limited that it can only supply activities that last less than sixty seconds. As no oxygen is used, this is an anaerobic energy system.

Short-Term Energy System

The immediate energy stores are rapidly depleted. After about sixty seconds, a second mechanism comes into play. What is used is glycogen, which as we know is the short-term energy store in the liver and muscles. It is here that glycogen is converted to glucose. The use of glycogen, known as glycolysis, results in the formation of the waste product lactic acid. This lactic acid accumulation is referred to as "the burn" in exercise. Oxygen is not being used in the synthesis of the energy phosphates, so this energy system too is anaerobic. Although essentially a short-term system, the anaerobic energy provided by glycolysis enables us to perform "all-out" exercises at intense speeds for short periods.

Long-Term Energy System

The short-term system can sustain the body the first two to three minutes. Once the immediate stores are depleted, glycolysis cannot generate enough energy to sustain prolonged exercise. This is where the system of aerobic energy transfer takes place. This energy is supplied by metabolic reactions that use oxygen. It would be incorrect to think that when the first few minutes of exercise were started, no oxygen was used. Oxygen uptake had been switched on, but during the first few minutes of all-out exercise, when the energy and power requirements are very high, the aerobic system cannot synthesize energy fast enough. During exercise of longer duration than all-out sprints, energy requirements are steadier and the aerobic system provides about 99 percent of energy.

What fuel does this system burn? While the immediate and short-term energy systems use muscle glucose in the form of glycogen, this energy store cannot last long, even though some glycogen is always essential. While we are using oxygen during the long-term or aerobic energy system, we are actually burning fat, for fat can only be burned in the presence of oxygen.

These are the three modes by which we obtain energy. Which one our body uses depends on intensity and duration of exercise. On many occasions, at different stages of the exercise, all three energy systems operate. Also, whether an exercise is aerobic or not depends on your level of fitness. The fitter you become, the longer you can perform an exercise. Therefore an exercise that previously was anaerobic for you (that you could not sustain for more than a few minutes) can become aerobic. Similarly, an exercise that is aerobic for you might be anaerobic for someone less fit.

Just because an exercise is done aerobically does not mean it can be done infinitely. Even with enough oxygen and our unlimited fat stores, we can still become exhausted. What determines the real point of exhaustion is lack of muscle glycogen. Once that is depleted, if you exercise all out you cannot go on.

Many benefits are associated with aerobic exercise. One is in the increase of oxygen uptake, which burns calories. This increased power of oxygen uptake is caused by an improvement in the heart rate, which enhances cardiovascular fitness. This is the other benefit of aerobics.

Oxygen Uptake

Our oxygen consumption determines our energy expenditure; therefore, the more energy we have to burn with the demands of exercise, the more oxygen we have to breathe. Our top capacity of oxygen uptake is called maximal oxygen consumption (max VO_2) or maximal aerobic capacity. It is the fastest rate at which we are capable of synthesizing energy aerobically. Our body is using oxygen alone to meet energy requirements in a "pay-as-you-go" system without incurring any oxygen debt. This max VO_2 can be measured only under laboratory conditions: it is the point where even when the exercise gets harder, we cease to consume proportionately more oxygen, and our uptake levels off and will not increase. After the max VO_2 has been reached, further energy is supplied once more by the short-term system of glycolysis with lactic acid buildup. The more we exercise aerobically, the more we increase our max VO_2 capacity and the longer we can exercise. Studies have shown that athletes have almost double the max VO_2 of a sedentary group.

Heart Rate

For max VO_2 or maximal aerobic capacity to increase, exercise must be intense enough to get the heart rate up to 70 percent of the maximum heart rate. This can be predicted by using a simple formula: 220 minus your age. Thus if you are 40, your age-predicted *maximum* heart rate would be 180 beats per minute. When you exercise aerobically, you are not aiming for the maximum heart rate but to get within the target zone or training sensitive zone. This is best if it is between a minimum of 70 percent and a maximum of 90 percent of the maximum heart rate. If you are 40, your target zone would be between 126 beats per minute (70 percent) and not above 162 beats (90 percent).

These figures apply to the time when you are exercising. After your warm-up, you should check your heart rate or pulse. The best way is to feel it at the wrist; if you can't manage it accurately try the carotid artery in the neck, but be careful not to exert too much pressure here. Count your pulse for ten seconds, then multiply by six, and you will know your heartbeats per minute. This is your resting heart rate. To give you a guideline, it should be below 50 percent of your maximum heart rate. If you worked hard in your warm-up, it may be a little elevated. On the whole, the fitter you are, the lower your resting heart rate.

Once you start exercising aerobically, your heart rate starts increasing. To ensure that you are improving your cardiovascular fitness, you should keep your heart rate at least 70 percent but not more than 90 percent of its maximum for twenty to thirty minutes. People in poor condition will need less time to see some benefit, but twenty to thirty minutes is practical and advisable for most people.

The increase in max VO_2, which is what you're aiming for, will depend on your previous fitness level. If you were very unfit, you could improve your max VO_2 by as much as 50 percent. Conditioned athletes, even with intensive training, sometimes improve by only 5 percent. How fit you are will also influence your recovery heart rate. The better condition you are in, the faster your heart returns to resting heart rate levels.

The benefits of aerobic exercise are numerous: better oxygen uptake and therefore increased endurance, better circulation, a more efficient heart, considerable energy expenditure, loss of body fat and thus weight reduction, and the "high" of energetic exercise. Almost everyone can enjoy these benefits as long as you work at your own level, paying attention above all to the heart rate and not attaining dangerous levels.

Muscle Strengthening Exercise

In qualifying different types of exercise, we must note that what differentiates them is their goal and their results. If you want to strengthen your cardiovascular system and lose body fat, aerobics are *essential*. You might also want to improve strength locally by toning certain muscles and, as a result, lose inches. Muscle-strengthening exercises will not burn calories as much as aerobics because they do not raise the heart rate considerably. The energy used for muscle-training exercise comes from the short-term energy system. This kind of exercise is therefore anaerobic. It is needed for intensive bouts, such as lifting a weight or doing a sit-up, which last only for a matter of seconds.

This kind of exercising is very impractical. An hour spent completing a weight-lifting program may only involve ten minutes of *actual* exercise. If you want to lose weight, muscle-strengthening should be a supplement to your aerobic program and not the sole means of exercise. With the invention of a new approach to muscle-strengthening exercise, however, benefits such as calorie-burning and cardiovascular fitness can also be obtained. This system is called circuit weight training. Instead of increasing the weight of what you are lifting, the overload, in order to work the muscle lighter weights are used for more repetitions. These are performed as quickly as possible. Once you have completed the whole training circuit, using all the weight machines, you start all over again and keep going so that you are in continual motion for twenty to thirty minutes. Thus it *is* possible for weight training to be aerobic, but you have to be moving very fast and continuously. The gym should be empty so that there is no waiting to use machines, and a trainer should be present. As you know, there are many simpler ways to enjoy cardiovascular benefits with ordinary aerobics.

Specifically, muscle-strengthening exercises consist of three different types. Isotonic training involves muscle contraction with movement. An example would be lifting weights, using barbells or dumbbells. Isometric training involves contraction of muscles without movement and is carried out against an object too heavy to move. The muscles generate force statically. The third is isokinetic training, where movements are performed with controlled resistance, as with exercise machines such as Nautilus equipment. Similar to the first category, isokinetics are considered superior. Whereas in normal weight training the muscles are not always working at maximum but instead attain a certain peak, isokinetically loaded muscles move with the same contraction throughout the movement. The word comes from *iso* meaning same and *kinesis* meaning movement in Greek.

Also included in the muscle-strengthening category are all the exercises popularly known as spot exercises or sometimes rather vaguely labeled calisthenics. All exercises performed against resistance, either with hand-held weights or weights worn on the body or using the weight of your own body, will build and strengthen muscles.

One of the reasons women become worried about this kind of exercise is that they feel they will become muscle-bound. Women just do not have enough male hormones, especially testosterone, to build bulky muscles. Unless you train several hours a day with extremely heavy weights as bodybuilders do, the results will be a stronger and better-defined body and no extreme bulges.

Recovery

When you have been exercising vigorously for twenty to thirty minutes, you are tired because you probably have acquired an oxygen debt and lactic acid has built up. There are two forms of postexercise recovery: passive and active. Completely passive recovery consists of lying down and minimizing energy requirements so that the oxygen debt can be paid off faster and oxygen consumption returns to normal. Other methods include cold showers, massage, certain body positions, and cold drinks. Active recovery consists of a cool-down period, usually featuring stretches or light exercises that help prevent muscle stiffness and cramps. Active recovery is better than passive because it keeps the circulation going and thus facilitates removal of lactic acid. With a good flow of blood carrying oxygen to the muscles, this waste product can be oxidized (combined with oxygen) and converted back into energy by metabolic process.

Now that we realize what recovery entails, we can see its importance. Exercise also affects the circulation. When the large muscles in the lower body are contracting, they are pushing blood up toward the heart. The heart returns this blood with equal vigor. When you suddenly stop exercising the heart is still sending blood to the muscles, but the muscles have stopped working and no longer return the blood. It then "pools" in the veins and takes some time to return to the heart. If you stop exercising gradually, with the aid of a cool-down, this will not occur. Also during the recovery period, your heart will return to its resting rate, and your muscles, which contracted during exercise, will get stretched out again.

When you are doing your cool-down, because your body has been warmed up by exercise your flexibility should be increased and you can afford to stretch that much further without risk.

Yoga can be very effective as a cool-down form of exercise. It is the perfect way of integrating mind, body, and spirit. It is gentle yet extremely powerful and, done correctly, will bring lifelong benefits. Excellent for all overweight and bottom-heavy individuals, it does not make you breathless and is not at all strenuous. If you work at it for several months, you will become flexible and confident of your agility, which will help enormously if you intend to exercise in classes or sports. Ten or even five minutes a day of yoga loosens the joints, stimulates circulation, and, most important of all, through deep yogic breathing, teaches you to relax.

8

The Venus Workout: What You Can Do for the Bottom-heavy Figure

Because I have been bottom-heavy for many years, I know from experience what the physical and psychological difficulties are when you're exercising. You feel self-conscious, awkward, and out of condition, even if you're not. Don't be prejudiced toward yourself; there is no physiological reason that you cannot be fit and bottom-heavy. The bottom-heavy build is characterized by a great deal of flexibility in the lower joints, which aids exercising. In any case, with increasing exercise you will find your body comes more into proportion. Fat on the hips and thighs does not preclude agility: it also doesn't mean you have let yourself go. These are simply ridiculous judgments made by ignorant people who know nothing about fat cells or distribution. There is no sport or exercise you *can't* do because of heavy legs, but there are plenty you can't do because of a negative attitude.

For most of my life I was positively terrified of exercising. My father's attitude toward sports verged on the paranoid. Considering that they were the people who founded the Olympic Games, it is ironic that most Greeks exhibit an aversion to sports and exercise. The national pessimism predestines all physical activity to end in disaster. The conviction that I would have a fatal accident not only didn't galvanize me into action, it left me paralyzed. Fitness, agility, and confidence have become a new way of life for me. I have discovered that I can move freely and gracefully and that all those activities I thought were impossible are now within my reach, even water skiing, which I once dreaded. I am still out of proportion but I am working toward a better shape, certain that I will attain it. Unlike some fitness gurus, I won't pretend to have conquered the problem. I still have a long, long way to go, and having a lot of weight on my legs makes some exercises harder for me. Heavy legs can often cause chronic stresses: pain in the tendons and in the calf can be the result of the weight your lower leg has to support. This can flare up after an aerobic workout that has a lot of jumping. As you become lighter and your muscles become stronger, the discomfort will subside and you will have more confidence and thus, you will find, more endurance.

The bottom half of your body is very strong because it contains some of the largest muscle groups. This is a positive thought to adopt, especially if you have spent your life thinking of the bottom half of you as alien to the rest, as something ugly, unhealthy, and out of condition.

The aim of the Venus workout is fivefold: to improve flexibility, cardiovascular fitness, weight loss, muscle strength, and shape. The program therefore recommends stretching for general flexibility, aerobic exercises for cardiovascular strength and for weight reduction, and a specific toning program for muscle conditioning and shape, which will burn calories. The most important achievement is to fulfill all these aims and to follow a program that includes a *balance* of these activities. If your time is short, it is better to follow a shortened but balanced program than to exercise sporadically, doing only one kind of exercise and for only certain parts of the body. The body is best kept in tune when it is being stretched and exercised totally, not in part. Therefore, the following pages offer you a balanced combination of stretches and exercises featuring the five fitness goals mentioned in Chapter 7.

Prevention Exercises—to reduce risks of injury

Warm-up Stretches ⎫
Cool-down Stretches ⎭—for flexibility and for general health

Aerobic Exercises—for cardiovascular fitness and weight loss

Muscle-Strengthening Exercises—for muscle tone and for shape

Prevention Stretches

These should be done very slowly and carefully. The whole purpose is to prevent injury that may be caused through rapid or sudden movement. You do not want to cause injury by bouncing or stretching the muscles. Doing an exercise wrong is doing it uselessly. You should study and learn the movements before attempting them and always exercise in front of a mirror so that you can see exactly what your body is doing. I also recommend the following tips:

1. Do prevention exercises preferably in bare feet (so you can feel the floor with your toes) or in light shoes such as ballet slippers. Wear loose and comfortable clothing, preferably nothing flowing so that you can clearly see your body and have full ease of movement.

2. Wear a headband to keep hair out of your eyes.

3. Play soft, flowing music when you do your stretches.

4. Wait at least two hours after a meal. If you have eaten a heavy meal, wait four hours.

5. Do the exercises slowly. Take your time and really *feel* the movement.

6. Never exercise on a hard, cold floor. Always use a mat or towel, even on a carpet.

Duration

If you do all the stretches slowly and carefully, the prevention exercises should take no more than ten minutes. A minimum program that is half the length has been included for those days when you are short of time.

Frequency

If you have never exercised before, even if you don't have problem areas, you should do only these exercises for a few days before commencing any program, just to strengthen yourself gently. Otherwise, if you have any pain or discomfort in your body, always do these stretches before exercising.

PREVENTION EXERCISES FOR THE BACK. MAXIMUM PROGRAM.
Remember the pelvic tilt from Chapter 7: pull in the stomach, tuck your buttocks under you, push your pelvis forward, and hold the position firmly, ensuring that there is a hollow in your lower back.

1. Stand tall, legs wide apart, knees slightly bent, hold pelvic tilt,

relax shoulders. Relax the upper body, bend forward, and let your head fall between your legs. Hang there relaxing your neck, shoulders, and spine, especially the lower back. If you can, rest your hands or arms on the floor; otherwise just reach down as far as possible. Feel the weight of the upper body pulling you down and keep your lower body tight for support. Slowly, as if stacking one vertebra on top of the other, roll up until you stand tall again. As you lift, bend the knees and remember that pelvic tilt.

2. Lie down flat on your stomach, stretching out your arms and legs in a straight line from your body. Slightly arching the back, lift your arms up in front of you as high as possible. At the same time, lift your legs up off the floor behind you as high as possible. Keep them hip distance apart and keep them straight. Really stretch the arms and legs. Go very easy on this. It does strengthen the back but there is a danger of pulling the muscles.

3. Get down on all fours. Inhale as you arch your back upward like a cat with your head hanging between your arms. Pull in the stomach muscles and the buttocks. Arms remain straight. Exhale and slowly collapse the back so it curves downward and, with the stomach also, is pressed toward the floor. Your buttocks are now stretched toward the ceiling and you are looking upward. Do this exercise several times. The movement should be flowing.

4. Lie on your back, knees bent, arms out to the sides. Cross the right leg over the left as if you were sitting and pull your crossed legs sideways down to the right. Turn your head to the left and keep your shoulder blades on the floor. Hold and repeat with legs to the left, head to the right. Then repeat both sides but with left leg crossed over the right.

MINIMUM PROGRAM. Exercises 1 and 4.

BACK STRENGTHENERS. MINIMUM AND MAXIMUM PROGRAMS.
Once you have done the prevention exercises for the back, you should begin strengthening it with the movements described here. The back is one of the most neglected areas when it comes to fitness. We pay attention to our arms, stomach, buttocks, and thighs and ignore the back. We want only to fight flab, not strengthen our very support system, the spine. A strong back is the secret to complete flexibility and to strength and endurance in many exercises, especially abdominal ones.

A big mistake many people make when exercising is how they bend down. Whether you are bending over your toes from a standing position or reaching over your legs when sitting up or in a straddle position, it is all too easy to bend only from the waist and consequently to round your back. This does nothing to stretch you and in fact strains the neck muscles. Always bend from the hip, thus increasing flexibility of the flexor muscles of the hip joint, vital for all exercises. If you bend from the hip, your back—lower, middle, and upper—will be completely straight. If you stretch every movement out of the pelvic area, you will improve its flexibility, strengthen your back, and not put stress on the neck and shoulders as you do when you round your back over.

Here are some exercises to help you achieve this.

1. Standing against a wall, make sure that the whole of your back and your shoulder blades are against the wall. Lift your knee to your chest and hug your leg into your body, always pressing your back into the wall. Repeat with other leg. You can do this exercise lying flat on your back and hugging your knee to your chest. The point is to keep the whole of your back flat on the floor.

2. It is best to do this exercise in front of a mirror so you can make sure your back is straight. Legs about shoulder width apart, turn your toes in slightly. Bending from the hip joint, bring the whole of your upper body down toward the floor, pushing the chest out. Stop once your back is completely flat, like a table parallel to the floor, in an L-shape with your legs. Push your shoulders back so that they are in line with your hips and bend your elbows. Once the position is correct, bend the knees and then straighten them. As you move up and down, the movement should only be in the hips and knees. The back should be completely straight and, as you straighten your knees, should even curve slightly downward with a dip like in a horse's back.

3. Sitting tall, both legs straight out in front, clasp your arms behind your back. Keep the arms straight and interlace the fingers. Palms should be facing inward. Keeping the back straight and the legs flat on the floor, lift the arms as high as possible.

4. Sitting tall, legs straight in front, bend your right leg and rest the foot on the floor. Twisting to the right, bring your left elbow to the outside of your right knee to pull the stretch further. Do not bounce but stretch around to the right as far as possible. Repeat to the left, bending the left leg, etc.

5. Sitting tall, legs straight in front, lift the right elbow up in front of your chin and support with the left hand. Keep your back very straight and legs flat on the ground. Hold the position. Then bring the right elbow behind the head and hold with the left hand, once again keeping the back straight. Repeat with the left elbow. This not only strengthens the back but also the frontal thigh muscles.

PREVENTION STRETCHES FOR KNEES. MAXIMUM PROGRAM.

1. Standing, bend your knees and place your palms on your knees. Pushing gently on the knees, rotate them several times in both directions to get all the kinks out.

2. Lie down on your back, pull your knees into the chest, and bend and straighten the legs to the ceiling. You are working on extending the leg while it does not have any weight on it. Thus the knee joint can stretch without pressure.

MINIMUM PROGRAM. Exercise 1.

PREVENTION FOR CALVES. MAXIMUM PROGRAM.

1. Sit down, bend your knees, and hug your right thigh to your chest. Straighten leg to ceiling. Vigorously point and flex your foot, then rotate your ankle in both directions. Repeat with left leg. The movements must be vigorous and deliberate.

2. Stand tall, legs wide apart, and bend over and walk the body all the way forward using your hands so you are supporting your weight on your hands and feet. With feet pointing forward, lift high on to the toes, then back down on to the heels. Go up and down, fast and energetically, and feel the burn.

Variation: Turn toes inward and do the same thing.

3. Stand about three feet away from a wall. Put the left foot flat on the floor, toes pointing forward. Place your right foot, which is flat with toes forward, one foot in front of the wall. Lean forward, pressing your arms against the wall, bending the right knee and stretching the left leg out behind you, pushing the heel to the floor and feeling the stretch in the calf. Then change legs.

MINIMUM PROGRAM. Exercise 2.

Warm-up Stretches

These stretches are preparatory movements designed to warm up the body before exercising. Before you exercise each time, you should stretch out your body, even if you exercise several times in the same day. A minimum selection of stretches is featured for those days when the full program will take too long. As a guideline, the full stretching program should last ten to fifteen minutes once you learn the moves. Don't make the mistake of thinking that stretching becomes less necessary the fitter you become. Actually, the opposite is true. While regular exercise does improve flexibility by loosening the joints and extending their range of movement, exercise contracts muscles. Your muscles therefore need to be stretched out frequently. A warm-up always raises body temperature so muscles work more efficiently and increases circulation to the muscles so more oxygen is available to them.

Stretching should be done with caution. When you overstretch, the body has its own protective reflex, which causes the muscle to contract in resistance to the stretch. When this happens, the muscle may tear. The reflex is an immediate reaction to the stretch. If you wait for between ten and twenty seconds after your initial stretch, you will find the body relaxes and a further stretch can be attempted. The right breathing is crucial here. When you exhale, the body will again relax and allow a further stretch. If you hold your breath, you hold your body in also, limiting its flexibility. Always exhale on the stretch.

Never bob or bounce. This type of ballistic stretching is not as effective as holding a stretch for thirty seconds, inhaling and exhaling as you progressively stretch further. The basic principle is to stretch until you feel your muscles tighten, then stop, wait until the protective reflex subsides, and go further. With each session of stretching the reflex will be extended; that is, you won't tighten up so soon. Stretch until you feel tightness, not actual pain. Be aware of your muscles' message: they may be telling you the exercise is hard (in which case persevere) or dangerous (in which case stop).

HEAD. MAXIMUM AND MINIMUM PROGRAM.

1. Stand tall. Roll your head very slowly around to the right, back, left, and forward, chin to chest. Imagine it as a very heavy

bowling ball you are rolling around. Reverse direction.

2. Stand tall. Reach your arms high over your head by your ears. Stretch up out of your rib cage. Pull in your stomach and buttocks muscles tight but keep your neck and shoulders relaxed. Look upward. Now stretch again but pull your head down, chin to chest.

JAWS. MAXIMUM AND MINIMUM PROGRAM.

Though we never think of it, the jaw can hold a lot of tension. Easy exercises to relax them are:

1. With the jaw open, push your tongue around the teeth and gums of both jaws.

2. Let your jaw hang down and consciously relax the muscles. This also releases the temples and will help relieve headache.

3. Extend lower jaw out, like a chimpanzee, opening your lips. Then relax it back again.

SHOULDERS AND ARMS. MAXIMUM PROGRAM.

1. Stand tall, feet shoulder width apart. Keeping the lower body controlled and tight, bend forward from the waist, keeping an extended and flat back. Keep arms in by your sides and keeping them straight, lift them up behind you, interlocking the fingers, palms facing inward, elbows facing out. You are making a bridge over your back with the arms.

2. Stand tall, feet apart. Raise your right shoulder and slowly roll it forward and down, back and up, rotating the entire joint. Alternate shoulders. Try the same movement in reverse direction, going backward.

3. Stand tall, feet apart, and reach both arms up. With very rapid movements, imagine that you are climbing a rope and grab with your hands, all the time reaching up out of your ribs.

4. Same position, bring arms down and reach them straight out in front of you. Open and close the fingers with *speed*.

MINIMUM PROGRAM. Exercises 1 and 2.

RIBS. MAXIMUM AND MINIMUM PROGRAM.

Stand tall, feet apart, upper body well pulled up, arms out to side, palms facing the floor. Keeping your hips still, move your ribcage over to the right side, as if your right arm were being pulled. Return to center. Repeat to left. The point is to extend the ribcage. The hips and lower body must remain still. The movement is from the ribs.

WAIST STRETCHES. MAXIMUM AND MINIMUM PROGRAM.

1. Stand tall, legs wide apart, toes pointing out. Slowly bend your upper body to the right side, running your right hand down the outside of the right leg. Keep your chest pushed out and facing squarely forward, shoulders back. Hold and slowly go down even further to the right. The lower body remains locked to give you support as you lift your upper body up to center again, always keeping your chest squarely to the front. Repeat to the left.

2. Stand tall, legs shoulder width apart, toes pointing forward. Arms are crossed in front of your chest and are bent, hands resting on elbows. Bend the knees and hold the pelvic tilt. With your lower body firmly locked in this position, begin to twist from the waist in a smooth flowing movement, first to the right, as far as you can go looking past your shoulder, and then around to the left. As you swing your upper body around from side to side, slightly bend your knees.

UPPER BODY. MAXIMUM PROGRAM.

1. Stand tall, feet apart, hands on hips. Bring upper body all the way forward, bending from the waist so that your back is completely flat and your upper body parallel with the floor. Rotate the upper body around in a complete circle, working on extending the movement. Rotate to the right several times and then to the left.

2. Same position, bring upper body forward and stretch for two counts, knees straight. Then bring it back, stretching back, hands firmly on hips, knees bent to take strain off lower back. (Do not do this exercise if you have a bad back.)

3. Stand tall, feet shoulder width apart, feet facing forward. Bend forward and rotate your upper body, reaching your right hand to the outer side of your left foot. Your left arm is extended out behind your body pointing upward and across to the right. When you first start to do the movement, you should keep the knees bent. If you have a bad back, continue to bend the knees even when you are familiar with the exercise. You should not fling yourself into the movement because then you will be using momentum. You should move freely and evenly in a swinging motion but be careful to control

the movement. Do not throw the arms, stretch them and reach your hand as far as you can on the outside of the opposite foot when you bend.

MINIMUM PROGRAM. Exercises 1 and 3.

BACK. MAXIMUM AND MINIMUM PROGRAM.
Stand with feet slightly apart, toes pointing forward. Slowly bend over and attempt to touch your toes or the ground in front, bringing your head in toward your knees. Keep your legs straight. Go as far as you can and hold the stretch for about fifteen to thirty seconds, then try and stretch again. Hold once more and slowly roll up, tightening your stomach muscles, holding the pelvic tilt, imagining that you are stacking one vertebra on top of the other. Once upright bend backward *as far as you can,* arching your back, hands on hips. If you have any pain with this stretch stop at once.

HIPS. MAXIMUM AND MINIMUM PROGRAM.
1. Stand tall, feet shoulder width apart, holding your pelvic tilt. Keeping the upper body tight, rotate your hips around in wide circles. Make the movement smooth and controlled. Do not fling the hips, roll them, first to the right a few times and then to the left.
2. Stand tall, feet together, hands on hips. Lift one leg high up in front of you, bending your knee into your chest. Return the leg and lift the other one. Do these lifts at a good pace and lean your chest into the knee, thus also working the upper body. Then do the same movement but lift the leg right out to the side of the body; this also works the hip flexors, the muscles in the groin.
3. Get down on all fours and reach your right leg out behind your body and then stick it out diagonally behind you to your left. Reach your leg as far as you can as if someone is pulling it, all the time supporting your weight with your hands and your left knee. Drop down onto the elbows so the whole of the right leg and the hipbone are pressed to the floor. Hold and repeat with the left leg crossed behind you diagonally to the right.

GROIN. MAXIMUM AND MINIMUM PROGRAM.
Sit down, bend your knees and bring your heels in toward your body, resting the soles of your feet against each other. Grasp the ankles and rest your elbows on the inside of your knees. Pull yourself

up tall and slowly push your knees open with your elbows, trying to touch them to the floor. Hold this position and feel the stretch.

INNER THIGHS. MAXIMUM AND MINIMUM PROGRAM.
Stand with your legs wide apart, feet pointing outward. Bend your right knee deeply and bring your hips as near to the floor as possible but not below knee level. You are supporting yourself with your hands on the floor in front of you. Stretch your left leg out to the side, the heel resting on the ground with the foot flexed. Press the right knee outward with the right elbow. This stretches the inner thigh. Bounce very slightly for eight counts and then shift weight on to the left leg, bending deeply at the knee and stretching the right leg all the way out to the side. (Do not do this exercise if you have bad knees.)

BUTTOCKS. MAXIMUM PROGRAM.
1. Sit cross-legged with the right foot over the left. Sit up tall, resting your weight on the buttocks and then slowly, as you exhale, bend forward, trying to reach the head to the floor. Hold and then release. Repeat exercise, crossing left leg over right.
2. Stand tall, feet together. Bend over and touch your toes. With your fingers resting on the floor for support bend your right knee and as you do so, push up the left hip and buttock, really stretching them. Do not hold for long. Repeat to the left. Do this exercise in a flowing motion, bending alternate knee and pushing opposite hip up.
3. Stand tall, feet together. Place your right leg over your left and bend down. Try to reach your calf, ankle, toe, or the floor. You will feel a stretch in the back of the leg. To maximize the stretch in the front of the leg, grasp the left knee from behind and push forward. Hold and then slowly come up. Repeat with the left leg crossed over the right.
MINIMUM PROGRAM. Exercises 2 and 3.

FRONT OF THIGHS. MAXIMUM PROGRAM.
1. In a sitting position, with your back straight, extend right leg in front of you, and *flex the foot.* Stretch left leg out to the side slightly and bend your left knee, push it down to the floor, keeping the left foot as close to the buttocks as possible. As you push your

left knee to the floor, push up your left hip. This will maximize the stretch along the frontal thigh muscle, the quadriceps. Lean back on both elbows for four counts and try and relax as much as possible. If the pain is unbearable or you get a cramp, release the bent knee slightly so that the lower leg is not tucked under so much. Raise yourself to a sitting position. Supporting yourself with your straightened right arm, reach forward with your left arm over the right leg. Really stretch for four counts over the flexed foot, going as far forward as possible, for four counts. Repeat to the other side, left leg straight, right leg bent, etc.

2. Stand with legs wide apart, feet facing forward. Lift right heel, rotate leg inward, and turn to the left with your whole body. Exhaling, bend over your left knee, making sure the knee is beneath the left shoulder. Place hands on the inside of your left foot for balance and stretch out your right leg behind you, pushing the heel toward the ground. Your left heel should be firmly on the ground and, if possible, your back straight, not rounded. After holding for fifteen to thirty seconds, stretch out the right foot on the floor, heel facing the ceiling. Release the posture by rocking your weight back on to your right knee and pushing up to a standing position. Now repeat this stretch on the other side.

3. Stand tall, feet together. Until you are sure of your balance, rest your right hand on a door, wall, or high-backed chair. Lift your right leg up behind you, bending at the knee. Grasp your right ankle behind your buttocks with your left hand and press the heel in. Hold, release, and repeat to the other side.

4. Kneel up on both knees and slowly lean all the way back, resting your weight on your hands, which are placed on either side of your heels. Drop your head backward and stretch as far back as you can. *If you have weak knees or a bad back, be careful with this stretch.*

MINIMUM PROGRAM. Exercises 1 and 3.

BACKS OF THIGHS. MAXIMUM PROGRAM.

1. Bend the right knee into the chest, pick up the right foot with both hands, grasping either the foot, ankle, or calf, depending on your flexibility. Straighten the leg upward to the ceiling and bring it in again eight times. Then try and straighten out the leg upward and in front of you, and bring it down to the ground, keeping it

completely straight, and still holding on at the calf, ankle, or, prefer-ably, the foot. Repeat with other leg.

2. Stand tall, feet together. Bend down and clasp your ankles with your hands. Pull your head toward your shins and hold. Then raise your chin, look up, and using little quick movements, press the lower back up and down and stretch your buttocks to the ceiling. Keep the legs straight.

3. Maintaining the above position, now walk your hands out in front of you as far as you can. Keeping your feet together, bend the left knee and straighten the right leg, pressing the heel firmly to the floor and stretching the tendon. Hold and then repeat with the left leg.

4. Stand with legs wide apart. Inhale and reach up, exhale and collapse forward, letting your head fall between your legs. Bend your knees slightly to prevent strain on the lower back. Straightening the left leg, bend the right, wrap your arms around your right thigh, and bring your head to meet your knee. Straighten right leg still trying to press forehead to knee. Bend right knee and release. Repeat over the left leg.

5. Lie down on your right side propped up on your right elbow. Bend the left knee so that it is facing the ceiling and bring left foot in as near as possible to the groin area. Reaching along the inside of your left thigh, clasp your left heel in your left hand. Then try and straighten the left leg upward to the ceiling, still holding on with your left hand. You may not be able to reach all the way at first but go as far as you can.

MINIMUM PROGRAM. Exercises 2 and 4.

CALVES, FEET, AND ANKLES. MAXIMUM AND MINIMUM PROGRAM.

1. Stand, feet shoulder distance apart, toes facing forward. Lift your heels off the floor so that your weight is on the balls of the feet. Go up and down rapidly; the purpose is to feel a burning sensation.

2. Lift one leg off the ground, point and flex the foot *vigorously* and do ankle rotations. Repeat with other leg.

3. This stretch can be done sitting down, with both feet, or stand-ing, with one foot. Stretch the foot, flexing it, then bend your toes tightly as if wanting to curl them around a pencil. Hold tightly.

In addition to these exercises for your feet and ankles, I recommend the following, especially if you suffer from fluid retention.

1. Massage your feet frequently. Pull the toes away from the foot gently but firmly and try kneading the balls and the soles. There are points on the foot that correspond to organs in the body, and taking care of the feet can improve the functions of these organs and of the circulation.

2. Raise your feet above your head, either in a shoulder stand or leaning them against a wall, every day for at least ten minutes.

3. Sleep with the foot of your bed raised about six inches to improve circulation.

Aerobic Exercise

As I said in the previous chapter, there have been a lot of misconceptions about aerobic forms of exercise. Aerobic refers to the long-term energy system used by the body when it is engaged in exercise lasting more than a few minutes. Thus "aerobic" is a term describing how the exercise is performed. Almost any activity could be performed aerobically if you performed it rapidly and vigorously enough to get within your target heart zone for twenty minutes.

Some exercises are more effective as aerobic workouts than others. I have not devised an aerobic workout for the Venus syndrome not because aerobics are ineffective for the bottom-heavy figure but because if you follow the guidelines here, you can select whichever exercises you prefer. Whereas toning muscles locally restricts you to certain movements, aerobic exercise offers much more variety, as the following list demonstrates.

Cross-country skiing

Soccer

Swimming (Swimming is aerobic if you swim vigorously and non-stop for twenty minutes. Your heart rate will probably be about ten points below your normal target zone because of the cooling effect of water on your body. However, the drag factor in the water provides resistance and makes swimming an excellent workout.)

Walking (briskly, moving arms vigorously)

All aerobic dance or aerobics classes (the benefit of these classes largely depends on how they are taught)

Bicycling

Running

Step-up exercises (Using blocks of wood, build two steps higher than normal stairs. Keep stepping up and back down again, fast. This is an inexpensive and very effective exercise "machine.")

Jumping rope

Disco dancing (fast and vigorous)

Duration

No optimum time has been established to improve cardiovascular fitness. Obviously the less conditioned you are, the sooner you will be working aerobically, within your target zone. A person who has not exercised may get his or her heart rate up to 70 percent of maximum capacity in three to five minutes. The fitter you get, the longer it takes for your body to work aerobically.

If you want to strengthen your heart and lose weight you should aim to get your heart rate up to 70 percent of its maximum for twenty to thirty minutes. Only if the exercise is excessively intense and totally nonstop can you get away with fifteen minutes. You have to be honest about this with yourself because when you're tired, it's all too easy to count in the warm-up and cool-down as part of the twenty to thirty minutes. You will be cheating yourself of the aerobic and caloric benefits if you do this. As soon as you slow down, even for twenty seconds, your heart rate falls off very quickly. So aerobic exercise must be sustained exercise. Because you're consuming much more oxygen to sustain you, you are burning considerably more calories when you work aerobically. For a *real* twenty to thirty minutes of aerobics an *average* calculated expenditure might be as high as three hundred calories.

With aerobics, your cardiovascular fitness will start to show results within one to two weeks. Of course your weight loss will depend also on the other factor of the energy equation, energy input, but if you are dieting, aerobics should help you lose weight quicker and will also reduce appetite for several hours after you do them.

Frequency

No optimum frequency has been established for aerobics. If you are very eager to lose weight, you may wish to work out aerobically five or six times per week. If your time is limited and you wish to do shape exercises also, it may be best to alternate days, say aerobics three times per week for twenty to thirty minutes plus warm-up and cool-down, and shape exercises three times per week for thirty to forty-five minutes plus warm-up and cool-down. That seems like a lot of time, but this is the program I undertook and it really did have results on what had been pronounced a hopelessly out-of-proportion body. How much time you spend is your decision: the rewards will be yours also.

Caution

Aerobic exercise makes your heart fitter but *in certain cases* it can cause excessive strain. Before beginning any aerobics program, do the following:

1. Check with your physician to see if your heart is healthy. However young and healthy you are, you lose nothing in making sure your cardiovascular system (including blood pressure) is in good order.

2. Choose a good teacher. Unfortunately, many so-called aerobics teachers do not know the slightest thing about exercise physiology. Aerobics, if not taught properly, may pose certain high risks, not only of injury to the limbs but also of possibly fatal accidents such as heart attacks. This may sound like an exaggeration, but it cannot be emphasized enough that if not correctly monitored, aerobics may do more harm than good. Correct instruction in aerobics should always advise the following:

   a. An adequate warm-up period (ten minutes *minimum)* and measurement of *resting* heart rate (it may be slightly elevated after warm-up).

   b. A gradual increase in workload or intensity to ensure you don't "burn out" too soon.

   c. Maintenance of the target heart zone rate for twenty minutes if possible. If you begin to feel tired you should slow down but not stand still. You may jog or jump on the spot and move your arms, which greatly contributes to increased heart rate. If you stop, a lot of blood that is being pumped to the large muscles in the legs will collect there. Keep the legs moving.

d. Correct breathing. Breathe rhythmically, in through the nose and out through the mouth.

e. A measurement of *working* heart rate *right after* the twenty-minute workout. You can see if you were working within your target zone. Do not wait even a few seconds, as heart rate falls rapidly.

f. An adequate cool-down period (ten minutes *minimum*), including stretches and exercises for the legs, such as knee bends, ankle rotations, and foot flexes, which help prevent pooling of blood in the legs (see Chapter 7).

g. A measurement of *recovery* heart rate—the bigger the difference between this heart rate and the working one taken just after exercise, the fitter you are. It takes your heart less time to recover and achieve near to its *resting* rate if you are fit.

3. Always wear sneakers to class and dress sensibly. There are several types of aerobic dance sneakers available now. Running shoes may be too heavy, and if they have toe supports or wedged soles, you may trip. If you wear too many layers of wool or plastic (foolish in any circumstances) you will become overheated and flushed and your body may take longer than necessary to recover. Go at your own pace. Do not be discouraged that others around you may be doing more. Your fitness level is what you should be watching and improving, so no distractions.

4. Wait two to four hours after a meal before you do aerobics. If you have eaten lightly (salad, fruit, etc.) two hours is *permissible.* If you have eaten anything heavier than that you must wait four.

5. During your workout, do not stop moving completely. If you have to stop, keep walking on the spot or kicking the legs and moving the arms.

The Venus Workout (Muscle-strengthening Exercises)

What to Expect

The exercises in this section are specifically designed to trim fat hips and thighs. In the first few weeks you will be increasing the thickness of the muscle fibers in those areas, thereby adding to your percentage of lean body mass. As muscle weighs heavier than fat you *may* gain weight at first, but after this gain stops and fat loss from the body's reserves starts, you will lose weight. As far as fat and inches are concerned, when muscle tissue increases, fat tissue volume *decreases,* although there is no difference in cell number and size. Also, as muscles are toned, they contract, and by "shrinking" this way the overlying fat is also made tighter.

Before we start, I would like to kill off the ridiculous notion that friction exercises will break down fat. I spent years bumping my behind and my thighs on uncarpeted floors in an effort to destroy fat cells. The only effect of banging fat against the floor were many ugly bruises. Fat cells cannot be broken down from outside, only burned up from inside.

When you are exercising for shape, contraction of the muscles causes a burning sensation. Because you are working anaerobically you are burning short-term stores of glycogen, whose end product is lactic acid. Eventually this lactic acid is removed from the system and oxidized, but while it is formed in the muscles you can definitely feel it. It means your muscles are working, which is why most popular exercise books recommend "going for burn." You should feel this sensation and persevere, working past it. Not only will you increasingly strengthen your muscles but also psychologically overcome defeat.

How to Make It Easier

Thought is creative. If you don't believe me, think how your mind can sabotage you and defeat your body before you even try to move. Instead, you can harness that mental power and get it to help you exercise. Think of how your muscles are working and toning every time you contract. Get to know the feel of your muscles, where your stiff and flexible areas are, and chart your progress and performance. This mental picture will reinforce your motivation and take your interest away from any discomfort you may be experiencing. Second, the correct breathing really does help. Always inhale through the nose and exhale through the mouth. Always exhale at the hardest part of the exercise: on the sit-up or as you lift your leg.

Selection of Exercises

The Venus workout features all the exercises that I have found, from personal experience, to be the toughest and the best for toning the hips, the thighs, and the buttocks. They really make those muscles work. They will at first make you sore but they will also make you slim. A wide choice of exercises is included. They have not been categorized into hips, thighs, and buttocks exercises simply because most of the exercises use several of the large muscles of the lower body. Some movements use isolated muscles, but most of the large muscles are arranged in groups, so most movements involve the use of all these groups. Instead of division per body part, the exercises are categorized by position: flat on back, sitting, all fours, etc. The best thing is to select exercises from each of these sections.

Duration

The duration of your workout depends on you. In the game of getting a beautiful body no one sets the rules but you. You decide how quickly you want results and then how hard you work. How long you exercise depends on two factors: how much time you have and how fit you are. If you are very pressed for time, the workout must be short but intensive. If you are unconditioned, you must start out more slowly and gently.

There is also a minimum workout. These exercises are the best ones to do if you have only a short time available. That does not mean that the rest of the exercises are not effective, simply that these are fairly key exercises that will work your muscles and give you a good variety of movement.

On days when you have more time, do the whole workout. At first this may seem daunting, but once you learn the movements it will become much easier because all your energy can be put into exercising rather than thinking about it. Read over the exercises and practice them several times. Then start doing them. To start off, do four repetitions of each exercise. Once you have done that for seven days *in total* (you may be alternating the day of your workout with an aerobic exercise day) you can graduate to six repetitions. After another total of seven days, do eight repetitions, and so on. This may seem slow, but it will ensure that you learn the exercises thoroughly and get them all done rather than doing more repetitions and collapsing before you're halfway through the program.

When exercising for muscle tone and shape, it is important to understand what your aim is. With aerobic exercise, the point is to breathe plenty of oxygen and thus burn calories. Therefore you have to stay in your target heart zone for twenty minutes minimum. With shape exercises your primary aim is to tone flabby muscles and thus firm the flesh on top of them. To achieve this, exercises must be done with control rather than with speed. You should make sure you are doing the exercise correctly, then check that you maximize the movement, stretching your range of movement and giving all your energy. Then you should build up the number of repetitions and only then, finally, go for speed, so that you also burn maximum calories while toning your body. Speed is your final aim, so concentrate on the repetitions first. My advice is that you always count in sets of eight; for instance, if you reach sixteen repetitions, count two sets of eight. If you start counting in double figures, it seems much more tiring. How long the workout takes depends on you. Don't rush it. It should take *at least* thirty minutes to be of benefit and may take as long as forty-five to fifty minutes.

Please don't forget that you must allow ten or fifteen minutes for warm-up and cool-down or recovery stretches. Add this into your time allotted to the shape workout. It will prevent injuries, aid your general health and well-being, and is essential for good performance of the shape exercises.

Frequency

As I said when discussing aerobics, if you are really committed to solving your weight and shape problem, you should combine an aerobic with a shape and body conditioning program. You can achieve this by doing an intensive aerobic workout (twenty to thirty minutes plus stretches) three days per week and an intensive shape workout three days (forty to fifty minutes plus stretches), alternating the days. Otherwise, every day you can do twenty to thirty minutes of aerobics plus thirty to forty minutes of toning, with, of course, all the necessary warm-up and cool-down stretches. In this way you get to work all your body's major muscles daily. This is a very full program and it is something to build up to. Always start a program slowly and gradually, never rush into it. If you are working with Nautilus or weight-lifting equipment, the alternate day plan is better because these methods overload the muscles, which need

to rest and replenish their glycogen stores. From personal experience,
I find the daily combination more exhilarating and more effective
for weight and shape reduction.

STARTING POSITION: FLAT ON YOUR BACK. MAXIMUM PROGRAM.
1. Roll up your knees into your chest and, keeping both shoulder
blades on the floor, roll your knees over to the right and turn your
head to the left. Hold for a few seconds and then reverse directions.
2. Bend your knees and hold a pelvic tilt. Keep your feet on
the floor, slightly more than hip distance apart. Clenching the buttocks, lift your hips and lower back off the floor as high as you
can go, resting your weight on your shoulders. Hold and lower very
slowly, pressing your lower back to the floor one vertebra at a time.
3. Do the same exercise, but as you lift your buttocks and hips
up, bring your knees together. As you lower your back, press the
knees out again.
4. Bend your knees, place your feet together, and lift your hips
and lower back off the floor, resting on your shoulders. Squeeze
the knees tightly together and lift your right lower leg off the floor,
the foot pointing toward the ceiling. Hold and then do the exercise
with the other leg.
5. Elevated variation. Same as 2 but support your body weight
on your feet and on your hands by pressing the palms on the floor
by your ears, fingers pointing away from the body, bending your
arms, elbows to the ceiling. Exhale as you reach the hips upward,
arching the back and letting the chest come up too. Your head is
off the ground if possible, hanging loosely backward. Hold and
squeeze and try and straighten out the arms. Keep pushing the body
higher and higher if possible. (Be careful if you have a bad back.)
6. Lie flat, hands by your sides. If you have difficulties with your
lower back or have most of your weight deposited on the lower
half, place your hands under your buttocks for support. Starting
low, just over the floor, hit your feet together rapidly. As you do
this, very slowly in a controlled motion, raise your legs up until
your feet point toward the ceiling. Keep your legs as straight as
possible, constantly hitting the legs together. Then, doing the same
movement, slowly lower the legs to the floor. The raising and lowering
should be done slowly, the hitting together of the heels fast. When
this exercise becomes easy, do not support your buttocks with your
hands, unless you have a bad back.

7. Once again, at first support your buttocks with your hands if you find this kind of exercise almost impossible. Bend the knees and bring them into the chest, then open the legs very wide in a V shape to your body. Press your knees outward with your hands as you bend the knees outward to the side and press your heels together. Then bring the legs together and lower very slowly with great control until they are just over the ground. Do not touch the ground.

8. Knees bent, feet together, bring the knees in to the chest, then straighten the legs up to the ceiling and lower in a straight line to just above the floor. The movement should be done smoothly. As in the previous exercises, if necessary, support your buttocks with your hands.

9. Legs straight out from body on the floor, open them in a V shape to your body. Lift both legs upward, making a semicircle with each, and when they are pointing toward the ceiling, join them together and lower them slowly in a straight line to the floor. After doing your set amount of repetitions, reverse the leg circles. Lift both legs up together to the ceiling, then separate legs, and each one forming a semicircle, lower to the floor and place legs together.

10. Legs are together on the floor. Imagine your legs are stuck together and circle them both in one direction about six inches above the floor. You are again lifting a lot of weight here so place your hands under your buttocks at first. After circling in one direction, reverse.

11. Legs together on the floor. Once again you may need to support your buttocks with your fists. Lift your legs about six inches off the ground and scissor, right leg over the left, left over the right, etc.

MINIMUM PROGRAM. Exercises 1, 8, and 9.

STARTING POSITION: SITTING TALL. MAXIMUM PROGRAM.

1. Supporting yourself with your hands behind your back on the floor, extend the left leg straight out in front. Pull your right knee into the chest and then extend it out over the ground but do not straighten it out completely. Be careful not to touch the ground with the leg. After finishing the right leg, do the left and afterward do both legs.

2. Leaning on hands and resting your weight on the feet, keep arms straight, knees bent, and hold body high off the floor but parallel to it. Kick out the right leg with a hop and extend it out over the

floor. Bring it in again with a hop and afterward kick out the left. Once you learn this movement, it should be done fast and smoothly.

3. Sit squarely on your behind, keeping your back as straight as possible and trying to resist the weight of the legs, which tends to make you lean back, fold your arms and bend the left leg, bringing in the left foot toward the groin. Lift the right leg, flex the foot, pointing toes upward, and swing first out to the right as far as possible, then way over to the left, touching the left knee. Do not swing the leg uncontrollably as you will then be using momentum. Be controlled in the movement. Do your repetitions and then switch to other leg.

4. Arms still folded, back still straight, left leg bent as before, stretch the right leg straight out in front. Flex the foot and lift the right leg up and down in a kicking movement, keeping the leg straight. Repeat with left leg.

5. Sit straight, legs straight out in front of the body, feet flexed. Reach your hands over your head and bend all the way forward, touching your toes. Hold this position for a few seconds and then, flexing the right foot even more tightly, lift your right leg up in a straight line from the floor as high as possible. This is a tough stretch and the leg may not go high, but persevere. Repeat with other leg.

6. Sit up straight, arms shoulder height and out to the sides, and using your buttocks as "legs" walk forward on them as fast as you can. Keep your legs and your back straight. Then walk backward.

7. Bend your knees and rest your weight lightly on your toes. Place the hands on the knees for balance. Point the right foot and bend and straighten the knee, lifting the calf out to the right side, hardly touching the floor in between. Then work the left foot to the left side. Afterward work both feet at the same time, bending both knees with toes pointed out to each side. If your balance is good and to get a better use of the stomach muscles, take your hands off your knees and hold your arms out to the side at shoulder height. Keep your back as straight as possible when doing this exercise. Lifting the weight of your legs will rock you back slightly but the more you resist, the harder you work the stomach.

8. Extend your arms and legs out in front of you. Pull the legs up, knees into the chest without touching the ground. Turn the legs, keeping them bent, to the right, touching the point where your buttocks meet the ground with your heels but without resting your legs on the floor. In this way your muscles are supporting your

legs' weight. Immediately, extend your legs out to the front again, without touching the ground. Repeat fast to the left and then side to side. Eventually when you master it, this movement is graceful and powerful.

9. Sit up with your legs spread apart as wide as you can without hurting your inner thigh muscles. Supporting yourself with your hands on the floor behind you, turn your body as far as possible to the right. Turn the hips also so that you are nearly doing the splits while facing your body over the right leg, your weight resting almost entirely on the left buttock. Lifting yourself up with your hands, turn the head, upper body, and hips completely around so that your right buttock and leg are now supporting your weight and you are facing over your stretched out left leg. The point of this exercise, even if you cannot do the splits, is to open up your hip joint.

MINIMUM PROGRAM. Exercises 2, 3, and 8.

STARTING POSITION: FLAT ON YOUR STOMACH. MAXIMUM PRO-GRAM.

1. Bring your legs together and reach forward with your arms. Exhale as you lift the head, lift and stretch the arms in front and the legs out and up behind you.

2. Same position but bend the right knee and lift as much of the thigh as possible off the floor, your foot pointing to the ceiling, and hold. Change legs.

MINIMUM PROGRAM. Exercise 1.

STARTING POSITION: ON YOUR SIDE, PROPPED UP ON AN ELBOW (unless otherwise indicated). YOUR LEGS SHOULD BE IN A STRAIGHT LINE WITH YOUR TORSO. MAXIMUM PROGRAM.

1. Raise your top leg and bring it forward, out to the side of your body and at a ninety-degree angle to it. Your inner thigh is facing the floor and your knee is pointing forward. Lift and lower the leg, keeping the foot tightly flexed. Lift as high as possible but keep the leg completely straight and do not move the hips to help the movement. Just work the hip and thigh. Change sides and repeat with other leg.

2. Same position as 1. Hold the leg about two feet off the floor, really stretching it out of the body, bend the knee, and kick in and

out vigorously with your lower leg. Keep the movement small but powerful. Do not fling the leg. Roll onto your other side and repeat with other leg.

3. Same position. Keep the leg about two feet off the floor and swing the leg all the way forward right out to the side of your upper body. Keep the leg straight and the hip still. Change sides and repeat with other leg.

4. With both legs together, swing the top leg all the way forward at ninety-degree angle to your body once again. Keep the movement controlled, do not fling the leg, and keep it straight. Immediately, swing the straight leg all the way back and behind you, bringing your heel up to the height of your hip, if possible. Do this movement very fast, getting a wide and extended swing. Change sides and repeat with other leg.

5. With both legs together, bend the knee of the top leg and place the foot on the floor in front of the groin area. If you like, hold on to the foot with your hand (if right foot then right hand and vice versa) and raise the heel so you are pressing onto the ball of the foot. Stretch out the bottom leg, making sure it is in a straight line with your torso, and lift the bottom leg. For the first few sets, point the toe, then for the next few, flex. Once you are familiar with the exercise, alternate pointing and flexing with every lift. Change sides and repeat with other leg.

6. With both legs together, bend the knee of the top leg, knee facing the ceiling, and grasp the heel with your hand. Your arm should reach along the *inside* of your thigh so you can grasp the foot. In a fairly rapid movement extend the leg up toward the ceiling, without letting go of your heel. Do this three times and on the fourth count, roll over gently onto your other side, grasp the heel of the other leg from the inside, and repeat.

Do the exercise slowly at first until flexibility improves.

7. Prop yourself up on both hands, arms straight, side of hips still resting on the floor. Lift the upper leg and push it backward so that you reach the toe to the floor behind the lower leg, which is resting on the floor. Now bring the upper leg to the front, flex the foot tightly, and touch your foot lightly to the floor in front of the lower leg, which is resting on the floor. Change sides and repeat with the other leg.

8. Same position as 7, but this time also lift the side of the hips

off the floor, supporting most of your weight on your hands, arms straight. Lift your top leg up and down, taking it as high as possible and keeping it straight. Change sides and repeat with the other leg.

MINIMUM PROGRAM. Exercises 1, 4, and 5.

STARTING POSITION: SHOULDER STAND. MAXIMUM PROGRAM.

Shoulder Stand. Lie flat on your back. Roll your knees into your chest in a fast movement and then roll your hips off the floor. Support your spine by bending your elbows and placing your hands on either side of your waist, and make sure your fingers support your middle back. As you push your body up higher, less of your back will be on the floor and eventually your fingers will be supporting the top of your back, near the shoulder blades. Your legs should be pressed together, held straight with your toes pointing up toward the ceiling. Your degree of strength and flexibility will determine how high you can go.

If you have neck or back problems, be very careful doing the shoulder stand and the following exercises. If you have any pain, discontinue them immediately.

Holding your shoulder stand, do the following exercises. While you are in this position, all movements must be controlled to maintain balance.

1. Move each leg alternately down and up in a circular motion as if you were riding a bicycle.

2. Open your legs wide in a V shape to your body and pull together again. Go as wide as you can.

3. Criss-cross the legs over each other. The movements should be small, controlled, and very fast.

4. Keeping your left leg still extended straight up to the ceiling, slowly lower your right leg behind your head. Keep the leg straight and lower as slowly as possible. Slowly raise the right leg, always keeping it straight, back up to meet the left. Change legs.

5. Once again keep the left leg straight and bend the right knee. Bring your right foot into the right groin and extend up and out to the right side. Do this movement rapidly and with control. Change legs.

6. Keeping both legs together, bend the knees and, twisting the hips as far around to the right as possible, bring the legs around also, heels trying to reach the buttocks. Pivot back to center and

raise yourself up again into the full shoulder stand position. Repeat twisting to the left and then up again. Once you learn it, the movement should be fast and flowing.

MINIMUM PROGRAM. Exercises 1 and 3.

STARTING POSITION: DOWN ON ALL FOURS. MAXIMUM PROGRAM.

If you have a sensitive back or knees, be careful. You may find it helpful to lower your body toward the floor and lean on your elbows rather than rest on your hands with your arms straight.

1. Lift your right leg, knee bent, up to the side just as a dog does at a lamppost. Repeat with left leg.

2. Same as 1. Once you have lifted your knee up extend the leg out. The front of the leg is now facing forward and the inside of your stretched-out leg is parallel to the floor. Then bend your knee again and return leg to the floor. Repeat with left leg.

3. Extend your right leg straight out behind you, the front of your foot resting on the floor. Lifting the leg as high as possible, keeping it straight, swing it in a strong, controlled movement over to the right side of your body at a ninety-degree angle. Do not touch the ground but immediately take the leg to the back again. The idea is to *lift and place* the leg, *not* fling it back and to the side using momentum. Do not let the leg touch the ground either at the side or at the back. Make the movement as large as possible. Repeat with left leg.

4. Variation: Instead of placing the right leg straight out behind you cross it over toward the left. This extends the stretch. Repeat with left leg.

5. Extend your right leg straight out the side and make wide circles with it, going forward. Flex the foot tightly. Make the movement as large as possible. Then reverse directions. Repeat with left leg circling again in both directions.

6. Extend the right leg straight out behind and lift the leg up and down as high as possible, pointing the toe. Do the same exercise with foot flexed. Repeat with left leg.

7. Extend right leg out behind and raise leg as high as possible. Knee should be higher than the buttocks. Bend the knee and kick out in small movements. You are only moving the lower leg in and out. Keep leg high. Repeat with left leg.

MINIMUM PROGRAM. Exercises 1 and 5.

STARTING POSITION: KNEELING UPRIGHT. MAXIMUM AND MINI-
MUM PROGRAM.

If you have weak knees or find these exercises painful, do not
do them. Never do them on a hard surface, and even on a carpet
put a thick mat or folded towel under your knees.

1. Hold a pelvic tilt and pull up your upper body. Really tucking
your buttocks under you, begin to tilt your body backward, keeping
a straight line from the knees to the head. Your whole body is moving
together, you are not bent anywhere but at your knees. Lean back
as far as possible and slowly start to tilt yourself back to an upright
position. At all times your stomach must be kept tight and your
buttocks clenched.

2. Arms folded, push your hips down to your right so that you
"fall" in a controlled motion and are sitting on the side of your
right hip and buttock. Your knees are still bent and your lower
legs are still resting on the floor pointing in a straight line from
your knees. Now pull yourself up to the starting position without
using your hands. Keep your stomach tight and your buttock and
thigh muscles contracted and push yourself up to the starting position. Immediately repeat and fall to the left. The movement should
be continuous and as smooth as possible.

STARTING POSITION: SQUATTING DOWN ON BOTH LEGS, HEELS OFF
THE FLOOR, SUPPORTING YOURSELF WITH YOUR HANDS. MAXIMUM
PROGRAM.

If you have weak knees, be careful with these exercises.

1. Stand up and spread your legs wide apart, toes pointing outward. Squat down, bringing your hips down to knee level if possible.
Walk your hands backward through your legs and place them behind
your feet. Press the elbows against the inside of the knees so that
you are pushing them out. Now bounce very gently up and down.

2. In the starting position, keep the knees together and bring the
hands wide apart on either side of the knees and support yourself.
Keep the feet close together, open out the knees as wide as possible,
and close them in again. Do this very rapidly, and when you feel
ready to hold your balance, lift your hands off the floor and continue
the exercise.

3. Bring your hands in close to the feet and support yourself.
Reach your right foot straight out behind you but do so with a

hop, in one clear, quick movement. Your weight is now on your hands and on your bent left leg. Pressing your weight on your hands, bring the right leg back to center with a hop and simultaneously stretch the left leg out behind you. As you do this faster and faster you will bring your buttocks into the air and straighten your arms, as they support your weight. This exercise should be done fast but it takes time to build up speed.

MINIMUM PROGRAM. Exercise 1.

4. *Advanced exercise.* This exercise is particularly hard and should only be attempted by people who have achieved a high fitness level and who have strong knees. It has been included because it really works *already strong* thigh muscles.

From the starting position *with your arms folded* jump up into the air and land in the starting position; that is, from a squat, you launch yourself into the air and come down again immediately into a squat.

BE CAREFUL ON THIS ONE!

STARTING POSITION: STANDING. MAXIMUM PROGRAM.

1. Standing against a wall and holding a pelvic tilt, keep the whole of your back, especially the shoulder blades, middle back, and your buttocks firmly against the wall. Slide your back down the wall so that you are in a sitting position with your back pushed against the wall and your knees bent. Your thighs will be bearing your body weight. If necessary push down on your knees with your hands, otherwise just keep your arms folded. Hold this position for as long as you can, and each time you do the exercise increase the time you hold the position.

2. Legs shoulder width apart, feet pointing slightly outward, go into a deep knee bend. Keep your heels off the floor, resting your weight on the balls of the feet. Reach your arms out in front of you, palms facing and interlocking the fingers.

3. Same exercise as above but as you improve, try and keep the heels on the ground. You will have to bend the knees deeper and bring the hips down more to do this. Again use your arms to balance yourself, stretching them forward and lacing the fingers.

4. Get a two-and-a-half-pound or a five-pound dumbbell (depending on your strength) or a heavy book. Hold the weight behind your neck, bending your elbows, pointing them to the ceiling, and

keeping them back. Step forward on to your bent right leg and lunge down as deeply as you can, keeping your hips squarely facing forward and your upper body erect. Your left leg is outstretched behind you. Pull in your stomach and buttock muscles. Go down as far as you can, all the time supporting the weight with your hands, behind the neck. Hold this position and instead of bouncing, push the right knee in tiny movements toward the floor until it is almost touching. Change legs. *If you have bad knees, do not do this exercise.*

5. Stand with your heels together, toes pointing out. Lift your right leg *straight* up to the side and tightly flex the foot. Get it as high as you can but keep the hips squarely facing forward and pull up the upper body. Hold this position, really pushing the leg up and to the side, and then return the leg and repeat with the left.

MINIMUM PROGRAM. Exercises 1, 3, and 5.

Recovery Stretches

The cool-down or recovery is just as important as the warm-up. Your body needs to return to normal after heavy exertion. You can help it by stopping your exercise gradually. If you just collapse onto the floor, you are not helping the heart slow down gradually nor are you aiding the blood flow to even out as it should after so much blood has been sent to the major muscles in the legs. Your muscles have contracted and they need to be stretched out.

MAXIMUM PROGRAM.

1. Lie down on your back and move your buttocks right up against a wall. Lift your legs up and rest them against the wall. Press your feet down firmly and, using the wall to support your weight, roll up into a partial shoulder stand. If you can, go up into a full one with your feet pointing to the ceiling, your head, neck, and shoulder blades on the floor and your hands supporting your spine.

2. From this position, keeping the legs together, bring them back down behind you and try and touch your toes to the ground behind your head. Keep the legs straight and keep supporting the spine.

3. Release this yoga position, known as the Plough, by bending your knees and letting them relax, bringing them into your shoulders. Slowly roll the body down, letting the vertebrae touch the ground one by one, all the time supporting yourself with your hands. Keep

the legs together as soon as your middle back is on the floor and straighten them to the ceiling. Now bring them down to the floor, keeping them straight, in one long, controlled movement.

4. Lying on your back, bend your knees and place the feet on the floor, shoulder distance apart. Place your hands behind your head and interlock the fingers. Imagining that your head is a heavy bowling ball, raise it slowly, letting its weight rest in your hands. Do not use the neck muscles. Carry your head all the way forward, letting the chin come to the chest. Hold and then release back down slowly.

5. On all fours, bring your elbows down onto the floor, letting your upper body go down toward the floor and your buttocks stretch to the ceiling. Now rock backward, bending the hips, pushing your buttocks backward and down, bouncing very slightly and stretching your arms out in front of you as far as possible, elbows on the ground.

MINIMUM PROGRAM. Exercises 4 and 5.

Jet Stretch: A Program for Those on the Move

One of the most important things about exercise is the routine. Your body is being worked on a continuous basis and the results are proof of this. Travel could easily disrupt that routine, however.

This need not be the case. You can actually create ways and opportunities for movement wherever you may be. An increasing number of hotels have jogging tracks, pools, gymnasiums, and some even have exercise videos available on their in-house television systems. All these can help reinforce your resolve to keep on exercising. Another way of maintaining your exercise schedule is to pack a leotard and an exercise cassette or a favorite selection of music. You can then do your exercises and stretches in your hotel room. Additionally, what makes me feel right at home in a foreign country is going to exercise class. Almost all American cities and many European ones now have some classes available at clubs or studios on a daily, non-membership basis.

SITTING IN YOUR SEAT EXERCISES
  1. Head rotations. Both directions.

2. Lift shoulders toward ears, tense for three counts, then relax and collapse.

3. Roll shoulders forward, then back.

4. Stretch hands out in front, open and close the fingers very fast. This is a very good one for promoting circulation.

5. Sit tall and then, bending from the base of the spine, fold your upper body, waist, and lower back forward over your knees, drop your arms to the floor, clasp your ankles, and let your head relax. Feel the stretch in the hip flexor muscles of the groin and in the lower back. Then slowly straighten from the base of the spine and roll up, one vertebra at a time.

6. Stretch your arms up over your head, fingers interlaced, and look up.

7. Pull your chin into your chest and pull it in with your hands clasped behind the neck.

8. Stretch your legs out in front of you and flex and point the feet.

9. Do ankle rotations in both directions.

10. Hold the feet just off the floor. Touch toe, then heel to the floor very fast, both legs at the same time.

STANDING EXERCISES

1. Walk up and down the aisles as energetically as possible, avoiding small children, older passengers, flight attendants, and trolleys. Swing your arms (discreetly) to get maximum movement.

2. Standing tall at the rear of the aircraft or wherever there is enough room, reach up first with the right arm then the left as if climbing a ladder.

3. Feet apart, toes pointing forward, bend to the right *side,* reaching to your right calf or knee with your right hand. Keep your whole body facing squarely forward and go down as far as you can, extending your left arm over your head as you bend to the right. Repeat to the left.

4. Stand, feet together. Interlock the hands behind your buttocks, palms facing the ceiling, elbows facing out, palms inward. As you bend forward from the waist with a flat back, reach the arms up behind you away from your buttocks. Take them as high as you can. This stretches out those stiff shoulder blades.

5. Holding on to something, bend the right knee. Clasping the

right foot behind you, pull it as close to your buttocks as you can. Change legs.

Do these exercises once every hour or two and you really will arrive in better shape.

Eat and Run: A Guide to Nutrition for Exercise

Until a few years ago, trainers, athletes, and even the general public thought you had to pack yourself full of protein to have more energy. Research on the subject has since shown that this was a misconception. Protein does not give you energy that is immediately available. Carbohydrates do. When exercise is moderate, carbohydrates provide about 60 percent of the immediate energy you use; however, as workload increases, they provide 100 percent of energy.

We store carbohydrates as muscle glycogen naturally. However, evidence suggests that in people who exercise regularly and whose muscle glycogen is thus often depleted, diet is of paramount importance in keeping these glycogen stores constant. A high-carbohydrate diet can actually increase the body's capacity to store glycogen and thus prolong endurance during exercise much more than a high-fat or high-protein diet.

If you eat a high-fat or high-protein diet, if you are crash dieting or hardly eating at all, the rate of glycogen synthesis will be very slow. Your physical performance will suffer as a result, for you will become exhausted more rapidly. In marathon running, which is a long-term exercise in that it requires endurance and you are using the long-term or aerobic energy system, you will fuel yourself at the start of the race with 90 percent energy from muscle glycogen and 10 percent from fat in the form of circulating free fatty acids in the bloodstream. By the end of the marathon, the picture is reversed, and 95 percent of energy is obtained from fat. *However,* an essential amount of glycogen is absolutely necessary for any exercise to be performed and maintained.

In practical terms, then, it does seem necessary to eat some carbohydrates. From an *energy* point of view, glucose used to be the preferred kind of sugar. As a monosaccharide it was supposed to be more readily absorbed. This is no longer believed, as other, more complex carbohydrates have been shown to dissolve just as readily.

Because complex carbohydrates offer better nutritive value for calories and have the added benefit of fiber, it is wise to include them in your diet, especially when you are exercising. Conversely, the high-protein fans claim that high-carbohydrate, low-protein meals result shortly afterward in hypoglycemia (low blood sugar), causing fatigue, dizziness, and weakness. High protein intakes supposedly maintain blood sugar and promote satisfaction for longer periods. Research has confirmed neither view definitively and the battle still rages. It seems, in the end, to be best to eat a balanced and healthy diet.

Another important factor is salt and water loss. In the hot weather, when the body needs more salt because it sweats more, the kidneys tend to conserve more salt when filtering the urine, and the sweat also becomes less concentrated. Overloading your body with excess salt in foods or tablet form just upsets this natural water balance. Lack of water, on the other hand, is very dangerous. You can never drink too much water. Any excess will be excreted.

Are there any miracle foods that aid athletic performance? Stimulants are usually not advised, with the possible exception of caffeine. Too much coffee may cause nervousness, irregular heartbeat, and may increase the risk of certain cancers; however, 330 milligrams of caffeine (the contents of approximately two and a half cups of regular, percolated coffee) help endurance and make exercise seem easier. Caffeine also seems to stimulate fat metabolism, so your body switches to burning fat quicker and preserves the carbohydrate stores of quick energy that are so essential.

Putting It All Together

This program is intended mainly as a guideline. It is recommended for the average person, while much of it has been designed specifically for the bottom-heavy woman. The program must be adapted to your specifications: your age, weight, standard of physical fitness, lifestyle, amount of free time, and, most important, what *you* like. As you exercise, you will become fitter and more flexible, so your program has to be updated every two months or so to ensure that the exercises you do constantly stretch and challenge you.

If you really want to lose fat from your lower body, exercise will do it. In conclusion, an effective program must consist of:

1. An aerobic workout three times per week working at 70 percent of your maximum aerobic capacity for at least twenty minutes.

2. The Venus workout, if possible the whole program (forty to fifty minutes), if not the minimum version (fifteen to twenty minutes), three times per week.

3. A warm-up period of at least ten minutes and a cool-down, recovery period of at least ten minutes.

This is an intense program: it demands energy but it will also *give* you energy: it requires determination but it achieves results. For years I suffered a negative body image, fear of ridicule, a stiff and painful body, and an inexcusable ignorance of my own physical strength and inner power. As soon as I began to move, all that changed for me.

Beware of expecting overnight changes. You are changing your *body*, not your mind, and it does take time. It is also important to be realistic. If you start out with very fat legs, the chances are that they will never be skinny, but they will become toned and defined. If you do have off days on your exercise program, forgive yourself. For most of us, exercise has to be incorporated into a busy schedule; it cannot take up the whole day. Let go of the anger and judgment and just start up again as soon as you can.

9

Drugs, Needles, and Nonsense: Some Desperate Remedies for Thinness

People will do anything to get rid of fat. Some will even risk their lives, most will jeopardize their health, and all of us will deplete our bank balances to banish the bulge forever. However, the bulge, as we know, has a nasty habit of returning, however drastic the measures we take may be. Nothing but a complete revolution of your eating and activity habits will keep it *permanently* at bay. Few of us realize this, and before we learn the truth we succumb to the many "easy" ways of losing weight and fat. These are rarely easy; in fact, they can be dangerous, painful, expensive, and harmful. In this chapter, we are going to examine the obsession for slenderness and analyze the often masochistic means that people use to lose fat. Just how effective are they?

Before you listen to the claims of all these miracle methods and products, remember the truth. Fat is an oily *internal* substance, it is not hard, it cannot be broken down by external means, by massages, machines, or lotions. The only thing that can "break down" fat in metabolic terms is a calorie deficit: you must take in less than you burn up.

When you read this chapter it may be tempting to adopt a judgmental attitude. It is all too easy to assume that such "easy" ways out are only for the weak-willed and impatient. We now know that the only way to lose weight and improve shape permanently *is* to diet and, most important, I believe, to exercise on a frequent basis. However, it took me years to reach this realization. Before that, *I* was desperate about the way I looked, desperate enough to try anything that promised slenderness. Therefore, to condemn those who believe in the "solutions" I am about to evaluate would be to condemn myself. In my fight against fat, I divorced myself from my body and was prepared to inflict any method on it in order to reduce. Because I remember what that feels like I am writing this book. In some way, I hope it will help you evaluate for yourself the treatments for weight and shape that are available and decide whether they are worth it.

Jaw Wiring

There are some weight reduction procedures that are so drastic that they can justifiably be performed only on very obese people. Jaw wiring is one of these. By very obese people I am referring to those whose degree of "overfat" is a health risk. The extremely or morbidly obese are 100 percent or more over their "ideal" weight as calculated from the life insurance tables discussed in Chapter 3.

Jaw wiring naturally requires a doctor's recommendation and is performed under local anaesthetia if requested. The jaws are wired together, giving the impression that the person is wearing braces. The diet consists of fluids, milk, or any blenderized diet. The jaws are usually wired for six to nine months. Losses are usually around 30 percent of the prewiring weight. The method does not guarantee against cheating, since overconsumption of high-calorie fluids can defeat the loss. Normally, though, the caloric intake is lower than what the patient was previously consuming and weight loss is inevitable. Another factor is the starting weight of the patient: the heavier he or she is, the more weight will be lost.

Naturally there are problems with jaw wiring. It is difficult for patients to speak and of course impossible for them to brush their teeth on the inside, although the wires are periodically removed for this purpose and regular dental checkups are required. The diet itself, often below nine hundred calories, needs to be supplemented with vitamins and minerals. More questionable is whether eating through a straw does anything to reeducate the patient in learning new eating habits and taking smaller portions once the wires are removed. The psychological problems could be considerable, although patients who want to have their jaws wired are usually very motivated and their successful weight loss is ample reward.

The major problem is keeping the weight off. The long-term results of jaw wiring seem to be mixed. Dr. John Garrow of Northwick

Park Hospital in England found that those with the best weight maintenance were patients who had a cord tied around their waist when their jaws were released, as a constant reminder of their new size. Every time they gained weight, the pinching cord reminded them that they were relapsing. Patients with no such "attached" memory rapidly gained back some or all of the lost weight.

Jaw wiring thus seems to be effective as long as it lasts, but once the wires are off the patient finds it difficult to continue the diet. Even though jaw wiring drastically reduces intake, it does not give a person the psychological assurance that his or her own eating behavior is changing out of choice and that this change can and will last.

Jaw wiring is the most cost-efficient method for drastically reducing weight in patients with a severe medical problem. It can, moreover, be used as an important adjunct before surgery on the stomach and intestines, which is to be discussed shortly.

Drugs

There is a very wide variety of "reducing" drugs available: hormones such as thyroxine, appetite suppressants, bulking agents, starch blockers, drugs that inhibit metabolism, and others.

Appetite Suppressants

Anorectic or appetite-suppressing drugs come in various strengths. Several mild brands are sold over the counter. One particular type, which comes in the form of a candy you suck before meals, makes you less hungry by elevating blood sugar levels just before you eat. Others work in different ways and could be dangerous if taken in unwisely large doses by obsessive dieters.

Prescription drugs are stronger. Amphetamines, commonly known as speed, are used less and less because of their excessive stimulation and addictive properties. Not all appetite suppressing drugs have a noticeably stimulating effect. Fenfluramine actually has a sedative effect. Both stimulant and nonstimulant types of appetite suppressants are particularly effective in the first few weeks of treatment; eventually, however, the effect begins to wear off, in some people quicker than in others.

Doctors used to disapprove of appetite-reducing drugs for several reasons: tolerance to the drug and eventual ineffectiveness, psychological dependency, lack of reeducation of eating habits, and possible unpleasant side effects such as insomnia, agitation, dry mouth, high blood pressure, palpitation, and anxiety. Actually, the picture need not be quite so bleak. Properly prescribed appetite suppressants *can* really reduce appetite and help people lose weight. It has even been suggested now that some anorectic drugs, especially amphetamines, have secondary effects on reducing fat storage, although this is not certain. The eventual slowing down of weight loss may have as much to do with the decrease in metabolic rate caused by sustained dieting as with tolerance to the drug and its reduced effect. The stimulant drugs tend to be more addictive than the nonstimulants, probably because of their euphoric "high," but there is yet no agreement among doctors as to whether patients actually do become dependent or not. It is certainly difficult to distinguish between a physical need for a drug and a behavioral addiction to it, which may be the bigger problem. The known side effects of most drugs are mild and are usually not dangerous. As for the criticism that a reduction in appetite does not actually help with eating behavior, it is unrealistic to expect a pill to reeducate the mind.

This is where the main problem lies. Many people may experience a lack of appetite while taking this kind of drug but may still eat more than they need because they like eating, the food tastes good, it gives them emotional security, etc. Appetite suppressants are valuable only in suppressing appetite. They cannot perform miracles and counteract the many other impulses that make us eat when we are not hungry. This being the case, I would only recommend the use of drugs for limited periods so that they can have maximum effect.

Hormones

One very popular method of treating obesity, usually in conjunction with diet, is the administration of hormones such as the thyroid hormone thyroxine. This is usually done in pill form. The most popular type of thyroxine is triiodothyronine. It is widely believed that these tablets act as metabolic accelerators and prevent the fall in metabolic rate that occurs with dieting. While they do actually speed up weight loss, studies have shown that lean tissue loss is increased and *not* fat loss. Ultimately this could be dangerous and does nothing to reduce adipose tissue, which is the aim of treating obesity. What can even happen is that after prolonged use of the pills in conjunction with diet, the body tends to adapt to the drug's effect on metabolism and the metabolic rate becomes sluggish despite and maybe even because of the thyroxine. Thyroid pills are only available on prescription and can make you jumpy and irritable, with side effects such as palpitations. If your doctor does prescribe them to you, he or she should be keeping a careful watch on your body protein losses and on your general physical condition. Thyroid pills are far less favored now in the treatment of obesity than they were a few years ago.

Diuretics

These are some of the most abused diet pills. Thankfully the stronger kind of diuretic is only available with a prescription, though a variety of over-the-counter pills are available. Diuretics are "water pills." They increase the amount of urine you excrete and thus get rid of excess fluid. Diuretics are prescribed for cardiac patients who suffer from high blood pressure and *may* sometimes be prescribed for dieters and for women before their period, when they are retaining extra fluid.

Diuretics will not and cannot help you lose fat. They can only make you lose water and thus *temporarily* lose weight. As soon as your body makes up its fluid balance again in reaction to the diuretic, you will regain the lost weight. It is very tempting to get rid of the bloated feeling that comes from water retention and from those depressing "water pounds" that you see on the scale but you could be doing yourself a lot of harm. Repeated use of pharmacological diuretics can do damage to the kidneys and to your general health. The main reason for this is that the extra output of water also contains valuable minerals such as sodium and potassium. These electrolytes are essential for the correct working of the body's millions of cells. Potassium loss causes bad muscle cramps, dizziness, and weakness.

I took diuretics frequently for several years. I realized that I was developing an addiction but I couldn't resist. I felt I had found an easy way to lose weight. Now I realize how wrong I was. There are plenty of safe herbal diuretics available as well as certain herbal teas that have a water-eliminating effect. Parsley also is an excellent safe, natural diuretic. It is *not* worth jeopardizing your general health to lose weight quickly.

Bulking Agents

These are a type of appetite reducer, sold without prescription, that contain fiber in the form of methylcellulose. This swells inside the stomach, making you feel full. The problem with these bulking agents is that the swelling occurs rather slowly, and you also need to take large doses to feel a sensation of fullness that would be adequate to reduce food intake. They are less effective than appetite suppressants although less dangerous.

High-fiber foods such as apples, celery, or raw carrots, which contain just as much fiber, would be just as effective and much easier and tastier to eat. The time it takes to eat such foods also permits the satiety centers in the brain to work, thus giving the signal of fullness in time for you to stop eating.

Starch Blockers and Similar Drugs

Starch blockers are pharmacological drugs that are supposed to work on carbohydrate metabolism. Most of them do this by inhibiting the enzyme pancreatic alpha-amylase, which breaks down starch into maltose, an intermediate product, and then into the simple sugar glucose, which is taken up by the cells and eventually is used for the synthesis of fat. If less starch is absorbed there is consequently less sugar in the blood after a meal (scientifically referred to as postprandial hypoglycemia). As a result of lower blood sugar, less insulin is released, and, because insulin is one of the most important hormones involved in fat storage, less insulin means less fat is stored. As scientists developed different variations of this drug, they realized that an agent that worked only on starch, which has a more complex molecular structure than sugar, would not be effective on a diet high in simple refined sugar, such as Western societies consume. Work has already begun on more thorough blockers that inhibit the enzymes sucrase and maltase as well as amylase.

The newest starch blockers have little or no effect whatsoever on refined carbohydrates, not to mention the million molecules of protein and fat we eat every day. The problem with using starch blockers is that people forget to be selective and to eat only starch in conjunction with the blocker. As a result they put on weight. Starch blockers have no effect on chocolate or mayonnaise or whatever else you may like to devour. Another drawback is that even if these drugs do effectively block alpha-amylase, other enzymes act on starch also and may, in the absence of alpha-amylase, do the job of absorbing starch just as well.

Starch blockers may be dangerous or at least detrimental to digestion. The unabsorbed nutrients pass through the intestinal tract and are then eliminated. None of their goodness has been absorbed. We have instead taken all our calories from fats and proteins, which are not as good for us as complex carbohydrates. A drug that inhibited lipid metabolism, the absorption of fats, would be a much more beneficial discovery for dieters. Work is actually being done on such drugs and also on those that inhibit glucose. Even if such thorough blockers are perfected, there would still be problems. All medicines that decrease absorption of food in the intestines prevent not only absorption of energy (calories) but also of essential nutrients, vitamins, and minerals. What we really need is a drug that selectively prevents or drastically reduces the absorption of empty-calorie foods.

Even though seemingly harmless, starch blockers can cause diarrhea, severe flatulence, and bloating.

Lipolytic Agents
Lipolytic (fat-releasing) agents as such do not exist, although many diet cures claim to be able to dissolve away fat without increasing energy expenditure or decreasing intake. This is, of course, impossible. Even if a drug or ointment existed that released fat from adipose tissue and had it circulating in the bloodstream as free fatty acid, where would it go? It would either be redeposited into another depot elsewhere in the body or it would be burned. If you are *not* creating a caloric deficit by diet or exercise, energy will not be burned and your fat stores will stay the same.

It's just as well that such a drug doesn't exist, because having a lot of circulating free fatty acid in the bloodstream is not a good thing. It may begin to deposit itself elsewhere than in fat depots; for example, on artery walls or in the liver. As for causing fat itself (rather than fatty acid) to leave the fat cells, this could well be fatal, as a fat embolism could occur. This is a fragment of fatty tissue that is carried by the blood toward the lungs. There it blocks the small arteries and can cause death.

The fact that obesity research is looking at *possibilities* like starch blockers is exciting even though there is still a long way to go. The discoveries are frequent yet their validity rarely, if ever, stands up to stringent scientific testing. While some finds merit a follow-up, others are outright hoaxes. Some good examples are the advertisements in magazines for magical capsules made from innocent, "natural" products that burn fat away in hours, even minutes. To further stretch the imagination and shrink our waistlines, one company advertised a "100 percent safe, natural dietary supplement that can be eaten with food—any food, even bread" and that would "turn your body into a giant fat-burning machine." If any of these incredible gimmicks really worked, eminent obesity specialists, in fact the whole medical profession, would approve them.

Cellulite

Cellulite can be treated at great expense in many specialized cellulite clinics in Europe and the United States. Many of these establishments are run by so-called world-famous diagnosticians, who remain totally unknown to the real obesity specialists, who have spent the best part of their lives studying metabolism and fat cells. In carefully worded advertisements, which bypass all scientific reality, we are told that losing fat from the hips and thighs can be accomplished quickly and painlessly. The mere application of gels and lotions containing miracle extracts from the mineral and plant kingdoms will just melt the fat away, "by accelerating the body's cleansing process," whatever that may be.

All this may sound plausible, especially if you are so obsessed by the size of your hips and thighs that you will believe any explanation of why they are large. For many years I read articles on cellulite with avid interest. I believed every word because I wanted to think there was an instant, simple cure for the part of my body I disliked. Only when I began my research on fat cells in different regions of the body did I understand how complex the matter was.

The claims of cellulite treatments simply cannot be proven to work scientifically, persuasive though they may sound. Doctors in England approached a company that manufactured a cream to treat cellulite. The doctors asked if they could do an experiment on the cream's effectiveness but they met with no reply. This does not exactly suggest the treatment's authenticity. Other treatments include circulatory aids, such as machines that use electronic currents to stimulate circulation. Another invention is "pumping boots," a plastic covering that covers the legs and deflates and inflates around them. I tried these boots, and even though the treatment felt good, once again there is no scientific evidence that stimulating local circulation can get rid of local fat. It just doesn't work like that.

Another very popular treatment for cellulite is body wrapping. These treatments can be expensive, as a course of them is usually recommended. You are measured and then swathed like an Egyptian mummy in elastic bandages that have been soaked in hot water and mysterious fat-melting solutions whose efficacy has not been proved by any reliable medical source. You sit for over an hour, the bandages are removed, and your measurements taken. You are supposed to lose a remarkable amount of inches. The type of inch loss achieved by wrapping treatments is false and temporary. It is caused by three factors: inaccurate measuring techniques, water loss, and indentation of the skin. In Chapter 7, I emphasized how measurements can vary and the importance of measuring yourself in the same place every time. Clinics make money on inches lost, so it is in their interest to make mistakes and let the tape measure slide here and there. Even if you pay close attention, the people who measure you can still obtain false results. If you are bandaged, you will sweat and thus temporarily lose pounds and inches, owing to water loss. Finally, if you have compressed your skin with a bandage, when you take it off the area that has been constricted appears smaller and tighter than normal. This effect wears off soon after, as the body fluids and tissues expand to their normal size again. In fact, body wrapping could actually impede circulation and cause thrombosis.

Other treatments for cellulite are the application of various plant extracts, such as ivy, onto the skin, which must then be rubbed vigorously with massage gloves. These rather vicious instruments leave the skin red and irritated from friction. They are supposed to speed up circulation, with the result that your blood will carry away "all the toxins and impurities" that cause you to look fat. Fat is what makes you look fat and even though rubbing hard on your skin will speed up circulation it won't do anything to flush your fat away. Attempts to sweat fat off, whether in steam or sauna baths, or by exercising or sleeping in plastic clothing, are equally ineffective. All they promote is water loss and thus a temporary loss of a few pounds.

Also erroneous is the premise that if you pummel fat, it will turn into a sort of pulp and disappear. I have not only known women who did this, I have done it myself. On the misguided recommendations of deluded cosmetologists in Switzerland, France, and Greece, I have been kneaded like a piece of white dough by painful massages, and have had my fat tunneled into by harsh underwater jets. Shall I tell you the results? Purple bruises, little red veins, soreness, desperation, a much-emptied bank account, and exactly the same amount of body fat.

Before totally dismissing cellulite treatments, perhaps one should evaluate their psychological effects. Although science pronounces these treatments worthless, they may help to support women in some ways. I researched most cellulite clinics by trying them personally. I concluded that the only real benefit was that women felt that they were actually *doing* something for a problem about which they felt helpless. Some of the clinics operate just for money but others believe in what they do. Most of the better clinics also advocate diet and exercise, and the treatments themselves make the women feel they are doing something extra. No passive treatment alone, however, can be effective in correcting such a little-understood problem as lower body fat.

HCG Injections

Human chorionic gonadotrophin is a hormone produced in the placenta of pregnant women. It is supposed to increase the mobilization of fat by acting on the hypothalamus, the weight-control headquarters in the brain. The hormone, if injected into nonpregnant women, is supposed to do the same thing. The miraculous property assigned to human chorionic gonadotrophin is not only that it is a mobilizer but that it especially frees fat stores in the lower half of the body.

HCG and another hormone called human pituitary gonadotrophin, produced by postmenopausal women, are not strictly sex hormones. When injected into people with normally developed sex glands, they do nothing to change the patient's sexual characteristics. HCG was first discovered as a treatment for the victims of Froëhlich's syndrome, a disease that retards sexual development in boys and that endows them, strangely enough, with a pear shape.

In theory the effectiveness of the HCG treatment on fat, and particularly fat on the lower half, is twofold. First, it decreases appetite so that you are able to follow a low-calorie diet and supposedly lose a pound a day. This weight loss can only be due to a water loss, for as we saw when we performed our caloric calculations, it takes 3,500 calories to lose one pound of fat, and to incur such a deficit of calories on a daily basis one would have to starve. Second, HCG is supposed to mobilize fat from the hips and thighs, and this is what you feed off. There has been no proof of this.

Injections of HCG are given daily for anything from twenty-three to forty days, and a very strict five hundred-calorie diet is pursued, consisting mainly of protein in the form of fish and lean meat, very few carbohydrates, and extremely small amounts of fat. A diuretic is usually given daily. I interviewed two doctors who had been giving the treatment in England. One, a plastic surgeon, claimed a 40 to 60 percent success rate with patients *during* treatment. However, he could not guarantee that bottom-heavy women, once off the very strict diet and not on HCG, would not gain all the weight back on their hips and thighs. The other doctor doubted that he would obtain the same good results without the stringent diet *and* the diuretic he was dispensing for water loss.

I have met some women who were on the HCG program. They reported remarkably good results both in terms of weight loss and improvement in shape. But as soon as the injections stopped and the diet ceased, they gained back the weight and resumed their shape. One of the reasons for this is the composition of the diet. The HCG diet is very high in protein and low in carbohydrates. This promotes water loss. As soon as a normal diet is resumed containing some carbohydrates, water is immediately retained and weight gained. This diet is *not* nutritionally recommended: it is deficient in many vitamins and minerals, and it is not fully balanced because of its very low fat content. Even though it sounds like the answer to every bottom-heavy woman's prayer, HCG is probably worthless.

Massage

Massage is certainly enjoyable, but pounds and inches are lost only by the masseuse. Massage stimulates the circulation, thereby accelerating and encouraging the body's natural healing process, but it cannot and does not dissolve fat.

Many clinics and beauty salons specialize in cellulite massages. This usually involves a very deep massage, which may be useful for relieving tension deep in the muscle fibers if you have been exercising very strenuously or are under a lot of stress. It can, however, do nothing to release fat, which as we know is locked in depots under the skin and deep within the body. The technique is called connective tissue massage, and it supposedly restores healthy circulation to the lower body so that the fat deposits can be mobilized. Of course circulation is important to all body functions, but it would be a gross oversimplification to say that it is the sole cause of obesity. It is a peripheral cause. However clearly the circulation flows, no fat can be used up unless you incur a caloric deficit.

The results of forceful and rough massage are bruises and blemishes on the skin, and possibly the risk of internal damage. Massage should be enjoyed because it makes you feel relaxed and rejuvenated. It cannot help you get rid of fat, nor can it do a lot for slackening skin. Skin progressively loses its elasticity with age as its collagen fibers slacken. Nothing can actually tone slackened skin, but the underlying muscles *can* be toned, by exercise, which will then give the skin a firmer appearance.

Fat Suction Surgery

In the past few years doctors in Europe and, more recently, in the United States, have been learning the technique of lipectomy (the excision of adipose tissue) assisted by suction. The idea of fat suction is not new. It actually originated from the suction methods used in abortion and dilation and curettage. The doctor draws lines on the patient's body while she is standing up, to see where the fat should be removed. Patients are sometimes injected first with a "chemical cocktail," the doctor's own secret brew of supposedly fat-dissolving enzymes. This potion is injected into the area that is to be reduced. This supposedly turns the fat cells into a liquid state.

A very small incision, often no more than a half to one inch, is made, and a relatively blunt-edged instrument called a cannula is inserted, which tunnels away to loosen the undesirable fat. The fat is then released in the form of an oily substance via a plastic tube that is inserted time and time again. Attached to the tube is a suction aspirator, so the fat is actually sucked out and not cut out, which would necessitate a much bigger incision. The amount of fat that is extracted is limited to approximately five pounds. If any more fat were to be removed, a blood transfusion would be necessary.

In fat suction, the patient is under general anesthetic and feels relatively little pain when she awakens (the patients so far have been mostly women but some men have also had the operation). There is also little discomfort and inconvenience during the recovery process, according to most reports by patients and doctors. Obviously the patient has not undergone the physical trauma of surgery, which takes so long to heal and overcome. Neither does she have large scars to contend with. These are the major selling points for fat suction.

Fat suction is presented as a fantastic alternative to conventional plastic surgery. An increasing number of plastic surgeons perform the procedure, and it has received phenomenal coverage from the press, who eagerly promote it as tempting fodder for a fat-obsessed public. The great advantage of fat suction is that it isn't really surgery; *in theory* little blood is lost, major veins and arteries are pushed aside out of harm's way, and other vital networks, such as the lymphatic drainage system, go unharmed. There is no postoperative pain, little stiffness and immobility, a short recovery period, and, most important of all, no scars. Fat suction fans claim that all that is lost is the yellow oily substance that fills out all the ugly bulges they claim you can't lose by diet or exercise. Are they telling the truth?

Suction-assisted lipectomy, to give it its correct medical terminology, sounded like the most seductive solution to fat hips and thighs that I had heard so far. Yet having had plastic surgery myself and been through the long, arduous process of recovery, I was suspicious of the claim that fat could be removed without any complications. I was not alone in my doubts, which were shared by many obesity specialists and also many plastic surgeons who will not perform the procedure. These doubts arise from the fact that it is extremely difficult, if not impossible, to remove fat without damaging vital tissues, structures, and networks that surround and nourish the fat. Even though the area is immediately bandaged and wrapped, the risks of internal damage are still high. It has not so far been explained how the suction can operate without destroying the membrane of the fibroblasts, which are millions of cells making up the connective tissue that holds fat in place. Other cells that are in close proximity to the adipose cells *must* be affected. Many surgeons are doubtful about doing it until it has been tried and tested many times. It is also possible that the suctioning can do local nerve damage. Many of the risks connected with plastic surgery, such as infection, internal bleeding, and filling of the emptied fat pockets with liquified fat that is in the area, apply to suction surgery.

Another very real aesthetic risk is that because the surgeon cannot actually see inside you while removing the fat, the suction may afterward leave a rippled effect. Even the surgeons who promote fat suction admit to this, claiming that women over thirty-five are more at risk as their skin is less elastic. The risk is a considerable one if you think that, logically speaking, if a great amount of fat is removed, the skin over it will lose its shape and not fit anymore. The advantage of plastic surgery is that it removes fat *and* skin, leaving a tightened surface. I noticed even with my own plastic surgery that the areas from which most fat had been removed has a tunneled, caved-in appearance, with slight depressions in the skin. This occurred particularly on the inside lower thigh, just above the knee. In fat suction, as the fat is sucked out from under the skin and the surgeon cannot see what is going on, it's extremely possible that the fat could be removed unevenly and leave troughs and depressions under the skin.

Even if the technique became perfected, the most important question is, does the fat come back once it is removed? We know that fat can come back at any time if your energy intake exceeds your output. So much then for the confident assertion made by some of those who practice fat suction that after puberty fat cells definitely stop increasing. However much weight you lose and however much fat is removed by suction or surgery, all of it and even more can be regained if you increase your intake and lessen output. As for whether fat cells can regenerate in a particular site once they have been removed, there is still a lot of controversy over this question, which is obviously of greater relevance to those of us who chiefly have a shape problem. I shall discuss this more in the next chapter, but it is safe to say that however many times you have plastic surgery or fat suction, if you don't control your weight by diet and exercise, the results will be reversed.

Fat suction is therefore no more a permanent solution than any other reduction method. As five pounds is the maximum amount of fat that can be removed, it is certainly not a solution to a weight problem, just as plastic surgery itself is not. If it is not followed up with correct eating habits and a regular exercise program, it will be a failure; you will gain weight and therefore replenish your fat stores. There is no foolproof way of losing fat forever. That requires a lifetime commitment to careful eating and vigorous exercise. All in all, one should be wary of the fat suction technique until it has been absolutely confirmed that no long-term harm is done to the surrounding tissues and major vessels.

10

Getting Slender by Surgery: The Most Drastic Approach to Getting Rid of Fat

There are two totally different types of surgery to get rid of fat. The first can be generally termed surgery of the stomach and intestines. These are major operations and are performed in various ways, using several different techniques. Their aim is to help people reduce food intake and thus lose weight. Plastic surgery, which is totally different in its aim, cannot help you lose weight, as the amount of fat that can be extracted is no more than a few pounds. What it does is recontour the body. Plastic surgery, especially if extensive, is just as serious a procedure as other types of surgery. It can be performed on the hips, thighs, and buttocks to extract fat locally and improve shape. Plastic surgery is discussed in more detail than stomach and intestinal surgery because I myself have undergone it and can speak from experience. It will also be of greater interest to the reader who has problems with fat distribution on the lower half of the body.

Surgery of the Stomach and Intestines

These operations are very severe and are performed only on those who are extremely overweight and who have tried every conventional method of reduction and still failed not perhaps to lose weight but certainly to keep it off.

Trying to describe the various kinds of operations in simple terms is complicated. There are two major categories of surgery, intestinal and gastric (stomach). The most commonly performed type of intestinal surgery used to be the jejunoileal bypass, which creates a shortcut through the small intestine. The main aim of this type of surgery is to cause malabsorption of nutrients, which thus cannot be stored as fat. However, it has been increasingly observed that the immediate dramatic weight loss after surgery results mostly from spontaneously reduced food intake, although why this is so is not yet certain. Patients tend to lose weight for about eighteen months after surgery, then they reach a plateau, and afterward they may gain back varying amounts of the weight they've lost. It is extremely rare for the patient to gain back all the weight.

There are some very unpleasant and in some cases dangerous side effects with the old types of intestinal surgery unless strict precautions are taken. These complications include loss of electrolytes such as sodium and potassium, which could impair heart function. Another risk is permanent kidney or liver damage. Not necessarily fatal are a variety of nutritional deficiencies, including protein loss and muscle wasting. Flatulence and temporary diarrhea also result. Intestinal bypass is reversible, so fatal damage can be avoided by undoing the intestinal loop. Much progress has been made with this operation, including newer, safer modifications, and many of the mishaps associated with it can be avoided if the patient is under lifelong doctor's supervision. With these advantages significant and sustained weight loss is possible.

Comparatively less risky and thought by some to be more successful in controlling food intake is gastric surgery. There are several different kinds of operations, but the two main variations are gastric bypass and gastroplasty. The bypass involves forming a small pouch and bypassing a large part of the stomach, similar to what happens to the heart vessels in coronary bypass and to the small intestine in intestinal bypass. Gastroplasty is a means of reducing the stomach by partitioning; it achieves the same small pouch as the bypass without actually excluding anything.

Both these procedures reduce the volume of the stomach so patients feel fuller sooner. Postoperatively, patients are given a liquid diet, and great attention must be paid to quantity. Excess intake may not only undo the staples that are used in the bypass but will also cause pain and vomiting and eventually permit weight gain. Patients gradually go on to solids again, paying attention to quantity and never drinking with a meal, which would cause distention. Because of the unpleasant feeling of fullness after eating, this operation is very successful in reducing food intake initially. An interesting fact is that after gastric bypass, patients seem to reduce their intake of certain foods more than others, especially high-calorie carbohydrates. This suggests that gastric bypass surgery may have secondary effects on absorption and digestion as well as on reducing intake.

An interesting but purely experimental method for limiting food intake is the insertion of balloons into the stomach. These are then inflated through some tubing and fill out the stomach, thus limiting food intake. The balloons can stay inflated for varying periods. Sometimes they spontaneously collapse, enter the digestive system, and are excreted. Experiments are now being done on extended use of these balloons. It is uncertain whether they will be able to stay in the stomach as long as six months without damaging the stomach or causing it to stretch.

Effective though these methods may be, they simply treat the *symptoms* of obesity. A more serious attempt has been made to get to the real cause of the problem: the regulation of appetite and food intake. Hypothalamic lesioning—brain surgery on the appetite center, which is performed frequently on rats—has also been tried on humans as extensively as ethics will allow. The results have been disappointing: loss of appetite was only temporary, which suggests the complexity of hypothalamic regulation.

Operations have also been done on the vagus nerve, which carries messages of hunger from the stomach to the brain. Some success was achieved here, even though stopping hunger sensations does nothing to address the behavioral problem of overeating that is not due to hunger.

Techniques have yet to be perfected, and even when they are, surgery of the stomach and intestines can be recommended only for people whose overweight may prove fatal. The operations do nothing to treat the actual cause of obesity. That still remains an elusive unknown, buried in its hypothalamic hideaway. Furthermore, these food reduction techniques could pose an additional problem to obese people who know only too well that their food intake seldom has any relation to feelings of hunger and satiety. For them a surgically produced restriction of intake is useless from a behavioral point of view: they will prefer to vomit and have pain than to stop eating. The misery and frustration of this pattern of eating can be imagined, though many patients tolerate it rather than being fat.

Plastic Surgery

Motivation

One of the reasons I wrote *The Venus Syndrome* was that I wished I had had such a book to consult before I decided to have surgery. I don't necessarily think it would have changed my decision but at least I would have had a better idea of what to expect. I hope that by sharing the experience of the surgery I will help anyone considering plastic surgery to know what to expect and decide what to do. Perhaps my explaining the motivations that led me to plastic surgery will illustrate why people are prepared to undergo the pain and risk to get rid of fat. Let me make one thing clear. I am not advising surgery as the ultimate and permanent method of removing fat. It is just an available means and as such deserves to be assessed.

When I first considered plastic surgery, there seemed no one able to help or advise me. In 1979 the whole topic was cloaked in secrecy and was considered by most people to be the self-indulgence of wealthy neurotics. My interest in the subject was bred from discontent about my figure but was also the result of greedily reading every magazine and newspaper article about it. For facts, I was dependent on journalism and myth, and sometimes I could hardly tell the difference between the two.

My efforts to obtain information from doctors were equally frustrating. A plastic surgeon in London refused to do the operation, saying that the extensive lymphatic drainage network system in the legs made surgery risky and liable to lead to circulatory complications and possible infections. His adamant discouragement typified the view of many doctors, especially British ones at the time: plastic surgery was a cop-out. The English belief in the stiff upper lip extended to other parts of the body too. If you had fat thighs you had to live with them or starve until they went away. Surgery was a serious business, hardly to be used on neurotic women with low self-esteem. I met with the same reaction from many other doctors. Each time I went to them for help, I met with discouragement. I remember how frustrated I felt. It seemed to me that no one ever understood the problems of an out-of-proportion figure, let alone had a solution for one.

Then, thankfully, a dear friend of mine, a New York kidney surgeon, came to the rescue. He had known me for years and came from the same fat-ridden Greek island as myself, so he had a good idea of my hereditary figure problem. He was the first person to support and confirm my idea that plastic surgery would be a constructive move, if it could work toward giving me a more positive image of myself. I believe the results of the operation gave me the incentive to do what I am doing today and what I shall continue to do for a lifetime: control my shape through diet and exercise. The operation was the first step in the direction of realizing that I could change my body image.

Undoubtedly the most important thing about plastic surgery is the choice of surgeon. Dr. Richard Stark, Clinical Professor of Surgery at Columbia University, who performed the operation on me, was introduced to me by my Greek surgeon friend. Together we first visited Dr. Stark with my father. The purpose of the visit was for Dr. Stark to assess my motivation and for me to ask him questions about what to expect. I shall always be grateful to him for his honesty and common sense. He told me he could not promise me the perfect figure but that he could vastly improve on what I had, provided I was willing to maintain and even improve the results afterward by a diet and exercise program. We discussed surgical procedure, length of recovery, and many other details.

During the consultation I cried. The misery and humiliation I had suffered as a result of being fat suddenly became intensified. Being interviewed about my case history stimulated self-pity. A painful process, it was nevertheless a catharsis, a final release of the past.

I had always seemed to be apologizing for the way I looked and trying to compensate for it by developing my intellectual abilities. Now I saw the possibility that all that could change; that I could have a reformed body and a reformed attitude. As I came out of the doctor's office into the crisp, sunny air of a New York October, I already felt different. I actually skipped for joy—in my mind's eye was a new person, someone who moved gracefully and energetically, without inhibition; someone free.

The best advice I can give anyone contemplating surgery would be to get your motivations clear. Accept total responsibility for your body and try and get a clear and realistic picture of how you want it to look. Having thinner thighs is *not* the key to inner happiness, but having a better shape and more positive self-image are contributing factors to being at peace with yourself. Don't expect *drastic* changes either physically or psychologically after surgery. The physical results take some time to show, and surgery cannot change your life unless *you* are prepared to change your attitude.

Choosing Your Surgeon

Let us assume you have checked your motivations (something only you can do) and made your decision. Next comes the important task of choosing a surgeon, someone you like and can trust and who, most important, has a proven track record. Either choose a surgeon through the American Society of Plastic and Reconstructive Surgeons or consult your family physician and with his or her guidance approach either the head of a large medical center or a particular surgeon who has been recommended to you. Prices for the surgery will vary according to the surgeon and the extent of the surgery. An extensive operation could cost as much as $10,000, while a more modified version might cost between $3,000 and $7,500.

There are many different kinds of plastic surgery, and one can become quite easily confused. Different surgeons have different specialties and you want to be sure that you select one who has had a lot of experience in reducing hips and thighs. Most leading plastic surgeons began their career in the field of reconstructive surgery, repairing birth defects, burns, scarring, and the ravages that cancer makes on the body. This is not only a surgical challenge but also an accomplishment on a humanitarian level. Many surgeons adapted and extended their reconstructive techniques to cosmetic surgery.

One important thing to remember is that plastic surgery itself cannot help you lose weight. Remedial surgery is usually performed on patients who have lost vast amounts of weight already, either through undergoing gastrointestinal surgery, jaw wiring, or diet and exercise. This kind of plastic surgery extracts the loose skin, making several tucks or folds to get it smooth and firm again. It does not entail the removal of fat.

Cosmetic or aesthetic surgery is the kind of plastic surgery with which we are most familiar. Surgery to remove fat from the body is referred to as body sculpturing. The standard procedures are lipectomy (removal of fat) and a lift and/or tuck process. These are performed on the abdomen, buttocks, arms, breasts, or thighs. Even though fat is excised, weight is not lost as a result of plastic surgery. Instead you lose inches, improve your shape, and have a firmer, tighter silhouette.

A Short History of Body Sculpturing for the Lower Body
The surgical procedures currently used on the hips and thighs are the culmination of many years of development and refinement of surgical technique. The first plastic surgery for the thighs that we know of was performed by John R. Lewis, Jr., of Atlanta, Georgia, who also performed a buttock lift operation in 1957. At first all that was attempted with the thighs was the reduction of irregular surface bumps. No one tried to remove fat until Ivo Pitanguy, the famous Brazilian plastic surgeon, performed a more extensive thigh operation in 1958. This removed the fat at the side of the upper thigh, popularly referred to as "riding trousers" or "saddlebag" bulge. Other leading plastic surgeons began performing such operations the following year.

Surgical Procedure
The principle of plastic surgery is to make an incision wherever there is a skinfold to hide the scar; for instance, in the groin or underneath the buttocks. Knowing where to make the incision is the most important part of plastic surgery, which aims for minimal scarring. My surgeon, Dr. Stark, a talented artist as well as skilled surgeon, visited me in the hospital the night before surgery and actually drew the lines of incision on my skin with a felt-tip pen. This must be done when the patient is standing as only then can a doctor get an idea of fat displacement.

The buttock and thigh lifts are two different procedures. The first is simpler as the buttocks offer a natural crease in which the scar can be hidden. Fat can also be extracted from the upper thighs through the same incision, but if the thighs are heavy all over, an incision can be made toward the back of the inner thigh down as far as a few inches above the knee. These scars are not visible if the patient stands with his or her legs together, although at other times the scars can be seen as there is no crease to cover them.

The amount of fat extracted and the sites of extraction will depend on the surgeon's judgment. During the visits to the surgeon, you discuss where you feel the fat should come out and the surgeon will tell you whether this is practical or not. During the surgery, certain conditions may prevail where the surgeon finds it unwise to extract fat from some sites, but this cannot be predicted.

It would be unrealistic to expect a significant weight loss after surgery. When I awoke and first managed to stand on the scale, I had lost only a few pounds. It is tempting to imagine that because the fat is lifted out you will emerge lighter, but what the extraction really does is make you lose inches. Not even extensive removal of fat cells can help you lose drastic amounts of weight. You will never be able to lose as much body fat with plastic surgery as you will with diet and exercise.

In plastic surgery the fat is removed from the subcutaneous layer that lies under the skin and over the muscle and its overlying membrane, the fascia. As we saw when discussing cellulite, the skin structure is what determines the bunched-up look of dimpled lower body fat, not the mysterious and inexplicable existence of cellulite. Dr. Stark explained it to me more graphically by telling me to imagine a sofa where the stuffing is held down by buttons. The fat cells are like the stuffing in the sofa, and the septa, the perpendicular separators that stretch from the deepest layer of skin down to the fascia, are like the buttons that pin down the stuffing. Skin looks dimpled because fat is pressing on it from underneath. When there is less stuffing between the septa, the pressure is relaxed and the surface skin looks less dimpled because it is less padded from beneath. What plastic surgery does is remove the fat and ease the pressure on the skin.

Stitching of the incision is also very important. My stitching was done with nonabsorbable nylon thread and a subcuticular (under the skin) technique, in which the thread was actually inside the incision, surfacing through the skin to be pulled out when everything had healed. On the buttocks, the stitching is reinforced because this is where there is most tension on the scars and therefore an extra risk of their stretching.

Risks and Complications

All surgery involves dangers; it is wise to discuss all your anxieties with your surgeon beforehand. A few words should be said about the particular complications resulting from plastic surgery for the lower half. Groin incisions take the longest to heal. As they are in a natural skin crease, they do not close as easily as wounds on a

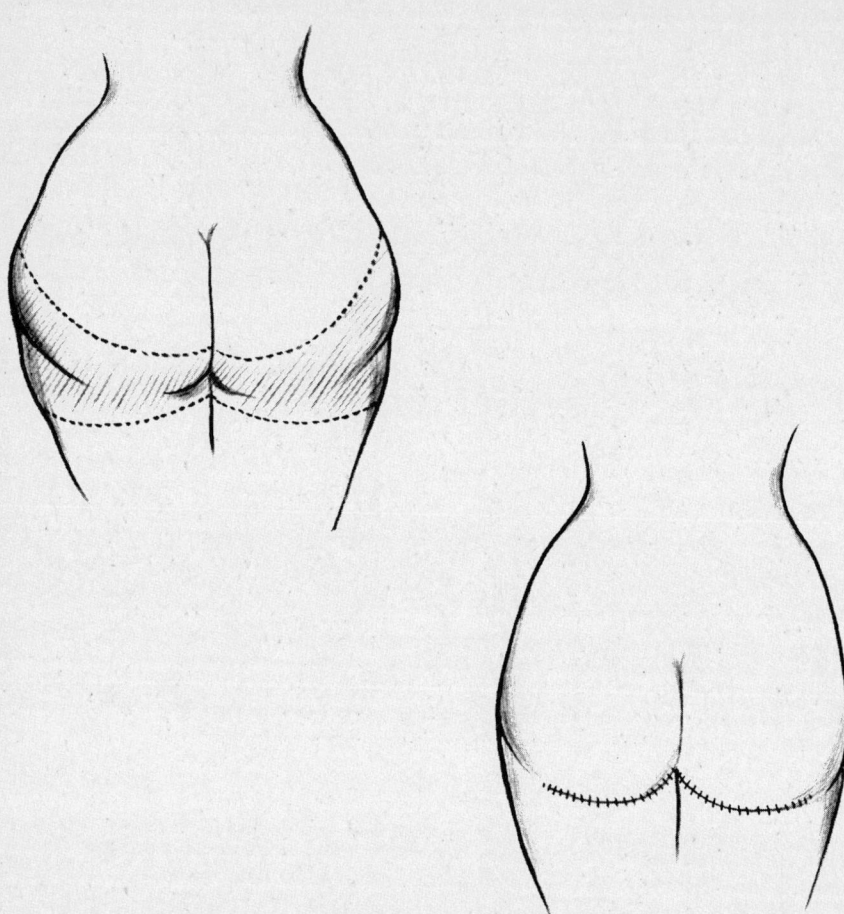

Figure 10 LINES OF INCISION AND AREAS OF EXCISION FOR THIGH AND BUTTOCK REDUCTION

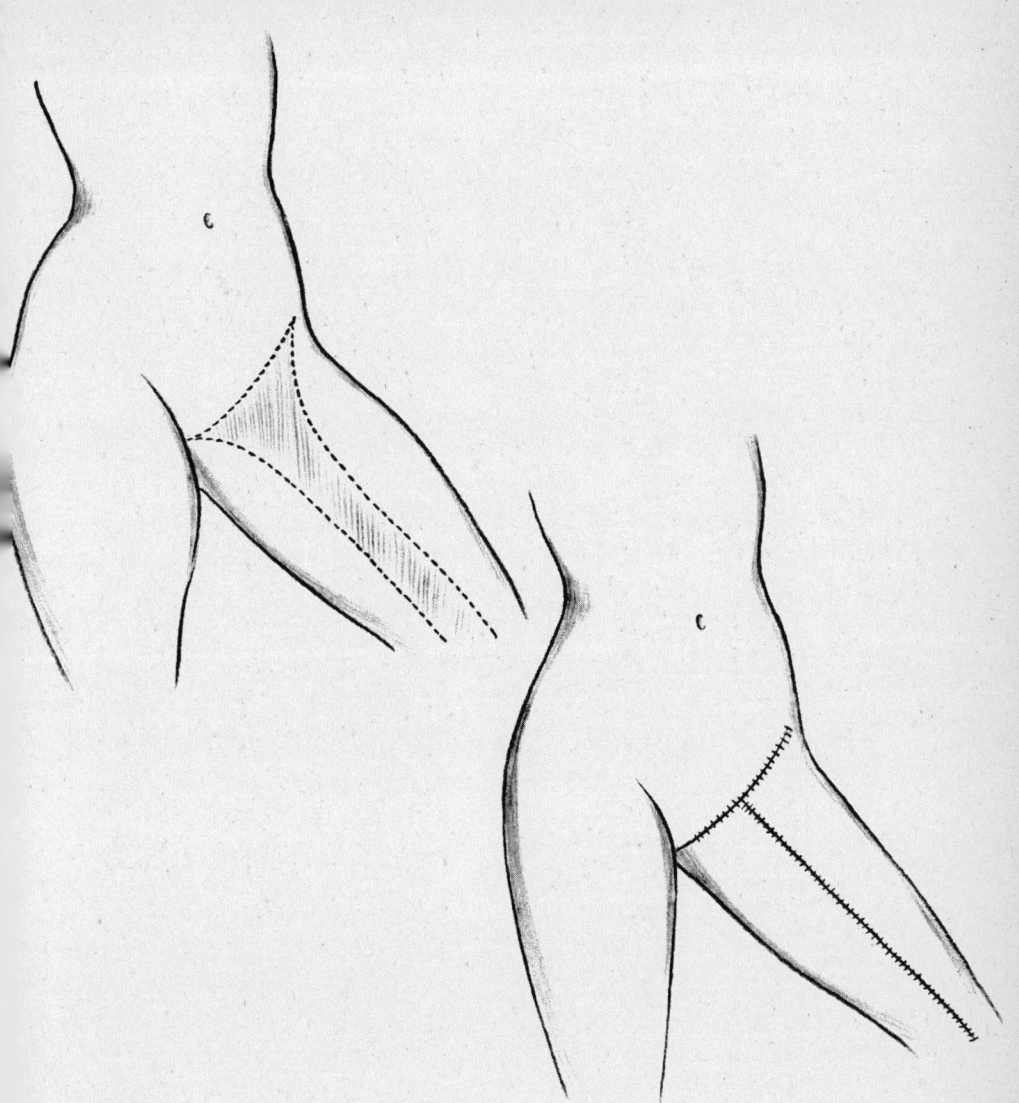

flat surface. Also they have less air getting to them and they tend to get hot and damp, especially if one is lying down all the time. That means they are an ideal breeding ground for bacteria. What sometimes happens, as it did to me, is that these wounds start healing from the inside by a process known as granulation. The wound heals internally but it still gapes open. Therefore it is very prone to infection and it has to be washed out regularly and thoroughly.

The second setback was a hematoma (a swelling containing blood). Some of the space left by the extracted fat tissue filled with blood that collected under the skin on the inner thigh near the knee. The hematoma disappeared after a few weeks, during which it became reabsorbed.

In some cases, there is also a risk of accumulation of wound fluid (seroma). When fat is cut out it leaves a vacant space, which can be filled by such fluid. In severe cases, this can result in infection. I had several nasty experiences when, even months after surgery, I would get a very high temperature. The problem was almost always the outer thigh, which would become very inflamed. Once it was treated with antibiotics the pain would decrease, but the first attack was not caught in time and fluid collected in an ugly bulge at the back of the thigh. Other rare but possible complications include malformation and occasional swelling of the genital area if groin incisions are made. This occurs because of severing of the lymphatic nodes in the groin area. Usually all swelling subsides a few months after surgery.

Recovery

The recovery period is different in every case. Sometimes it can take as few as ten days in hospital and a few weeks at home. In my case the recovery was a longer process because of complications. Throughout this time I required nursing, as my range of movement was very limited. If you undergo extensive plastic surgery, as I did, take it seriously. If you think you can just walk into the hospital, have your fat cut out, and walk straight out again, you are mistaken. I am not saying this to scare you. Clearly your recovery depends on the length and extent of the surgery. But surgery it *is,* with all its attendant discomforts. I felt weak for several days after the operation because of blood loss. I had been under anesthetic for almost five hours, so it took me several days to recover from that. I suffered from all the normal symptoms following surgery: nausea, soreness, stiffness, constipation, flatulence. In addition to all these, the most uncomfortable aftereffect of plastic surgery on the lower body is swelling of the legs, which took a long time to subside.

At the same time, my expectations deflated. I had secretly expected to see dramatic changes; to awaken in the recovery room and look down at pencil-thin thighs. Instead I saw what resembled heavily bandaged tree trunks because my legs were so very swollen from the surgery. I realized then that one of the most important qualities you need when you make the decision to have surgery is patience. For the first few days, and in some cases, weeks, you must stay flat on your back; sitting is forbidden because it would stretch the scars too much. Getting up to walk the first few times was a major maneuver, requiring several nurses, a general clearing of the room lest I fall, and a lot of willpower. Dizziness made it difficult to stand up, which in itself was quite an ordeal. The nurses had to make sure that I didn't bend my body at all lest I strain the stitches. On the first attempts I was yanked by my legs and levered up like a skateboard onto my heels, all without bending.

What I want most to convey to anyone who is contemplating plastic surgery is that there is a tremendous difference between how you actually feel and how you expect to feel. Any difference in shape did not become evident for at least six weeks, when the swelling finally went down. Another major issue is disappointment. I had wanted Dr. Stark to take out as much fat as possible and I must admit I felt disappointed to see that there was still an awful lot left. It is important to understand that body sculpturing concentrates precisely on sculpture, on achieving an acceptable contour, and not just excising fat. Enough fat must be left to fill out the appropriate places and create an aesthetically pleasing shape.

Plastic surgery can help your shape but *not* your weight. This aspect is sometimes inadequately emphasized by doctors. Because I was almost totally motionless, I certainly wasn't burning up my calories through activity, and even though one must eat a balanced and nutritious diet for healing purposes, my eating patterns certainly did not improve postoperatively and I gained weight. Psychological factors and boredom certainly didn't help either.

The emotional recovery from this kind of surgery is just as important as the physical. I experienced drastic mood swings after surgery, sometimes feeling elated, other times very down. That is fairly normal after surgery, as the energy levels in the body are heavily depleted and the body needs time to adjust. Once I returned from the hospital, things improved. I could move around more easily and was able to sit down without worrying that the scars would split. I began to see a difference in my body and my mind. The bandages had been removed, the swelling had gone down, and I began to try on all my clothes. The greatest thrill was putting on a pair of gray velvet pants that had not fitted me for years. Only then, standing in front of the mirror, did I realize what the surgery had achieved.

Scarring

A few plastic surgeons I talked to said they would not operate on the thighs because of the extensive scarring. Many women fear plastic surgery for this reason. The way I look at it is that scars, especially if they have healed well, can be concealed by various skin creams; fat cannot. If you fear that scarring will disfigure you, this operation is not for you. Even though plastic surgeons attempt to cut on a skinfold, the extent of this kind of surgery, especially across the buttocks and the inside thighs, makes the visibility of scars inevitable.

Scars increase in strength over a three-month period, as the healing tissue builds up. With this kind of surgery, the first stitches can be removed within the first week, though some stitches can be left in for as long as two months, as mine were, to assist in supporting the scars. After a period of strengthening, the scar undergoes a process known as maturation, when it softens and flattens out. One of the complications that plastic surgeons watch for is that the scar will become keloid. That means it overgrows and the surface becomes red and bumpy. Plastic surgeons often use a technique known as dermabrasion to flatten keloid scars. This exposes new cells in the scar and makes it the same color as the surrounding area.

The Return of the Prodigal Fat Cell. Are the Effects of Plastic Surgery Permanent?

Up until recently, it was supposed that the number of fat cells in the human body stopped increasing sometime around the age of eighteen. This is no longer accepted. If it were the case, removal of fat cells by plastic surgery might have proved a definite and permanent solution to both weight and shape problems because it would reduce not only localized fat but also total fat cell number, which is thought by some to help decrease food intake. This all looks pleasingly simple, yet, as research has advanced, the picture has become more complex. We know now that fat cells can enlarge and multiply at any time and, worse still, that they never die. This means that even if fat cells are excised by surgery, if you subsequently eat more than your energy requirements you will form new fat cells to store the excess fat.

A very interesting study was done on five patients who had lost large amounts of weight by conventional dieting. They had reduced the size of their fat cells but not the number. Extensive plastic surgery was then performed and a large percentage of the patients' excess fat cells removed. There were no indications that this removal had any effect in preventing future weight gain and at least one of the patients returned to the weight she had been before dieting.

If you gain some weight after plastic surgery, will it go straight to the area from which fat was removed? As usual, it is difficult to answer this question with any degree of certainty. As far as animal studies are concerned, after surgical removal of fat, rats showed a regeneration of fat cells in some depots within six months and not at all in others. In humans, it does not *seem* likely that fat cells can develop again in the same area. What may happen is that fat cells in the surrounding area may increase in size or number and get pushed toward the site of the operation, therefore making the area fatter.

All I can say is don't wait to find out. As the regeneration of fat on site is not certain, it's not worth taking the risk of gaining too much weight after surgery under any circumstances. I didn't follow my own advice and afterward slowly gained almost thirty pounds. My thighs never bulged out as they had before, but my lower half did not escape the weight gain, although the weight I put on was fairly evenly spread and this time I found I gained more weight on my face, arms, and stomach.

Should You Have Plastic Surgery?
Plastic surgery is a serious business, and the aftereffects, even though temporary, are not pleasant. You may experience swelling, soreness, and stiffness even a year afterward. I do not regret my operation but I do recommend that you give serious thought to other methods

of reduction beforehand, such as long-term diet and exercise. If plastic surgery is your final decision, choose your surgeon carefully and find out as much as possible about what to expect from the operation. Don't feel guilty about taking an easy way out; it is harder than most people think. Credit yourself with the courage of making such a move, but never expect from the scalpel what only you can do for your body. The *maintenance* of the surgery's result is up to you alone.

4

Healing the Problem

11

Body-Mind: Re-creating an Essential Connection

Are You Ready for This?

When I first began to write this book, the scientific realities about weight and shape were what fascinated me. Once I had glimpsed the complexity of the disorder, my earnest, almost feverish intention was to make people realize the injustice and ignorance with which obesity was viewed. I wanted to clarify not only that overeating was *not* the sole cause of obesity but also that it might not be a cause at all, possibly only a result. The main cause, if there was one, seemed to be that fat people used a minimum of fuel or food to maintain life and economically stored the rest away as fat. From a metabolic point of view, thin people were far more careless. They used up most of their fuel and gave off heat as a by-product while storing the minimum as fat.

As my scientific research continued and I came to accept these biochemical truths, their deeper, metaphysical implications became apparent to me. The more the physiological facts seemed to indicate a hypothalamic hypothesis or cellular defect as the root of obesity, the more I began to see it on a psychological level as a refusal to let go of food. In symbolic terms, it seemed as if fat people were almost trying too hard. Their metabolisms were working overtime, spending a lot of effort in clinging to the maximum amount of calories. Thin people stayed thin by releasing and letting go of what they ate: on a deeper level, by not worrying about it.

Even though my primary intention has been to be faithfully accurate about the medical condition of overweight, an equally strong intention is to express my feelings on how our body and mind interact. If this concept offends you, I assure you that nothing written here contradicts what has gone before. It just embellishes it and offers a deeper dimension. No opinions are being forced on you: I believe that the reader of a book reads only what he or she is ready to see. All I am presenting are my impressions on how the mind affects the body and on how our attitude can affect our figure.

How Much Is Overweight a Psychological Issue?

Years ago obesity specialists and a judgmental public scoffed at the possibility that there were psychological reasons for being fat. Now even the most eminent, not to mention the most unimaginative, doctors admit that there may be mental and emotional causes of obesity. The issue is a delicate one. Are inner conflicts the cause of overweight or are these complexes and anxieties that fat people have the result of their being fat?

Doctors have not been able to agree about the relationship between fat and the psyche. Maybe the truth belongs to a more esoteric dimension and therefore eludes the proof of clinical evidence. Let us first examine the issue on a biological, in fact, anatomical level. When we are talking about the mind, do we mean the brain, and what is the connection between the two? It looks as though they are quite intimately related on a physiological level, for the hypothalamus, the part of the brain that controls appetite, also controls our moods. It is still a mystery why happiness causes hunger in some and starvation in others, and misery can lead to bingeing or total abstinence. Until more is known about the influence of the hypothalamus on our moods, we should not discount that our physiological appetite centers and the psychological triggers of our eating behavior are intricately linked.

What Makes Us Eat?

Although the paths of research are various, there are two fundamental theories about what causes excess intake in fat people. These can be summed up as the "push" and "pull" theories. The push theory is basically behavioral; people stuff themselves with too much food because of external factors. The pull theory suggests that a metabolic error at some level causes the body to pull in more calories despite the person's good intentions. These theories offer a neat antithesis, yet neither can be proved to the exclusion of the other.

For a long time psychologists have been trying to isolate the obese personality and characterize particular eating behavior patterns that separate the fat from the thin. This has proved impossible. Many popular beliefs about fat people's eating behavior are unfounded. One of them is that the obese are supposed to eat more when anxious. A study using threat of electrocution as an anxiety stimulus found that this is not true. Much research must yet be done on the effects of anxiety on appetite and weight before any conclusions are accepted. Paradoxically, since if the obese eat more when they are anxious, they must *be* anxious, a common idea prevails that thin people are nervous and fat people calm.

Do nervous people have higher metabolic rates? Because everyone's metabolic rate is so different, it is hard to generalize. Mentally disturbed patients do not have higher metabolic rates, but an uncomfortable although not unbearable degree of anxiety, such as that experienced in the dentist's waiting room, has been shown to speed up metabolism to a certain degree. When I asked Dr. Philip James, then head of the Dunn Clinical Nutrition Centre in Cambridge, England, what the relationship of anxiety was to weight, he stated that it was slight and dubious. Anxiety can cause weight loss *in some people* by subconsciously altering their eating habits and distracting them from thinking about food. When worried, these people tend to eat more quickly, which leads to bad digestion, intestinal malabsorption, diarrhea, and wastage. They may also tend to be more active. Others, however, react to anxiety in a totally different way, by substantially increasing food intake and perhaps decreasing activity. A further possibility is that different kinds of anxiety in the *same* person will have a different effect on appetite, depending on the cause.

Other evidence suggests that instead of mood determining intake, certain food influences our mood. It has for some time been suspected that carbohydrates make us feel sensually satisfied, but we now know why. Carbohydrates accelerate the passage of an amino acid called tryptophan into the brain. This then raises the level of a brain chemical called serotonin, which makes us feel happy and calm. If we don't eat enough carbohydrates, for example when on a high-protein diet, we may tend to become nervous and irritable because of reduced serotonin levels.

The abundance of theories on eating behavior tends to be very confusing. So little is known about the perception of hunger and satiety signals that it is ridiculous to state for certain that fat people are not aware of them or that they purposely or unconsciously avoid them. It is perfectly possible that fat people *do* have hunger sensations but they are not discretely aware of them because they feel them constantly. Hunger could be a constant and thus normal state to the obese person, not a distinct stimulus felt at certain times.

None of these assumptions really means anything. However well we think we may understand eating behavior, it really will not help us at all to understand the clinical condition of overweight. To say that overeating causes overweight is, as one specialist pointed out, about as illuminating as saying that drinking too much is the cause of alcoholism. If obese people didn't genuinely feel such a need to consume food, dieting would be a mildly unpleasant but totally manageable exercise.

Rather than separating internal and external stimuli, perhaps it would be more realistic to suppose that they coexist and that in the obese their cooperation leads to excessive intake.

Not only fat people have an attachment to food. We all do. Furthermore, mealtimes are social events, where our hosts are constantly persuading us to overeat. In many Middle Eastern countries, and also in Greece, to eat well at a dinner party is a social necessity, a gracious sign of appreciation to the hostess. Eating is an undeniably pleasant activity: it is a basic act of receiving nourishment. It is both satisfying and comforting. Moreover, to most of us food is freely available, and, as most lonely people know, eating is a particularly convenient pastime because you do not need a partner.

Food for Thought and Thoughts on Food

Our relationship with food is a profound and primitive one: even before birth we receive nourishment in the womb. From the moment we are born the preparation of food for us, our receiving it, and the feelings that go with eating are closely associated in our subconscious with feelings of love and the satisfaction of getting what we want. Precisely because we have been eating every day of our lives and feeling so many different emotions while we perform that act are all these connections present.

Advertisements for food on television and in the press have latched onto our subconscious process of equating food with love and security. The conscientious mother who prepares a meal does so because she "cares." Her family is therefore obligated by the many hours she has spent in the kitchen to show appreciation. If they don't eat heartily, they reject her. Similarly, how is a man expected to show a woman how much he cares? By taking her out to an expensive restaurant. How do you calm your baby, persuade your child to behave, and reward your dog for his never-failing fidelity? Food, food, food! Anodyne, tranquilizer, and persuader, food is something to which no insomniac, neurotic adult, or hyperkinetic infant is immune.

There is no denying that more than being just a basic need, food is one of the joys of life. What is a mystery is why so many people, especially women, abuse food. Extreme instances of this are such eating disorders as anorexia nervosa, which involves sometimes fatal starvation. Apart from their psychological torment, for anorexia is a mental and emotional problem, victims suffer extreme symptoms. As they are usually near to normal weight or sometimes under even at the beginning, they have no fat reserves, as an obese faster does. Their bodies become cold, with bluish or red blotches, and they develop lanugo, a soft downy hair all over. They may develop dangerously low blood pressure and intestinal problems. Not only are they starving or seriously undereating, but they also often take insufficient liquids and no vitamin and mineral supplements.

Equally unpleasant is bulimia, in which grotesque binges are violently followed by purgation, such as vomiting and massive doses of laxatives or diuretics. No less serious examples are the millions of overweight women and men who are allowing food to rule their lives instead of just enjoying it.

This is where I think we can usefully begin to differentiate between the thinking of thin and fat people. Such an examination may reveal another reason, in addition to metabolic, cellular, and possibly behavioral differences, why some people get fat and others don't.

The very term "psychosomatic" arouses intense feelings of suspicion in some people. What the term really indicates is a bodily state that has been brought into existence, in varying degrees, by the mind. To grasp this concept, we have to accept the close connection between body and mind, which we so often deny. In our obsession to label, we do not really differ from our ancestors. Just as they thought that carnal passions and the forces of darkness were associated with the earth mother's bulbous form while spirituality and purity were confined to the innocent regions of head and heart, so also do we cut off soma from psyche. Our mind may be alert and clear, but our body uncontrollably expresses primitive sensuality and instinct. We have to cease this tidy compartmentalization if we are to understand that we are whole. The concepts of psychic and somatic causation are *not* incompatible. It is possible for many levels of meaning and explanation to exist. By saying that our thoughts about food are partly responsible for our turning it into fat, we need not discount the validity of the scientific origins of the disorder.

I have come to believe that it may be the heavy emotional charge we put on food, all the guilt and suppressed feelings attached to it, that helps to make us heavy. Even once fat and now thin people have not conquered their problem if they have still not changed their attitude as well as their body. They may be thinner, but the mind and not the body determines how we think, and if we still have heavy thoughts about food we still have a fat person's consciousness. Such thin-fat people are merely thin on the outside and fat inside. They maintain a low weight by a restrained pattern of eating. Their appetites are held in check by fear of food. They do not maintain a lower weight without excessive effort as naturally lean people do, they are merely reduced obese people, not people converted to a healthy body image. They are still afraid.

Fear is the key word. The fat person fails to understand that food itself is innocent and harmless; what makes you fat is your fear and guilty obsession with it. Dieting is a very poor cure for the obsession; you may cut down your intake successfully but guilt is still attached to the food that you *do* eat. Consequently food is still your obsession.

Both anorexics and fat people use food, admittedly in dramatically different ways, to act out their fear, guilt, resentment, anger, and whatever other emotion they dare not express otherwise. If these painful feelings could be acknowledged and examined, which might

dissipate them, anorexics and fat people could have a healthy relationship with food, consuming it in quantities they would be able to
determine as adequate, and could feel satisfied after eating. Once
you are free of fear, food is no longer threatening.

How Do Our Thoughts Shape Our Body?

Personal experience has shown me that by first changing my attitude
about my body, I was then able to change the body itself. All our
lives, we have been indoctrinated with the belief that physical illness,
overweight included, is an independent entity beyond our control.
We feel like victims. Until we realize that our body is intimately
connected with the mind, we will be hung up on "external" means
of healing ourselves; that is, all the means that do not come from
within ourselves.

Your thoughts, ideas, and emotions *do* affect your body. When
we cannot express strong emotions, we stuff them down and absorb
them into our body tissues. We accept the origins of "tension" or
"nervous" headaches, neck, and back problems, yet we refuse to
see that fat may also be a symptom of stress. Fat may be an extreme
physical manifestation of suppression: by covering the body with
it, we seek to smother the pain and cushion the fear. That emotions
actually do feel physically heavy is even apparent in our languages.
In English, responsibility weighs us down, in Greek the verb "to
be bored" means to be heavy or burdened. If you can see the body
as the outward expression of what you are feeling within and accept
it and learn from it, then and only then can you work on changing
it by letting go of the pain and anxieties inside.

Certain philosophies see the body as a field of energy. Buddhism
has identified certain *chakras* or force centers in the body. Each of
these chakras (the word means wheel in Sanskrit) vibrates with energy
drawn from the universe, and when they are awakened, they are
like whirlpools of energy transmitting from one center to the other
throughout the body. Another spiritual concept to do with the body
is that of the aura, which is a field of electromagnetic energy around
the body.

There is also a scientific justification for the energy concept. Think
of energy balance: intake, output, and storage are all seen in terms

of energy. When we are carrying too much fat we feel the opposite of energetic: we feel heavy, sluggish, immobilized, and blocked. Yet fat is still energy; it's just that instead of using it to celebrate life, we have stored it and blocked it.

Let us hypothesize that fat on the hips and thighs is blocked energy. Any feelings connected with the lower half of the body, which is the sexual center, may threaten and frighten us, especially as we are growing up as young women. An unconscious desire to suppress or deny sexual feelings, also possibly a desire to be pregnant or fear of being so, could be indicated on a psychosomatic level by a bottom-heavy pattern of fat distribution. A psychiatrist at one of London's leading psychiatric hospitals told me that even anorexics, who are skeletal, fear they are bottom-heavy.

This part of the body is not only our sexual core but also a life center. It is the seat of the root chakra, the first energy circle of the body and the receptor for the whole body of a special force fire from the earth. The site of this chakra is over the fourth sacral vertebra, over the coccyx; in other words, the behind. We may tend to forget just how fundamental a part of us our seat is until we consider such expressions as "You bet your ass," which is synonymous with "You bet your life." This identification of the lower half with the forces of mother earth is a very primitive one. While the upper half of the body is associated with the soul and the spirit, the lower half is considered to be the possession of the all-powerful and all-devouring mother goddess. Do we have perhaps some subconscious memory and perhaps even fear of this? Is this why we are so distressed at feeling our wide hips and large thighs in contrast to our thin and well-proportioned upper body?

Healing Yourself

Permanent physical change can only happen when thought patterns are altered. I hope that this discussion has done something to demonstrate that if your thoughts change, your body will also. Only you can change those thoughts, and the positive effects will be greater than those obtained from any drug or surgery. I have divided these "thought therapies" into two sections. The first deals with conventional methods of changing your attitude toward food and eating behavior. The second section features holistic treatments, which restore the body-mind link that we have so neglected.

Conventional Methods

Behavior Modification

Behavior modification aims at reforming eating behavior and induces you to decrease your food intake by observing and changing that behavior.

Such programs consist of several components. One is a monitoring technique using food diaries. Some people find that recording everything they eat and how they felt as they ate it will deter them and cause them to reduce intake. Apart from recall problems, this method is difficult to maintain for long periods without cheating or slacking off. Also, just writing down what you eat does nothing to absolve you from the guilt you may feel afterward.

Very popular indeed and thought to be one of the most successful aspects of behavior modification are support groups. This method may be better than the food diary because sharing a problem automatically reduces it; however, group support might work better for people who are extroverts than for shy people. Other elements of the behavior modification program teach people to control external temptations and minimize the food-oriented stimuli around them, to eat more slowly, exercise more frequently, learn more about nutrition, and change their attitude and body image.

Something rather different is aversion therapy. This is a punitive method in which you are induced, by a variety of unpleasant methods such as electric shock, nausea induction, and unattractive mental imagery, to develop an aversion to food while you are in the act of eating your favorite dish. Sometimes this treatment also involves verbal punishment and harsh criticism. Aversion therapy can be effective, but in many cases self-hate is already what makes a person eat, so this form of traumatic therapy will just reinforce a self-destructive pattern.

Behavior modification can work only if you believe that response to external cues or influences such as mood determines what you eat. I think that this is true *some of the time* but that most of the time we eat out of deeper psychological reasons. You may examine all the reasons for your eating behavior, acknowledge them, record them, and then still go ahead and eat. Even when behavior modification is successful, weight loss is disappointingly slow; however, recent studies show it is successfully maintained, which is a very promising aspect.

Psychotherapy and Psychoanalysis

Fat people find these treatments very slow and expensive ways of losing weight. That may be one reason that there are so few obese people in therapy or analysis. Most of them believe that their problem is fat and that once they lose weight, they will have no problem.

Sometimes *after* weight loss problems become much more apparent now that fat is no longer seen as their cause. Therapy is effective in helping fat people adjust to their new body image. However, therapy and analysis are both such gradual and subtle processes that they may take years to unlock the fear in people's minds and unlock the energy in their bodies. What is needed to deal with such problems is forms of therapy and treatment that seek to treat the mind and resultant bodily state through the body itself.

Holistic Treatments: Rediscovering the Body-Mind Connection

To those who are unfamiliar with it, holistic medicine may seem suspicious, vague, and threateningly mystical. That is how I saw it until I actually experienced some of the treatments. Then I understood that the term refers to a method of treating us as a whole. It treats the body, our physical vehicle, the mind, our controller, and the soul, our spiritual and higher self. The majority of treatments are performed on the body but may have far-reaching effects in the mental and spiritual spheres. Some examples are acupuncture and acupressure, reflexology and iridology (study of the person's condition through the feet and eyes, respectively), and aromatherapy (massage with essential oils). All holistic treatments are based on the belief that by treating the body, one treats the mind, which originally created the bodily state. The body simply incorporates what the mind thinks. The shape of our lower half reflects our relationship with mother earth and the ground itself and our reactions to sex.

Our hands mirror and represent our relations with each other; they are our chief area of physical communication with our environment and other people. Our head reflects our communication with our mental and spiritual spheres.

The idea of wholeness and connection between the mind and body has been much forgotten and neglected in our world today. Instead of a mind-body partnership, there is conflict. Sadly enough, this develops very early in life. Our education resists, inhibits, and punishes the body. We are supposed to control ourselves. But what is this self-control? It is the miserable opposite of a comfortable feeling of self-mastery. It is a force from outside and as such it is deeply resented. We are obligated to subdue our physical freedom and from childhood to wear the psychic straitjacket of proper behavior, which is soon to become the armor of self-defense.

When we leave the disciplinary institutions of home and schoolroom, the strict parent or teacher is now our mind. The mental and physical, emotional and spiritual aspects of our life are totally compartmentalized and a little of our precious time is disjointedly devoted to each. Yet this very conscious effort to include everything actually indicates what a schism exists in our lives between the mind and body. Millions of people in the United States are striving to snatch a few hours to keep fit. In the belief that this is better than nothing, their life consists of two extremes: a sedentary lifestyle violently contrasted with a vigorous, often punitive workout schedule.

Most people think that to have a beautiful body you have to suffer. If you have that attitude about your physical being, your achievements will have been inspired only by a threatening and masochistic sense of enforcement, mistakenly called discipline, and you will judge your lack of achievement as lack of willpower. If your mind and body were truly integrated, as united parts of a whole and total you, and if your mind were positively focused on having a beautiful body, it would happen in a more relaxed, more effortless way. It would be easy and natural for your body to act on what your mind believes. Nothing will work for you in your life unless you believe it will. Once the mind has embraced the idea, acting on it ceases to become an effort. As it has been integrated as a thought and as thoughts are automatically creative, it *becomes* into existence, it no longer needs to be consciously willed.

In his illuminating book *Fear of Life,* the psychotherapist Dr.

Alexander Lowen expounds his theories on "being" and "doing," which indicate how we are split within ourselves. He says that our happiest, and unfortunately increasingly rarest moments, are spent in the "being" mode, where we experience ourselves as God's creations. As created human beings, we are enough as we are, just being, we do not have to do anything or prove anything. Most of our lives are spent, however, in the "doing" mode, and this is where we experience anxiety. We have taken over from God and do the creating. We are no longer enough as we *are*, we have to do, perform, prove, impress. All this effort produces exhaustion, panic, and self-doubt.

We have undoubtedly lost the mind-body connection and the sense of wholeness over the centuries. I believe one way of restoring it is by working on the mind through the body, as these treatments, described in the following sections, propose to do. Admittedly, there is no scientific proof that these therapies dislodge fat from the hips and thighs that no diet, exercise program, or surgery has been known to do completely effectively. The main purpose of holistic treatment is to remove the negative energy you focused on your body and replace it with positive. You can then adapt that to physical means of altering shape—diet and exercise.

Bioenergetics

One of the best known body-mind treatments is bioenergetics. Created by Dr. Alexander Lowen, bioenergetics aims to solve psychological problems and stresses by relieving chronic muscular tensions and releasing blocked energy fields, usually by working on the spine. If you follow a sequence of bioenergetic exercises, involving stretching and bending, the energy fields are brought more into alignment and flow freely throughout the body. Many people have experienced enormous relief from depression, anxiety, and chronic pain in the back and other areas.

Bioenergetics is a therapy for both mind and body. Its aim is to help patients get in touch with their heart, with the part of them that loves and wants to be loved. Dr. Lowen describes how we have created defenses to protect our heart and how bioenergetics works to release them. In one way it does this mentally, using normal verbal therapy, but then, because of the shortcomings of this method, goes beyond and works on the body. Bioenergetic therapists read your muscular tensions, your posture, and your spinal condition as a testimony of what you have been feeling all your life. Then they work to release this by a system of exercise that includes deep breathing and is designed to release the flow of energy throughout the body.

Rolfing

Another popular holistic therapy is rolfing. This is a form of body manipulation that works on the fascia, the connective tissue that permeates the body's tissues and gives it form and structure. Because it concentrates on such deep tissues, if not done properly it can be very painful. The aim of rolfing is not to evoke pain but to bring about freedom and balance in the structure. Another one of its purposes is the releasing of mental pain. At a time that I was feeling a lot of turmoil, I underwent a course of treatments called body synergy. This is similar to rolfing only in that it works with deep tissue. As pressure was applied to the lower half of me, the pain was overwhelming. It seemed to penetrate beyond a physical level, and I began to react to it with my psychic being as well as my body. The sadness from the recent loss of my father became, for the first time, associated with the sadness I felt about my relationship with the lower half of my body. I cried and screamed during most of the treatments, and I must admit that after them I felt lighter and at the same time more grounded. By that I mean I felt my body's relationship with the earth differently. I felt much safer and physically better balanced as I walked.

Grounding is also a fundamental part of bioenergetics, and I would like to explain what it is. Women more than men often experience a sensation of unsteadiness in their feet and legs, allied to a fear of falling. Bottom-heavy women often experience this very acutely. They feel especially humiliated and threatened by the idea of falling and feel anxious about many movements that principally involve the legs. I often felt that my legs were solid but not strong. These therapies made me feel that my legs fully supported me.

It took me a long time to feel safe enough in my body to try rolfing. As I was being rolfed, powerful but subtle pressure was being exerted on my body. I felt the tissues expand and open, like the petals of a flower. The effect lasted for about twelve hours after the session. During this time I was still a little anxious, as the rolfing accentuated all my physical sensations, but once I realized that I could not only cope with that but that I appreciated the liveliness and sensitivity of my body, I felt no more fear. During the rolfing sessions I began to understand how we determine the body's structure and thus our quality and range of movement from early childhood. Our choice of clothes, especially shoes, our posture, the kinds of activities we perform, and most of all our mental and emotional states all form our body and influence the way it works. Many of these factors could subtly effect fat distribution, which in turn has other effects.

These body-mind treatments work on very subtle levels, and perhaps no remarkable physical change will be felt. What they will do is free your energies so that you can go on to effect remarkable changes that are physically apparent. What I experienced was the increasing certainty that my legs could be integrated with the rest of my body, which was slim, alive, and beautiful. In retrospect, I now realize that all the phases of treatment I went through for my legs, even the plastic surgery, contributed to giving me an enhanced body image and brought me to a state of self-confidence and self-realization that is enabling me to reform my own body without pain and sacrifice.

Rebirthing

Rebirthing differs from these treatments in several ways. It is not quite as specifically body-oriented as rolfing or bioenergetics. On a physical level, rebirthing is a deep-breathing technique in which you learn to breathe deeply and smoothly through the chest, finally attaining a complete circular breathing rhythm with no interruptions between inhaling and exhaling. It is a yoga of the breath. As such it is a body-mind treatment, for through using your lungs you awaken the rest of your body. As early as my second rebirthing session, my breathing initiated an intense tingling sensation in the body. While the rebirther who helps you achieve your breathing rhythm does not actively work on your body, you are working on it very subtly through the force that actually keeps it alive, your breath.

Rebirthing puts you in touch with your moment of birth and suggests that your birth trauma gave rise to the negative feelings you have about yourself. Breathing the stuff of life actively brings up the fear of death. Once you confront this fear and feel safe with it, knowing that it cannot kill you, remarkable things can happen in your life and to your body. I have actually lost weight during rebirthing sessions, and there have been many astounding reports about this. By recreating your birth and releasing your fear of death, you can resurrect your own body, lifting it from a deadened, painful state to full aliveness and expression.

12

The Rebirth of Venus

Your Body Reborn

Most people believe that changing your shape is impossible; you are the victim of your body type. We think that the best we can hope for is a lifelong struggle to eat less, move more, and eventually we will be rewarded with losing weight. Even the so-called miracles for shape, plastic surgery and fat suction surgery, seem daunting disappointments—sometimes dangerous and always ultimately ineffective as a foolproof guarantee against future weight and fat gain. This viewpoint is extremely negative and uninspiring, yet it is commonly held. Even if we don't actually hate our bodies, we envy the lucky few who are entirely at ease with theirs.

What most beauty books forget to tell you is that you too can be one of the lucky few. A new body, a new life, and a new you are within your reach. It is your right to feel completely free and light in your body, *no matter how much* you weigh or what shape you are. Once you have achieved a love of the body and a *feeling* of lightness, you can take the physical steps to mold the body to the weight and shape you desire.

Learning Self-Acceptance

Self-acceptance should not be confused with complacency. Accepting your body as it is in the present will enable you to have a better body in the future, but simply tolerating your present body and having no motivation to change it is *not* acceptance. Liking yourself as you are doesn't mean you have to stay as you are forever. You don't need to remain fat just to prove something. If you feel that your body would be better if it were a different shape, go ahead and change it. Remember also that *self*-acceptance is precisely that: it should not be dependent on the approval of others. Whether society approves or disapproves of fat is not important. What is vital is to examine your own point of view. What advantages does your fat give you? What does it excuse and protect you from? It must have some value, otherwise you would not have put it on in the first place.

Is It Really Okay to Be Fat?

Society has seemed recently to be radically changing its mind about fat. Even the most authoritative voices of doom, the much-revered life insurance tables, have had to modify their message and issue new, more lenient ideal weight tables. Some research has shown that the very thin and the very fat die younger and that if you are moderately overweight and healthy, it will not affect your chances of longevity. Instead of insisting that fat is the root of all evil, doctors are now paying more attention to threats such as high blood pressure and high blood cholesterol levels, conditions that sometimes accompany overweight but that can also easily occur in normal or even underweight people.

Even on the fashion front, fat is becoming more acceptable. A much greater and more attractive variety of clothes is designed for larger women, and the nationwide enthusiasm with which this choice has been received indicates that fat women are fashion-conscious. One of the country's retailers of larger-size clothing has become the third fastest expanding public company in the United States in the past decade. Larger models are finding more and more work because women are being encouraged by seeing clothes worn by women with whom they can identify.

The attitude that has spawned agencies employing fatter models, such as Big Beauties and Other Dimensions, is that fat is fine. I have no argument with that if you are *sure that you really do believe it.* However, I urge you to examine your motives with ruthless honesty. If you think that being fat is an act of defiance, of showing society that it cannot brainwash you with its skinny ideas, you care more for society than for yourself.

In the infancy of the human race, fat was awarded much significance. It was equated with survival, warmth, and wealth. Because of the association with mother earth, the lower down on the body the fat was, the more significant. Gradually, however, as worship was transferred from the earth goddess to a patriarchal religion, the pear shape began to lose its mystery and its power. The development of the study of human anatomy follows a similar course. In the Middle Ages, the Greek physician Galen considered the sexual organs to be the seat of energy, so the lower half was of great importance as the center of the body. In post-Galen, pre-Elizabethan times, the center moved upward, and the liver was thought to be the seat of power. An Arabic mother will still affectionately call her child "the center of my liver." Finally, in Elizabethan times, with the discovery of the circulatory system, the heart was pronounced the center of the body, and so the focus had moved entirely to the upper part of the body.

Today fat is of less significance. It is no longer a survival issue as it was in the past. Yet we continue to be obsessed with it. To some extent that is because our bodies have not been able to keep up with our minds. Women no longer need more fat than men to survive. In fact, women are expected to develop bodies like men, strong and streamlined, if they are to perform the same jobs with the same efficiency and wear the same kind of clothes. What we forget is that the human body evolved over millennia and that to expect to dispense with fat as the anachronism our society views it to be could very well be presumption on our part. We should have a little more respect for and patience with our bodies. Happiness is not the attribute of any particular body type. It does not come from being fat or thin but from having inner peace. When you have reached a true understanding of yourself, you will find that your body will eventually mirror that harmony.

The Complete Cure: Learning to Release Your Fat

Just remember that on a very subtle level, your thoughts about your body created that body. If your thoughts about your body become light, loving, and positive, the body will change. It has no choice— the mind controls it. Your mind is for thinking and your body for feeling. That is how your thoughts are experienced in your body and they are held there for years and years, until they are released. Only the mind can command that release and the command is, "Love yourself as you are," "Be kind to yourself." Unless this really happens, any physical changes will be the enforced result of struggle and effort and they will be temporary.

We have been brainwashed with the idea that a beautiful body is the final result of years of sweat, starvation, and effort. Thus we give way to the confusion and desperation on which the diet industry thrives. I know that it is easy to feel helpless if you are fat. I used to feel that I was trapped inside a body that did not reflect who I really was. While I held on to that thought and reinforced it with energy, no matter how thin I became through dieting and exercise and no matter how much trimmer the surgery made me, my body image was caught in despair and hate. Instead of that helplessness I now have faith that I can release my body from the heaviness I inflicted on it.

Letting go of your fat mentally can seem an abstract process. The first step is complete honesty. When you go to eat, simply ask yourself, "Am I hungry?" If the sensation really is that healthy one of hunger, its fulfillment shouldn't make you guilty. If the answer is No, congratulate yourself for being so honest and *do something else*. If you are tired, eating will make you feel worse. Instead, try something that will improve circulation and make you feel refreshed, such as exercise, yoga, or a massage. You could always try sleeping, a very good way of avoiding a binge. If you are bored instead of hungry, again exercise can dispel the feeling and turn it into a positive, energetic one. Phone calls, seeing a friend, going to the movies, reading a book are all good substitutes, but devote yourself completely to that activity. I mean that the film should *not* be accompanied by butter-soaked popcorn nor the exciting book by an equally enthralling chocolate bar. Finally, if you turn to food when angry, try screaming, hitting a pillow (as opposed to something more animated), and writing down all the things that made you mad. These techniques will not only prevent or at least postpone eating but make you more aware and more able to release your emotions without needing food.

Another way to lose weight is to lighten your attitude. Relax around food: after all, it is not leaving the planet. Have you ever noticed that when on a diet, you become obsessive about food and can think of nothing else? If you imagine for a moment that you can eat and drink whatever you like and lose weight, you will automatically loosen up and relax. Food will be a pleasure to you and not a cause of panic. The lighter you get in attitude, the lighter in body and the more light and positive in thought.

Remember to always be patient; it took years of negative and unloving thoughts to create the body you have now and it may take a little while to change. How long it takes depends on your willingness. In turn, your desire to change depends on how quickly you understand that it is safe to let go of your fat.

Thoughts for a Beautiful Body

Trust your body: surrender control to it. I found that when I was dieting strictly and forcing myself to exercise when my body felt stiff and exhausted, I would not get fast results. However, when I followed my body's instructions, eating when I was hungry and doing the kinds of exercise that felt right, I lost twenty-six pounds and my body became much firmer and more supple. When people who hadn't seen me for a year or so would ask in astonishment, "What did you have to do to lose weight?", I would have to rack my brains for a serious answer. My truthful answer is, "Nothing except what *felt* right." Your body knows what you should or shouldn't be doing, so pay attention to how you're feeling.

Part of surrendering control is being willing to let your feelings come up. If you can feel your anger, sadness, frustration, or whichever other emotion is suppressed, your body need not suffer anymore. A practical way to begin this is to be more relaxed in life and surrender more to your feelings. If you feel sad express it; if you feel joyful and mischievous, go ahead and play. When people offer you a choice in something, assert your preference. A very common pattern is to say "I really don't mind" when you really *do* mind. Then you feel neglected and unsatisfied, resentful that no one has listened. You can easily stuff down all those feelings with food when it would be much easier on your body to express what you want. What you are afraid to communicate is weighing down your body.

Good ways of relaxing and feeling safe enough to fully experience the body are having regular massage, swimming, and soaking in a warm bathtub or preferably a hot tub. A more intellectual method, which is also part of the rebirthing technique, is using affirmations. An affirmation is a positive thought about yourself that, when written a number of times, replaces your negative thoughts. Affirmations must be written frequently because you want them to sink into the subconscious, which usually continues its negative thought patterns. Each time you write an affirmation you should leave room on the opposite side of the page for a response column, in which you should express whatever resistance you have to the affirmation; for instance, "I don't believe it" or "If only that were true, but it isn't." Go on writing your affirmation and responding to it until your resistance goes away and your response is neutral. You may become impatient with or doubt the efficacy of using affirmations. I can assure you from personal experience that they work because you are engaged both in the physical act of writing and in the mental activity of thinking, so both body and mind are working for you. As you write the affirmations you can visualize them. This will strengthen the thought even more in your mind.

Listed below are some affirmations I thought up myself, which I found helpful. Their aim is to help you feel safe in your body, united with it, safe enough to feel its complete aliveness. When you have that kind of perfect relationship with your body, your fat will no longer have any purpose. You will lose it more easily than you ever thought possible.

1. My body is a safe place for me to be.
2. I am at peace living in my body.
3. I feel completely comfortable in my body.
4. I love every cell in my body. I am one with it.
5. My body and mind are in perfect union.
6. My body is strong, healthy, and powerful.
7. My body expresses my internal beauty and freedom.
8. All parts of my body are connected. I love them all.
9. Both my lower and my upper half are connected to my inner beauty.
10. I forgive myself for cutting off the lower half of my body.
11. My body is divine, pure, and innocent.
12. My body is perfect just as it is.
13. My body is most desirable to men/women.
14. I am now creating the body I have always wanted.

Treasure Maps

You can help create the body you want through visualization. A good way to do this is to make a treasure map of your ideal body. Cut out parts of a body from magazines; the arms you want, the breasts, the thighs, the bottom. Be realistic: don't choose someone with very long thin legs if yours are short and heavy; instead, choose body parts that could be yours if you improved your own a little. Patch the parts together, put *your* face in the picture and keep it in your closet, bathroom, or underwear drawer, not on the refrigerator door, for that just brings up guilt every time you go there and we know how destructive that can be.

Venus Reviewed

I began this book by invoking some ancient statues. I was drawing a parallel between a contemporary configuration that displeases thousands of women and a prehistoric art form that exaggerates woman's fertility, sexuality, or simply her curves. Just as we don't know why these ancient figurines are so fat, so also are we partially ignorant of why some women put on weight below the waist. It could be hormones, it could be genetics, and racial factors play their part. A metaphysical, and some may say far-fetched explanation, is that all fat is unexpressed fear and some people may tend to hold fear in a part of the body in which sexuality is centered and which has greater contact with the earth. All these are just hypotheses. We all have different bodies in different shapes and sizes. Some of us are satisfied but most are not. Many of us allow despair and disapproval to run our lives. Fat has become an obsession.

Becoming fat is easily done but difficult to understand. Yet unless we use our mind to find out the many diverse, complex, and often contradictory reasons why we deposit fat and deposit it in certain places, we shall be eternal victims of bodies that we hate. As our vehicle on this planet, the body deserves better treatment: we owe it love, respect, and attention.

Now when you look at your body or at another's, whatever the shape may be, suspend your judgment. You behold a work of wonder, a machine that technology cannot surpass. Instead of condemning it for having too much fat, see it for what it is and what it could be, when trained and perfected by sensible nutrition, frequent exercise, and most important, appreciation. In seeking to perfect our figures, we must first perfect ourselves. Instead of separating the body from the mind, we should be working on the total self. There is one prerequisite, though. As Venus is the goddess of love, remember each day to love yourself; only then can change become possible.

Epilogue

Once upon a time, only in my dreams was I dancing. Only in my fantasies was I graceful, thin, and moving as if on air. Now I know that I can make that image come true for me in every sphere of my existence. The miracle can happen, the longed-for can be real. This book is *dedicated* to all of you who have had anxiety about your body. It is *addressed* to that part inside of you that knows you can have the body you want, and that knows that you are, in reality, already beautiful.

Acknowledgments

For helping the book on a creative, metaphysical level:

I was fortunate enough to meet and be befriended by Dr. Jonas Salk while working on this book. His understanding, wisdom, philosophy, and very special essence imparted themselves to me the several times we met and discussed the inner process that was taking place as the outer one of writing progressed. If it had not been for his nurturing of this inner process, it might well have been omitted from this book and neglected within myself. Both *The Venus Syndrome* and my soul have been enriched as a result of knowing Dr. Salk.

The Venus Syndrome is dedicated to my editor, Louise Gault. I received incalculable assistance and immediate cooperation from all the people mentioned below; however, Louise provided the unceasing support and encouragement that enabled me to complete the book. She gave me not only advice and enthusiasm but, more important, the gift of self-confidence, of believing in what I had to say and in my ability to express it.

I am lucky to have as my mother a very exceptional person. Myrto, whose patience and serenity are always examples to me, has all my thanks for her support. My brother John has also been very helpful.

My cat Orlando did everything he could to hinder my progress. Sitting on the manuscript, spilling various liquids onto it, and playing with pens, erasers, and other paraphernalia, he posed both a threat and a challenge. For this stimulation and for his company, I have promised him a bowl of caviar as a reward.

For helping the book on a factual and organizational level:

Dr. Sami Hashim, Chief, Division of Metabolism and Nutrition, St. Luke's-Roosevelt Hospital Center, New York City, gave me facts, inspiration and the foreword to this book. He believed in me, worked long hours with me until I understood the points he was making, and always infected me with his lively mind and manner. He was as liberal with his brilliance as with his time: for both I am most thankful.

Dr. Margaret Ashwell, working now at the Dunn Nutritional Unit in Cambridge, England, helped me immeasurably not only with the majority of the facts but also with the painstaking task of correcting each chapter. An eminent researcher, she has the unique talent of being able to explain even the most complex processes. For her endless patience and for her incredible teaching ability, I thank her with all my heart.

Dr. John Kral, Director of the Division of Surgical Metabolism, St. Luke's-Roosevelt Hospital Center, New York City, helped me tremendously in many ways and over a long period of time. Without John's meticulously accurate explanations, his methodical corrections, and his dedicated and understanding grasp of obesity, there would have been no chapters on obesity in general, nor on gastrointestinal surgery or plastic surgery. For his caring influence, insistence on accuracy, and always sound advice, I am eternally grateful.

Dr. Alexander Sotiropoulos is the Greek kidney surgeon I mentioned in the book. If it wasn't for Alex's kindness and humanity, I would not have had the courage to have plastic surgery. If it wasn't for his enthusiasm, his willingness to introduce me to all the doctors mentioned here, and his whole-hearted belief in what I had to say, there *really* would be no *Venus Syndrome*.

Some of my most heartfelt thanks go to the people who helped produce the physical book itself. Hilarie Levion should be congratulated not only on being able to decipher my writing but also for typing so quickly, accurately, and frequently. With eternal good nature, she typed and retyped the chapters until she became more familiar with them than I was. I also want sincerely to thank Rae Derke, Sheryll Wilcox, Steve Frangos and Judy DiMauro, Areti Sotiropoulou, Mary Botsaris, and last but not least, Carol Noah in London. Their ingenuity, organization, and encouragement helped me track down useful information, keep excellent files, and refrain from panicking.

Dr. Joel Grinker took an avid interest in the book early on. When she was Associate Professor in Dr. Jules Hirsch's laboratory of Human Behavior and Metabolism at Rockefeller University in New York City, she passed on a wealth of valuable information and gave me many valuable contacts for my research.

Dr. Richard Boies Stark, Clinical Professor of Surgery (Plastic), College of Physicians and Surgeons, Columbia University, New York, and Founder and Attending Surgeon of Plastic Surgery Service, St.

Luke's-Roosevelt Hospital Center, New York City, not only trans-
formed me physically but also gave me a wealth of information about
fat on the body's lower half. He was patient, cooperative, and helpful.

Ruby Macmillan was a resourceful and conscientious research
assistant when the book was in its crucial stages. She typed, filed,
and investigated and was also great company. To her I am deeply
thankful.

To Dr. Bill McArdle, Department of Physiology, Queens College,
Flushing, New York, for his enthusiastic support and information
on exercise physiology, I am thankful.

Dr. Adam Drewnowski, previously at Rockefeller University, was
extremely helpful in the field of eating behavior and food preferences.

Dr. Ahmed Kissebah, Professor of Medicine and Pharmacology,
Medical College of Wisconsin, was helpful in sending his most recent
papers on regional differences amongst fat cells.

Thanks to Dr. Stewart Yudofsky, Institute of Psychiatry, Columbia
Presbyterian Hospital, New York City, who has worked with one
of the most celebrated figures in the field of psychiatry and obesity,
Dr. Hilde Bruch. He put me in touch with her work and gave me
some fascinating information.

I am also grateful for cooperation and information from:

Dr. Charles Brook, Department of Pediatrics, Middlesex Hospital,
London, England.

Mr. Christie Davies, Department of Sociology, University of Reading, England.

Professor Christos Doumas, Museum of Archaeology, Athens,
Greece.

Dr. David Galton, St. Bartholomew's Hospital, London, England.

Dr. Michael Gillmer, Nuffield Department of Obstetrics and Gyne-
cology, Radcliffe Hospital, Oxford, England.

Dr. Hubert Lacey, Department of Psychiatry, St. George's Hospital, Tooting, London, England.

Dr. Anthony Leeds, Department of Nutrition, Queen Elizabeth
College, London, England.

Mr. John Onians, Department of Art History, University of East
Anglia, Norwich, England.

Dr. Jerome B. Posner, Department of Neurology, Memorial Sloan
Kettering Hospital, New York City.

Professor Colin Renfrew, Department of Archaeology, University of Southampton, England.

Professor William Ross, Department of Kinesiology, Simon Fraser University, Burnaby, British Columbia, Canada, who greeted my request for information with unheard-of enthusiasm.

Mr. John Schetrumpf, Fellow of the Royal College of Surgeons, London, England.

Dr. Jackie Stordy, Department of Biochemistry, University of Surrey.

Dr. Ernest Wynder and Dr. Kristina Laakso of the American Health Foundation.

For those who helped me realize and reshape my body:

Mrs. Voyiadzis, whose teaching in ballet and gymnastics is always an inspiration and who makes Athens mornings bearable.

Joe Scifo, for his encouragement, patience, and perseverance. He trained me in fitness for over a year in New York, in which time I improved my fitness, my strength, and my self-image.

Sondra Ray for gently liberating me from my fears.

Alex Lukeman for rolfing me with care and attention.

Last and certainly not least, John Gordon, my witty and gifted dance teacher in London who made me understand the boldness and elegance of movement.

Bibliography and Suggested Reading

Much of the information in this book has been obtained through private communications with doctors, clinicians, therapists, and many others who have been acknowledged. Some information was also obtained at medical conferences. Otherwise I have, to a great extent, drawn on the following list of books and periodicals. Many of these are of a specific medical nature, others of more general interest.

Books

ASHWELL, M. "The Regulation of the Size and Nature of Energy Stores in Man." In *Clinical and Scientific Aspects of the Regulation of Metabolism,* Vol. II. Ed. M. Ashwell. Boca Raton, Fla.: CRC Press, 1980.

————, M. DURRANT, P. WARWICK, AND J. GARROW. "Obesity." In *Nutritional Problems in Modern Society,* Ch. 7. Ed. A. Howard. London: John Libbey, 1981.

BANNER, L. *American Beauty.* New York: Alfred A. Knopf, 1983.

BELLER, A. *Fat and Thin.* New York: McGraw-Hill, 1978.

BENNETT, W., AND J. GURIN. *The Dieter's Dilemma: Eating Less and Weighing More.* New York: Basic Books, 1982.

BRODY, J. *Jane Brody's Nutrition Book.* New York: Norton, 1981.

BRUCH, H. *Eating Disorders: Obesity, Anorexia Nervosa, and the Person Within.* New York: Basic Books, 1973.

CHASE, C. *The Great American Waistline.* New York: Coward, McCann and Geoghegan, 1981.

CHERNIN, K. *The Obsession: Reflections on the Tyranny of Slenderness.* New York: Harper and Row, 1982.

CLARK, K. *The Nude.* Garden City, N.Y.: Anchor Press, Doubleday, 1956.

Committee on Dietary Allowances Food and Nutrition Board. *Recommended Dietary Allowances,* 9th ed. Washington, D.C.: National Academy of Sciences, 1980.

CORBIN, C. *Nutrition.* New York: Holt, Rinehart and Winston, 1980.

DEUTSCH, R. *The New Nuts Among the Berries.* Palo Alto, Calif.: Bull, 1977.

DIAMOND, J. *Your Body Doesn't Lie.* New York: Harper and Row, 1979.

DUFTY, W. *Sugar Blues.* New York: Warner Books, 1976.

EYTON, A. *The F-Plan.* Middlesex, England: Penguin, 1982.

GALTON, D. J. *The Human Adipose Cell: A Model for Errors in Metabolic Regulation.* London: Butterworth, 1971.

GIDEON, S. *The Eternal Present, The Beginnings of Art.* Oxford: Oxford University Press, 1962.

GOODHART, R., AND M. SHILS, EDS. *Modern Nutrition in Health and Disease,* 6th ed. Philadelphia: Lea and Febiger, 1980.

GREENWOOD, M., ED. *Obesity. Contemporary Issues in Clinical Nutrition 4.* New York: Churchill Livingstone, 1983.

GREER, G. *The Female Eunuch.* New York: Bantam, 1972.

HOUSTON, J. *The Possible Human.* Los Angeles: J. P. Tarcher, 1982.

KRAL, J., AND L. GORTZ. "Recent Developments in the Surgical Treatments of Obesity." In *Obesity: Pathogenesis and Treatment.* Eds. G. Enzi, G. Crepaldi, G. Porza, and A. Renold. London: Academic Press, 1981.

LAVER, J. *A Concise History of Costume.* London: Thames and Hudson, 1969.

LEADBEATER, C. *The Chakras.* Wheaton, Ill.: The Theosophical Publishing House, 1927.

LOWEN, A. *Bioenergetics.* Middlesex, England: Penguin, 1976.

———. *Fear of Life.* New York: Macmillan, 1980.

LURIE, A. *The Language of Clothes.* New York: Random House, 1981.

MACARDLE, W., F. KATCH, AND V. KATCH. *Exercise Physiology.* Philadelphia: Lea and Febiger, 1981.

MAYER, J. *Overweight.* Englewood Cliffs, N.J.: Prentice-Hall, 1968.

MILLER, S., WITH J. MILLER. *Food for Thought: A New Look at Food and Behavior.* Englewood Cliffs, N.J.: Prentice-Hall, 1979.

MINDELL, E. *Earl Mindell's Vitamin Bible.* New York: Warner Books, 1981.

MORGAN, E. *The Descent of Woman.* New York: Bantam, 1973.

———. *The Aquatic Ape.* New York: Stein and Day, 1982.

MORRIS, D. *The Naked Ape.* New York: London: Jonathan Cape, 1967.

ORBACH, S. *Fat Is a Feminist Issue.* New York: Berkley, 1979.

ORR, L., AND S. RAY. *Rebirthing in the New Age.* Millbrae, Calif.: Celestial Arts, 1977.

PEARSON, D., AND S. SHAW. *Life Extension.* New York: Warner Books, 1982.

PRITIKIN, N. *The Pritikin Program for Diet and Exercise.* New York: Grosset and Dunlap, 1979.

RAY, S. *The Only Diet There Is.* Millbrae, Calif.: Celestial Arts, 1982.

RODIN, J. *Controlling Your Weight.* London: Century, 1983.

———. "The Externality Theory Today." In *Obesity.* Ed. A. Stunkard. Philadelphia: Saunders, 1980.

ROLF, I. *Rolfing: The Integration of Human Structures.* Santa Monica, Calif.: Dennis Landman, 1977.

RONSARD, N. *Cellulite: Those Lumps, Bumps and Bulges You Couldn't Lose Before.* New York: Bantam, 1975.

RONY, H. *Obesity and Leanness.* Philadelphia: Lea and Febiger, 1940.

ROSS, S. *Fasting.* London: Pan, 1978.

STUNKARD, A., ED. *Obesity.* Philadelphia: Saunders, 1980.

————. "Psychoanalysis and Psychotherapy." In *Obesity.* Ed. A. Stunkard. Philadelphia: Saunders, 1980.

STARK, R. "Extremity Lifts." In *Aesthetic Plastic Surgery.* Ed. R. Stark. Boston: Little, Brown, 1980.

TANNAHILL, R. *Sex in History.* London: Hamish Hamilton, 1980.

VAUGHAN, W. *Low Salt Secrets for Your Diet.* New York: Warner Books, 1982.

WATT, B., AND A. MERRILL, with assistants. *Composition of Foods. Agricultural Handbook No. 8.* Consumer and Food Economics Institute, Agricultural Research Service. Washington, D.C.: United States Department of Agriculture, revised 1963, reprinted 1975.

WILSON, G. "Behavior Modification in the Treatment of Obesity." In *Obesity.* Ed. A. Stunkard. Philadelphia: Saunders, 1980.

YOGANANDA, P. *Autobiography of a Yogi.* London: Rider, 1969.

Periodicals

ASHWELL, M. "Brown Adipose Tissue: Relevant to Obesity?" *Human Nutrition: Applied Nutrition* 37A: June 1983.

————, S. CHINN, S. STALLEY, AND J. GARROW. "Female Fat Distribution—A Simple Classification Based on Two Circumference Measurements," *International Journal of Obesity* 6:143–52, 1982.

BORBERG, C., M. GILLMER, E. BRUNNER, P. GUNN, N. OAKLEY, AND R. BEARD. "Obesity in Pregnancy—The Effect of Dietary Advice," *Diabetes Care* 3:3, 1980.

BÖRJESON, M. "The Aetiology of Obesity in Children. A Study of 101 Twin Pairs," *Acta Paediatrica Scandinavica* 65:279–87, 1976.

BRODY, J. Personal Health Column, New York *Times,* March 16, 1983.

CRAWTHORNE, M., AND J. ARCH. "The Search for Peripherally Acting Drugs for the Treatment of Obesity—A Review," *International Journal of Obesity* 6:1–10, 1982.

CROCKETT, G. "Jaw Wiring: 21 Cases Seen over 6 Years," *International Journal of Obesity* 6:218, 1982.

EDELMAN, B., AND O. MALLER. "Facts and Fictions About Infantile Obesity," *International Journal of Obesity* 6:69–81, 1982.

FRISCH, R. "Nutrition, Fatness, Puberty and Fertility," *Comprehensive Therapy* 7:7, 1981.

GARNER, M. "Fat Suction Surgery—Fad or Fact?" *Self* 34, 38: May 1982.

GRIFFITHS, M., AND P. PAYNE. "Energy Expenditure in Small Children of Obese and Non-obese Parents," *Nature* 260:698–700, 1976.

GRINKER, J. "Obesity and Sweet Taste," *American Journal of Clinical Nutrition* 31:1078–87, 1978.

———, K. MARISAK, AND R. FISCHER. "Sweet Intake as a Function of Infant and Maternal Size," *Olfaction and Taste* VII:331–34, 1980.

HALMI, K., E. MASON, J. FALK, AND A. STUNKARD. "Appetite Behavior After Gastric Bypass for Obesity," *International Journal of Obesity* 5:457–64, 1981.

HASHIM, S. "Obesity, Drugs and Formula Diets," *Postgraduate Medicine* 30:3, 1961.

———, AND K. PORIKOS. "Food Intake Behavior in Man: Implications for the Treatment of Obesity," *Clinics in Endocrinology and Metabolism* 5(2):503–16, 1976.

HOWARD, A. "The Historical Development, Efficiency and Safety of Very Low Calorie Diets," *International Journal of Obesity* 5:195–208, 1981.

JACOBSON, B. "Cellulite," *World Medicine* 101–5: May 1975.

KIRTLAND, J., AND M. GURR. "Adipose Tissue Cellularity: A Review. 1. Techniques for Studying Cellularity," *International Journal of Obesity* 2:401–27, 1978.

———. "Adipose Tissue Cellularity: A Review. 2. The Relationship Between Cellularity and Obesity," *International Journal of Obesity* 3:15–55, 1979.

KISSEBAH, A. "Relation of Body Fat Distribution to Medical Complications of Obesity," *Journal of Clinical Endocrinology and Metabolism* 54(2):254–60, 1982.

KRAL, J. "Surgical Reduction of Adipose Tissue Hypercellularity in Man," *Scandinavian Journal of Plastic Reconstructive Surgery* 9:140–43, 1975.

KROTKIEWSKI, M., A. ANIANSSON, G. GRIMBY, P. BJÖRNTORP, AND L. SJÖSTRÖM. "The Effect of Unilateral Isokinetic Strength Training on Local Adipose and Muscle Tissue Morphology, Thickness and Enzymes," *European Journal of Applied Physiology* 42:271–81, 1979.

———, P. BJÖRNTORP, L. SJÖSTRÖM, AND U. SMITH. "Impact of Obesity on Metabolism in Men and Women. Importance of Regional Adipose Tissue Distribution," *Journal of Clinical Investigation* 72:1150–62, 1983.

KRUT, S., AND R. SINGER. "Steatopygia: the Fatty Acid Composition of Subcutaneous Adipose Tissue in Hottentots," *American Journal of Physical Anthropology* 21:2:181–88, 1963.

LEWIS, J., JR. "Correction of the Thighs: The Thigh Lift," *Plastic and Reconstructive Surgery* 37:494, 1966.

NÜRNBERGER, F., AND G. MÜLLER. "So-called Cellulite: An Invented Disease," *Journal of Dermatology and Surgical Oncology* 4:3, 1978.

PITANGUY, I. "Surgical Reduction of the Abdomen, Thighs and Buttocks," *Surgical Clinics of North America* 51:479, 1971.

POLLITT, E., R. LEIBEL, AND D. GREENFIELD. "Brief Fasting, Stress and Cognition in Children," *American Journal of Clinical Nutrition* 34:1526–33, 1981.

SIMEONS, A. "The Action of Chorionic Gonadotrophin in the Obese," *Lancet* 2:946–47, 1954.

SJÖSTRÖM, L., AND T. OLSSON. "Prospective Studies in Adipose Tissue Development in Man," *International Journal of Obesity* 5:592–604, 1981.

VAGUE, J. "The Degree of Masculine Differentiation of Obesities," *American Journal of Clinical Nutrition* 4:1:20–31, 1956.

VAN ITALIE, T., AND J. KRAL. "The Dilemma of Morbid Obesity," *Journal of the American Medical Association* 246(9):999–1003, 1981.

WAXMAN, M., AND A. STUNKARD. "Caloric Intake and Expenditure of Obese Boys," *Journal of Pediatrics* 96(2):187–93, 1980.

WEINER, J., AND R. WEINER. "Biological Aspects of Some Indiginous African Populations," *South Western Journal of Anthropology* 19(2):168–76, 1963.

Index

Page numbers in *italics* indicate illustrations

Abdominal exercises, 163, 175

Acetoacetic acid, 52

Acupuncture and acupressure, 248

Acyl Co-A, *55*

Adenosine monophosphate (cyclic AMP), 58

Adenosine triphosphate (ATP), 58, *59*

Adenylcyclase, 58

Adipoblasts, 70, 71

Adipocytes, 70, 71

Adipose precursors, 70, 71

Adipose tissue, 51, 53, 63, 106
   brown versus white, 64, *65*
   enlargement of, 66–67
   location of, 26–27
   See also Fat

Adolescence, 21, 66
   anxiety in, 77–78
   growth and change in, 76–78

Adrenocorticotropic hormone (ACTH), 61

Aerobic exercises, 147, 153, 164–68, 173, 185–88, 191

Affirmations, 259

Age, 63, 68
   and body composition, 80
   and metabolic rate, 49

Air travel, 78, 100, 202–4

Alcohol, 90, 92, 108
   and appetite, 113
   and water retention, 78

Allergy, 93–94, 96

Alpha-amylase, 212, 213

Amenorrhea, 76

American Society of Plastic and Reconstructive Surgeons, 227

Amino acids, 51, 88, 102

Amphetamines, 39, 209, 210

Anaerobic exercise, 165, 166, 167, 169

Androgens, 26

Ankles, 111, 184–85

Anorexia nervosa, 39, 76, 77, 243, 244, 246

Anxiety, 136, 241, 250
   in adolescence, 77–78

Appetite, 46–48
   and alcohol, 113
   in babies, 72–73
   and exercise, 144
   and fertility, 76–77
   regulation of, 44–45

Appetite suppressants, 209–10

Apple-Cider Vinegar Diet, 93–94

Archimedes, 28

Aromatherapy, 248

Art, 11–12

Artificial sweeteners, 47
Atherosclerosis, 21
Attitude
  and dieting, 85–86, 99, 100
  and exercise, 137–38, 154–56,
    172, 189, 206
  See also Psychological factors
Aura, 245
Aversion therapy, 247

Babyhood, 79
  obesity in, 67–68
  overfeeding in, 72–73
Back, 160, 162–63, 174–75, 175–
  77, 181, 192, 197, 250
Basic metabolic rate (BMR), 147–
  49
Behavior modification, 247–48
Beta-hydroxybutyric acid, 52
Beverly Hills Diet, 93–94
Bicycling, 151, 186
Big Beauties, 255
Biochemical abnormalities, 42
Bioenergetics, 250–51
Birth control pills, 66, 78
Birthweight, 73
Black women, 19–20
Blood pressure, 21, 40, 93, 111
Blood sugar, 91, 104–5, 156, 209
Body composition, 27–30, 146–47
Body density, 27–29
Body image, 76, 143, 226, 256–58
Body sculpturing, 7, 227–28
  See also Plastic surgery
Body synergy, 251
Body wrapping, 215
Bones, 143
Boredom, 75, 92, 136, 233
Bowels, dropped, 22–23

Brain, 42, 44, 52
Breakfast, 135
Breast-feeding, 73, 80
  See also Lactation
Breathing, 156–57, 171, 178, 188,
  189, 252
Brown adipose tissue, 64, *65*
Brown rice, 92
B_6 Diet, 93–94
Bulimia, 243
Bulking agents, 209, 212
Burning sensation, 166, 189
Buttocks, 182, 190

Caffeine, 94, 114, 205
Calcium, 89, 93, 94, 110, 113, 136
Calories, 44n., 75
  in alcohol, 113
  and dieting effects, 87–89, 90,
    94, 95, 96, 98, 109, 115–17,
    119
  and energy balance, 49–51
  expenditure of, 149–51
  and nutritional needs, 108
Calories Don't Count Diet, 90–92
Calves, 162, 177, 184–85
Cancer, 40, 107, 114
Carbohydrates, 47, 51
  dietary need for, 101, 104
  and dieting effects, 87–88, 90, 95
  and energy, 204–5
  and mood, 241
  and starch blockers, 212–13
  See also Complex carbohydrates
Carbonated beverages, 132
Cardiovascular exercise. *See* Aerobic exercises
Cascade, 53, 58, 71
Catecholamines, 61

Cellulite, 5, 22–26, 214–16, 229
Cellulitis, 23
Cereals, 92, 113
Chakras, 245–46
Chewing, 134
Childhood, 74–76, 143
Chinese foot-binding, 15
Chloride, 91, 110
Cholesterol, 91, 106–7, 133
Circuit weight lifting, 169
Circulation, 185, 215, 216, 218
    and alcohol, 113
    and body shape, 21, 22–23
    and exercise, 142–43, 170–71,
        178
    regional differences in, 20, 63
Clothes, 15, 17, 252, 255
    for exercise, 158, 160, 164, 174,
        188
Coffee, 92, 114, 132, 205
Combination diets, 93–94
Complex carbohydrates, 51, 204–
    5
    and dieting effects, 90, 91, 92–
        93
Computerized axial tomography
    (CAT scans), 31, 67
Connective tissue massage, 218
Constipation, 91, 133
Cool-down stretches. *See* Recovery
    exercises
Corium, 24
Cortisol, 61
Cultural factors, 4, 43–44

Dancing, 164–65, 186
Death, fear of, 252–53
Dehydration, 91, 95, 111

Dental cavities, 47
Depression, 42–43, 250
Detoxification, 98
Diabetes, 21, 40, 63, 105
Diarrhea, 94, 213, 233
Dietary (environmental) obesity,
    42, 43–45
Diethylstilbestrol, 77
Dieting
    and attitude, 85–86, 99, 100
    and body proportions, 86–87
    and exercise, 136–38, 146, 186
    fad diets, 89–98, 99
    failure of, 85
    and food obsession, 244
    and metabolic rate, 49, 87, 89,
        117, 119
    physical effects of, 81, 87–89
    and water intake, 112
    See also Diets
Diet pills, 209–14
Diets, 7, 41, 71
    balanced, 100–17
    combination, 93–94
    composition of, 118–33
    high complex carbohydrate, 92–
        93
    high-fiber, 93
    high-protein, 94–96
    structure for, 117–36
    and water retention, 78
    See also Dieting
Diet soda, 132
Diseases, 20, 21, 40
Diuretics, 211–12, 217
Dr. Atkins' Diet, 90–92
Drinking Man's Diet, 90–92
Drugs, 62, 209–14

Eating behavior, 73, 134, 240–45
Electrolytes, 91, 95, 96, 98, 211, 223
Endocrine disturbances, 43
Endorphins, 46, 104, 143
Energy balance, 49–51, 66, 81
Energy fields, 245–46, 250
Energy output, 147–52
Energy systems, 165–67
Environment, 71, 73, 75
Environmental obesity, 42, 43–45
Enzyme Catalyst Diet, 93–94
Enzymes, 53, 109
Epinephrine, 58
Estrogen, 20, 57
  and adolescence, 76–77
  and menopause, 80
Evolution, 12–15, 18
Exercise, 100, 136
  and adolescence, 78
  and appetite, 144
  and attitude, 137–38, 154–56, 172, 189, 206
  and body composition, 146–47
  and childhood, 75
  and diet, 136–38, 146, 186
  and metabolic rate, 80, 145–46
  and mind-body integration, 249
  and nutrition, 204–5
  physical reasons for, 142–43
  and pregnancy, 80
  safety of, 139–40, 164
  and shape, 152–53
  types of, 160–71
  value of, 7, 21, 137–42
  Venus workout, 173–206
  and water retention, 79
Exercise clothes, 158, 160, 164, 174, 188

Exercise machines, 169, 191
Externality theory, 48

Fad diets, 89–98, 99
Falling, fear of, 251–52
Fashion models, 17, 255
Fasting, 95, 97–98, 102, 136
Fat
  biological value of, 13–15
  as blocked energy, 256
  and body composition, 27–30
  and dieting effects, 87
  distribution of, 19–22, 30–34
  and evolution, 12–15, 18
  and exercise, 142
  mental release of, 256–58
  and metabolic rate, 48–49
  and regional cellular differences, 62–63
  release of, 53, 58–62, 205
  re-storage of, 62
  social significance of, 15–18, 255–56
  storage of, 26–27, 53–58
  See also Adipose tissue; Fat cells
Fat cells
  and dieting, 81
  endurance of, 72
  expansion of, 66–67, 69
  recruitment of, 71–72
  types of, 69–71
  See also Fat
Fat distribution score, 31, *32, 33,* 34
Fatigue, 78, 155, 156
Fats, 51, 92
  craving for, 47
  dietary need for, 101, 102, 106–7
Fat-suction surgery, 218–21

Fatty acids, 51, 89
Fear, 244, 245, 251–53
Fear of Life, 249
Feet, 79, 162, 184–85, 188, 251
Femoral rotation, 162
Fenfluramine, 209
Fertility, 14, 76–77
Fiber, 118, 212
    and dieting effects, 91, 93
Fibroblasts, 70
Finland, 62
Fluid retention. *See* Water retention
Food for Thought, 115
Food groups, 101
Force-feeding, 73
F-Plan, The, 93
Free fatty acids, 51
Friction exercises, 189
Fruit diets, 94

Galen, 256
Gall bladder disease, 40
Garrow, John, 208
Gastrointestinal disorders, 93, 94, 213, 233
Genetic factors
    and babies' appetite, 72–73
    and body shape, 1, 19–20, 47, 63, 71, 81
    and childhood obesity, 74–75
Genetic obesity, 42, 43–44
Glucagon, 61
Gluconeogenesis, 60, 88
Glucose, 52, *57,* 87, 204
Glycerol, 51, *55, 56,* 57, 59, 60, 89
Glycogen, 51–52, 57, 87, 88, 152, 204

Glycolysis, 166
Golden Door, The, 7
Gout, 89
Grapefruit Diet, 90–92
Greece, 4, 19, 43–44
Groin, 181–82
Grounding, 251
Growth, 66, 74–78
Guilt, 42, 136, 244, 247, 260

Hair follicle, 24
Hashim, Sami, 41
Head, 178–79
Health food, 112–13
Health spas, 7–8, 136, 138–39
Heart disease, 40, 139–40
Heart rate, 167–68, 186
High complex carbohydrate diets, 92–93
High-fiber diets, 93
High heels, 20
High-protein diets, 90–92
High-protein liquid diets, 94–96
Hips
    and dieting, 86–87
    and exercise, 181, 190
Holistic treatments, 248–53
Hormones, 1, 20–21, 53, 109
Hormone-sensitive lipase (HSL), 58–*59,* 60
Hormone therapy, 209, 210–11
Hottentots of the Kalahari Desert, *16,* 17
Human chorionic gonadotrophin (HCG) injections, 216–17
Hunger, 242
    and appetite, 46–48
    external cues to, 48
    and physiological stimuli, 45–46

Hyperplasia, 67–68
Hypertrophy, 67, 68
Hypoglycemia, 105, 205
Hypothalamic lesioning, 224
Hypothalamus, 44–45, 66, 216–17

Infant obesity, 67–68
Injury, 160, 162, 164, 187, 191
Innervation, 63
Insomnia, 133
Insulin, 21, 105, 212
    and fat storage, 55, 57–58, 60,
      61
Insurance company statistics, 40
International Conference on Obe-
      sity, 12
Intestinal surgery, 222–24
Iridology, 248
Iron, 109, 110, 113, 136
Isokinetic training, 169–70
Isotonic training, 169
Italy, 19

Jaws, 179
Jaw wiring, 208–9
Jewish women, 19
Jogging, 151, 164
Joints, diseases of, 40
Junk food, 47

Kelp Diet, 93–94
Kempner's Rice Diet, 92–93
Ketone bodies, 52, 89
Ketosis, 52
    and dieting effects, 89, 91, 95,
      96
    from fasting, 97
Kidneys, 52
    and dieting effects, 91

and diuretics, 211
and fasting, 97
and intestinal surgery, 223
and protein excess, 102
and salt, 111
Kidney stones, 89
Kissebah, Ahmed, 21, 63
Knees, 162, 177, 199, 200, 201

Lactation, 13–14, 79–80
Lactic acid, 166, 170, 189
Last Chance Diet, 95
Lecithin, 109
Lecithin Diet, 93–94
Legs, 172–73, 233, 251–52
Lewis, John R., Jr., 228
Linn, Robert, 95
Lipectomy, 227
    suction-assisted, 218–21
Lipolysis, 53, 58–62, 109
Lipolytic agents, 213–14
Lipoprotein lipase (LPL), *54, 55,*
      62
Lipoproteins, 107
Liquid protein diets, 94–96
Liver, 51–52, 60, 88
    and cholesterol production, 106,
      107
    and intestinal surgery, 223
    and protein excess, 102
Lowen, Alexander, 250

Macrobiotic Diet, 92–93
Macronutrients, 101–7, 110
Magic Mayo Diet, 90–92
Mandels' It's Not Your Fault
      You're Fat Diet, 93–94
Massage, 218
Mattress phenomenon, 24, *25,* 26

Maximal oxygen consumption
    (max VO₂), 167
Mayer, Jean, 144
Measurements, 157–58, *159*
Megadosing, 109, 110
Menopause, 66, 80
Menstruation, 13, 211
    and fluid retention, 111
    and iron loss, 109
    onset of, 76–77
Metabolic rate
    and anxiety, 241
    and caffeine, 114
    and dieting, 47, 87, 89, 117, 119
    and energy balance, 49–51
    and exercise, 80, 145–46
    and hormone therapy, 210–11
    mechanics of, 48–49, 80
    and nicotine, 114
    nightly lowering of, 115
Methylcellulose, 212
Micronutrients, 101, 107–11
Miller, Saul, 115
Mind and body, 3, 35
    See also Attitude; Psychological
        factors
Minerals, 93, 94, 95, 98, 101, 110
Mineral water, 132
Mirror, 161, 174, 176
Mitochondria, 64, *65*
Monounsaturated fats, 106–7
Muscles, underdeveloped, 21
Muscle strengthening exercises,
    168–70, 173, 188–201

Nautilus equipment, 169, 191
Neck, 160, 197
Nigeria, 17

Nitrogen, 91, 97, 102
Nutrition, 204–5

Obesity, 27, 34
    childhood, 74–76
    as disease, 41–42
    and exercise, 143–47
    and fat re-storage, 62
    infant, 67–68
    overweight versus, 39–41
    and pregnancy, 79–80
    and psychological factors, 240–
        45
    stigma associated with, 41–42
    types of, 42–45
Oral contraceptives, 66, 78
Other Dimensions, 255
Overfeeding, 72–73
Oxygen uptake, 167

Parsley, 212
Pelvic tilt, 160–61, 174
Peptic ulcers, 94
Pitanguy, Ivo, 228
Pituitary gland, 44–45
Plastic surgery, 6–7, 137, 220, 221,
    222, 235–36, 254
    choice of surgeon for, 227–28
    long-term effects of, 234–35
    motivation for, 225–27
    procedures in, 228–29, *230–31*
    recovery from, 232–34
    risks and complications of, 229,
        232
    scars from, 228, 234
Plateau during dieting, 119, 135
Polysaccharides, 104
Polyunsaturated fats, 106–7
Postmenopausal women, 20, 80

Posture, 19–20, 160, 252
Potassium, 91, 110, 136, 211
  and lean body mass, 29
Preadipocytes, 70, 71
Pregnancy, 13, 14, 21, 78
  and obesity, 79–80
Prevention stretches, 160, 161–63,
  174–77
Pritikin Program, 92–93
Progesterone, 57
Prolactin, 57
Pro Linn, 95
Protein, 51
  in calorie-controlled diets, 119
  dietary need for, 101, 102–3
  and dieting effects, 87–89
  and energy, 204, 205
  and fasting, 97
  high-protein diets, 90–92
  liquid protein diets, 94–96
Psychological factors
  anxiety, 77–78, 136, 241, 250
  biochemical abnormalities in-
    duced by, 42–43
  body image, 76, 143, 226, 256–
    58
  and body shape, 245–46, 256–59
  boredom, 75, 95, 136, 233
  and breast-feeding, 73
  and childhood self-esteem, 75–76
  and desperate remedies, 208,
    209, 216, 233–34
  and dieting, 114–15, 133, 136
  and eating patterns, 241–45
  guilt, 42, 136, 244, 247, 260
  importance of, 8, 66, 240–41,
    260–61
  self-acceptance, 254–55
  and self-healing, 246–53

Psychotherapy and psychoanalysis,
  248

Racial characteristics, 19–20
Rebirthing, 252–53, 259
Recovery exercises, 170–71, 173,
  188, 191, 201–2, 206
Reflexology, 248
Regional cellular differences, 62–63
Reproductive functions, 76–77
Restaurants, 134–35
Ribs, 179–80
Rolfing, 251–52

Salt, 92, 93, 100, 115, 118, 132, 133,
  135, 205
  and water retention, 78, 79, 110–
    11, 112
  See also Sodium
Saturated fats, 106–7
Sauna, 156, 216
Scars, 228, 234
Scarsdale Diet, 90–92
Self-acceptance, 254–55
Self-healing, 246–53, 258–59
Septa, 24
Serotonin, 241–42
Sex differences
  in body composition, 30, 31
  in metabolic rates, 48
  in subcutaneous fat structure
    and skin texture, 25, 26
  in water-retaining tendencies, 91
Sex hormones, 20–21, 26, 57
  and adolescence, 76–77
Sexuality, 14–15, 246, 248, 260
Shinsplints, 162
Shopping, 133
Shoulders and arms, 179

Sims, Ethan, 44, 47
Sitting, 22
Skin, 6, 92, 218, 229
  and dietary fat, 106
  texture of, *25*, 26
Skinfold thickness test, 30, 74
Smoking, 108, 114
Sodium, 91, 110–11, 211
  See also Salt
Somatostatin, 57
Spain, 19
Spine, 19–20
Spirituality, 97, 248
Spot exercises, 170
Spot reduction, 152–53, 157
Starch blockers, 209, 212–13
Stark, Richard, 7, 226, 228, 229,
  233
Steatopygia, *16*, 17
Step-up exercises, 186
Stigma, 41–42
Stimulants, 205
Stomach surgery, 42, 222–24
Stress, 78, 92, 100
  stretch versus, 163–64
Stretching, 142
  prevention stretches, 160, 161–
  63, 174–77
  versus stress, 163–64
  warm-up stretches, 161, 163–64,
  178–85, 187, 191, 206
Stretch marks, 6
Stromal vascular cells, 69, *70*
Stylites, 97
Subcutaneous fat structure, *25*, 26
Suction-assisted lipectomy, 218–21
Sugar, 92, 104–5, 204
Support groups, 247
Support stockings, 79

Surgery, 209
  fat suction, 218–21, 254
  of stomach and intestines, 42,
  222–24
  See also Plastic surgery
Sway back, 19–20
Swedish twin studies, 43
Sweetness, 47, 73
Swimming, 140, 142, 152, 160,
  164–65, 185

Taste, 47, 73
Tea, 92, 132
Testosterone, 77, 147, 170
Thighs, 24, *25*, 31, 34, 77
  and dieting, 86–87
  exercises for, 182–84, 190, 200
  and lactation, 80
Thirst, 110–11
Thrombosis, 215
Thyroid deficiency, 43
Thyroxine, 209, 210–11
Total body potassium counter, 29
Traumatic obesity, 42–43
Travel, 78, 100, 202–4
Triglyceride, 51, 52, 53, 55, *56*, 58,
  59, 61, 106, 109, 143
Triiodothyronine, 210
Tryptophan, 241–42

U.S. Recommended Dietary Allowances (R.D.A.), 108, 110

Vagus nerve, 224
Vascularization, 63
Vegetarian diets, 112–13
Venus of Willendorf, 11–*13*
Very low density lipoproteins
  (VLDL), *54, 55*

Vibrator belts, 153–54
Visualization, 260
Vitamins, 92, 98, 101
  and dieting effects, 93, 94, 95
  need for, 107–9, 113

Waist stretches, 180
Walking, 142, 151, 152, 164, 185
Warm-up stretches, 161, 163–
    64, 173, 178–85, 187, 191,
    206
Water intake, 79, 112, 132, 135,
    136, 205
Water loss, 87, 91, 97–98, 205,
    216

Water retention, 135
  and body shape, 21, 22
  causes of, 77, 78, 111, 118
  and diuretics, 211–12
  prevention of, 78–79
Weighing oneself, 100
Weight, 34, 39–41
  See also Obesity
Weight lifting, 165, 169
Weight tables, 74, 255
Willendorf Lectures, 12

Yoga, 97, 156, 171, 201

Zinc, 110, 113